DISCARD

RENEGADE DREAMS

Renegade Dreams

LIVING THROUGH INJURY IN GANGLAND CHICAGO

Laurence Ralph

THE UNIVERSITY OF CHICAGO PRESS ‡ CHICAGO AND LONDON

LAURENCE RALPH is assistant professor of African and
African American studies at Harvard University.

The University of Chicago Press, Chicago 60637
The University of Chicago Press, Ltd., London
© 2014 by The University of Chicago
All rights reserved. Published 2014.
Printed in the United States of America

23 22 21 20 19 18 17 16 15 14   1 2 3 4 5
ISBN-13: 978-0-226-03268-9 (cloth)
ISBN-13: 978-0-226-03271-9 (paper)
ISBN-13: 978-0-226-03285-6 (e-book)

DOI: 10.7208/chicago/9780226032856.001.0001

Library of Congress Cataloging-in-Publication Data
Ralph, Laurence, author.
Renegade dreams: living through injury in gangland Chicago / Laurence Ralph.
pages cm
Includes bibliographical references and index.
ISBN 978-0-226-03268-9 (cloth: alkaline paper)—ISBN 978-0-226-03271-9
(paperback : alkaline paper)—ISBN 978-0-226-03285-6 (e-book)
1. Gang members—Illinois—Chicago. 2. Gangs—Illinois—Chicago. I. Title.
HV6439.U71457 2014
364.106′60975311—dc23   2013048756

renegade dream |'reni̯gād drēm|: *an aspiration rooted in an experience of injury that reimagines the possibilities within injury*

CONTENTS

✳

Divine Knights Gang

CHRISTOPHER ANDERSON
Member of the Anonymous Knights, a subset of the Divine Knights; Tamara Redding's nephew, Patrice Anderson's cousin

OTIS BALL (MR. OTIS)
Longtime member of the Divine Knights; Emma Ball's husband

ERVING RUSSELL BEAMER
Former Supreme Chief of the Divine Knights

ERIC CHILDS
Former member of the Divine Knights; community activist

MARCUS COOPER
Member of the Anonymous Knights; student at Jackson High School

RONNIE HARRIS
High-ranking Divine Knights official in the 1980s; Shawn Harris's father

SHAWN HARRIS
Gang leader of the Bandits, a subset of
the Divine Knights; Ronnie Harris's
daughter

DARIO HOPFIELD
Member of the Anonymous Knights,
a subset of the Divine Knights

PETE HUGHES
Member of the Anonymous Knights,
a subset of the Divine Knights

TIKO HUNT
Member of the Anonymous Knights,
a subset of the Divine Knights

STERLING JOHNSTON
Member of the Divine Knights

STEVE KEARNS
Member of the Roving Knights, a
subset of the Divine Knights; Fatima
Kearns's older brother

KEMO NOSTRAND
Gang leader of the Anonymous
Knights, a subset of the Divine
Knights

COLT PRATT
Member of the Anonymous Knights,
a subset of the Divine Knights

JOHN SAGE
Member of the Roving Knights,
a subset of the Divine Knights;
footworker

HENRY TODD
Member of the Divine Knights; army
veteran

REGINALD "RED" WALKER
Leader of the Roving Knights, a
subset of the Divine Knights

Eastwood Community Church

DENNIS ABNER
Employee at Delivery Development
Corporation; member of the Eastwood
Community Church

HANNAH BRADY
Youth worker at Eastwood
Community Church

CURTIS GAINES
Assistant pastor at Eastwood
Community Church

TRAVIS JACKSON
Microsoft employee; an "Eastwood
Future Legacy"

PASTOR TIM MONTGOMERY
Head pastor of Eastwood Community
Church; CEO and founding president
of the Rebirth Rehabilitation
Center and Delivery Development
Corporation

MONICA NAMBA
Bible-study instructor at the Eastwood
Community Church's Outreach
Program

MICAH NOBEL
Singer in the Rebirth Rehabilitation
Center Choir

GRACE REYES
Member of Eastwood Community
Church; Noel Reyes's wife

NOEL REYES
Member of Eastwood Community
Church; heroin addict; a former
official in the Divine Knights; Grace
Reyes's husband

GEORGE SARATOGA
Longtime member of the Eastwood
Community Church

TANEESHA SCOTT
Pastor Tim's personal assistant; an
"Eastwood Future Legacy"

BRIAN SMITH
Business consultant for the Delivery
Development Corporation; an
"Eastwood Future Legacy"

JOAN STEWART
Member of the Eastwood Community
Church; owner of a rehabilitated home

JEREMY WOODALL
Singer in the Rebirth Rehabilitation
Center Choir

Temple Worship Service

OLIVIA ARNOLD
Participant in the Eastwood
Community Church's Temple
Worship Service

FATIMA KEARNS
Member of Eastwood Community
Church; participant in the Temple
Worship Service; Steve Kearns's
younger sister

PETER OLSON
Participant in the Eastwood
Community Church's Temple
Worship Service

BLAKE PIETZ
Participant in the Eastwood
Community Church's Temple
Worship Service

AMY O'NEAL
HIV patient; participant in Eastwood
Community Church's Temple
Worship Service; Sue-Anne Green's
daughter

Chicago Public School Students and Teachers

PATRICE ANDERSON
Student at Brown High School;
Tamara Redding's niece; Christopher
Anderson's cousin

CECILE DRAKE (MR. DRAKE)
Teacher at Brown High School

ROBERT EDWARDS
Principal at Brown High School

GRAHAM FLYNN (MR. FLYNN)
Teacher at Brown High School

TASHA LITCH
Student at Brown High School;
Danny Silver's girlfriend

KWAME "COOK" ROBINSON
Student at Brown High School;
Danny Silver's best friend

DANNY SILVER
Student at Brown High School;
member of the Divine Knights; Tasha
Litch's boyfriend; Kwame "Cook"
Robinson's best friend

JEMELL WATERS
Student at Brown High School

Government Officials

PAUL BARNETT
Illinois state representative; ally of the Eastwood Community Church

AARON SMALLS
Employee at the City of Chicago's Planning Commission

DEBRA PEELE
Alderwoman for the district in which Eastwood is located

Neighborhood Coalition

TAMARA ANDERSON
Member of the Neighborhood Coalition; Christopher Anderson's aunt; Patrice Anderson's aunt

IDA CONWELL (MRS. CONWELL)
Member of the Neighborhood Coalition; longtime Eastwood resident

MARGARET DICKERSON (MRS. DICKERSON)
Member of the Neighborhood Coalition; longtime Eastwood resident

CHRISTINA HALL
Employee at the Justice Institute; ally of the Neighborhood Coalition

FRANCINE PEARL (MRS. PEARL)
Member of the Neighborhood Coalition

Crippled Footprint Collective

TONY AKPAN
Member of the Crippled Footprint Collective; disabled ex–gang member

DWIGHT DAVIS
Member of the Crippled Footprint Collective; disabled ex–gang member

OSCAR DYSON
Member of the Crippled Footprint
Collective; disabled ex-gang member

AARON SPARKS
Member of the Crippled Footprint
Collective; disabled ex-gang member

DARIUS GILBERT
Member of the Crippled Footprint
Collective; disabled ex-gang member

Gangsta City Entertainment

BORIS "PRECISE" KATZ
Member of Gangsta City
Entertainment; member of the
Divine Knights

DARRYL "BLIZZARD" TREMONT
Member of Gangsta City
Entertainment; member of the Divine
Knights; Tosh Tremont's nephew

KENNETH "EXPO" SHIPLEY
Member of Gangsta City
Entertainment; member of the
Divine Knights

JONNY "CHAMP" WILSON
Member of Gangsta City
Entertainment; member of the
Divine Knights

Other Eastwoodians

EMMA BALL
Longtime Eastwood resident; Otis
Ball's wife

JUSTIN CONE
Eastwood resident; disabled ex-gang
member

MARK BUCKLEY
A health worker at Healing Hearts

NICKY CONROY
Eastwood resident; Susan Hutchison's
aunt

FRANCO "DR. DEEP" CARR
A local Chicago rap artist

SUE-ANNE GREEN
Heroin addict; Amy O'Neal's mother

BENJAMIN GREGORY
(MR. GREGORY)
Bible-study instructor at the West
Side Juvenile Detention Center

CYNTHIA HUTCHISON
War veteran; heroin addict; Susan
Hutchison's mother

SUSAN HUTCHISON
Eastwood resident; Darryl "Blizzard"
Tremont's girlfriend

JIMMIE "SCOOTER" MATTHEWS
Inmate at the West Side Juvenile
Detention Center

LAURENCE RALPH
Anthropologist; community and gang
ethnographer

NELSON RANDALL
Probation officer; leader of the
Eastwood Youth Action Committee

PASTOR RAY STEPHENS
Head pastor at the House of Worship

REED "BULLET" TAYLOR
Rapper from the West Side of Chicago

KATHY TREMONT
Eastwood resident; Darryl "Blizzard"
Tremont's sister

TOSH TREMONT
Disabled ex–gang member; Darryl
"Blizzard" Tremont's uncle

✳

This book centers on a West Side Chicago neighborhood called Eastwood. I lived there from 2007 to 2010 and have returned countless times
since. My days in Eastwood taught me many things: how to build social bonds, how to listen to people's desires, and how to learn from the
ways people imagined alternative futures. In fact, my collaborators were
so open about their experiences—so profoundly vulnerable—that I felt
compelled to take my own dream more seriously. I wanted to write an
ethnography. But I didn't want my work to trade merely in theoretical
language, since my collaborators weren't trained to understand such ab-
stractions. I wanted to craft my research and writing out of the people-
centered evidence that I was uncovering all around me; and I wanted
it to be meaningful and useful for everyone who was gracious enough
to share their perspective with me—people whom you'll soon meet—
non-academics like Justin, Mrs. Pearl, Mr. Otis, Amy, Tamara, Tony,
and Tosh. Inspired by their projects, I, too, wanted to produce something that was wrought from a communal experience, something that

could transcend the barriers of expertise, something that truthfully articulated the hidden potentials embedded in injury.

Some Eastwoodians were impressed with my ability to capture what they said. Others were curious about why I dwelled on particular residents' experiences and not others. I used these follow-up meetings to tease out the assumptions that I was making as well as those of my collaborators. I began to see my transcriptions as a springboard for future conversations even when I used a recorder at public events like high school assemblies and anti-violence forums. When I finally began to write this book, from hundreds of scenes and conversations that I had pieced together, bit by bit, over a three-year period, I felt comfortable capturing speech as I heard it, because my process was collaborative, every step of the way.

Of course, this wasn't always an easy collaboration. At times Eastwoodians did not agree with my representation of their voices. One Thursday afternoon in February 2008, I shared a transcript of a digitally recorded conversation with members of a political action group called the Neighborhood Coalition. The conversation was from a strategy session of coalition members that took place at a local coffee shop. Mrs. Pearl was speaking about how Tiko, a young gang-affiliated Eastwoodian, could help raise awareness about an upcoming rally at City Hall. What she said sounded to my ears like: "Tiko can help us wit passing out dem flyers. He's always at our meetings, tryna figure out what he can do."

When I showed Mrs. Pearl the transcript of the conversation, she changed "wit" to "with," "dem to "them," and "tryna" to "trying to." Even though she agreed that my recounting of her dialogue accurately depicted what she actually said and how she actually sounded, she explained, "Some things are just right," and what I had given her to read wasn't. To make matters worse, she chided me: "You're supposed to be educated, boy." She even shook her head.

Watching Mrs. Pearl's disapproving face, I was presented with a dilemma. On the one hand, it was important for me to represent speech as I heard it. Most of my collaborators, regardless of race, spoke in what linguists refer to as African American Vernacular English (AAVE) as opposed to Standard American English (SAE).[1] Because of this, I wanted to represent the richness of AAVE as a spoken language in a way that did justice to its depth and beauty. On the other hand, if I addressed Mrs. Pearl's concerns and standardized her voice, I would have been left with an uneven recounting of people's dialogue. (When I presented my transcripts to younger residents, they had no qualms about my representation of their speech.) In the end, Mrs. Pearl and I found a middle ground. I would retain AAVE's grammatical conventions for every person in the book, such as the use of "they" instead of "their," and "ain't" instead of "isn't." But I would restrain my urge to be creative with my spelling of urban colloquialisms.

There were other issues. Sometimes Eastwoodians preferred not to have a particular quote attributed to them; I always respected these wishes. At times I decided to paraphrase what I had initially written in quotation marks and changed identifying characteristics of people and organizations upon request, creating composites. The Eastwood Community Church, for example, is actually a composite of more than one church on the West Side of Chicago. And since some religious leaders were uneasy about my depiction of strife within their organizations, "Pastor Tim" is a composite of more than one pastor. Likewise, in my effort to document the criminal exploits of several different gang leaders, "Kemo Nostrand" is a composite character.

I should also mention that as I began to draft dialogue and scenes, I noticed that they were taking shape as narrative essays. In my opinion, this mode of exposition conveyed what I witnessed in Eastwood most accurately. Still, I was afraid that my polished vignettes could potentially betray the messiness of social life in Eastwood. To rectify this imbalance, I eventually decided to start each chapter with a one-page ethnographic field note, reproduced from the notebooks I scribbled in relentlessly during my years in Eastwood. Oftentimes, these field notes reappear in different form throughout the chapters to suggest the process by which my initial, incoherent observations became developed analysis.

Because of all this—my negotiation with Mrs. Pearl about how to convey dialogue, my use of composites, and my apprehension about painting too perfect a picture of social life in Eastwood—Tosh, a resident with whom I developed a close relationship, liked to brag that the book he was writing about his own experiences in the gang was more real than mine. Even though he, too, availed himself of pseudonyms when referring to gang members, he used the gang's real name and I didn't. And he represented speech as he deemed fit.

I eventually decided that (despite Tosh's taunts) I couldn't reveal the name of the gang, and by extension people and organizations in the community, without betraying the trust of others in Eastwood. Indeed, anonymity was the condition that made much of my work possible.[2]

Anyone hoping to find quick references to Chicago's notorious gangs and infamous neighborhoods in this ethnography will be disappointed—as will anyone skimming the pages to find glossy snapshots of gang members. What is real about this ethnography—what hasn't been altered or rendered anonymous—are the events that I describe and the voices of my collaborators. Their voices bring to life the activities that take place on Chicago's street corners. Their voices bring dimension to people's identities and life struggles. Their voices paint a portrait of the variegated desires that stem from imagining life anew.

It's fitting in this regard that the painting that begins this book— Kehinde Wiley's work *The Chancellor Seguier on Horseback* (2005)— accurately captures the spirit of what it means to have a renegade dream. Wiley, a critically acclaimed portrait painter, is renowned for his heroic portraits that capture the status of young urban blacks in contemporary culture through reference to Old Master paintings. Adapted from a seventeenth-century Charles Le Brun painting *Chancellor Séguier at the Entry of Louis XIV into Paris in 1660*, Wiley's rendition blurs the boundaries between traditional and contemporary modes of representation by restaging the figures, and thus creating a fusion of period styles. Dressed in modern army fatigues and sweatpants, bandannas and baseball caps, T-shirts with airbrushed rappers and Air Force One sneakers, the figures in Wiley's composition are beautifully anachronistic. Yet the genius in Wiley's work is that it leads us to question: Why can't urban African Americans assume the delicate harmony and militant posture reminiscent of a Renaissance master? This book seeks to similarly restage urban blacks within societal institutions and fields of power from which they are often presumed to be excluded. Despite the statistical odds against their dreams coming to fruition in such a context, I foreground the resilience it takes for black Chicagoans to keep dreaming anyway.

Kehinde Wiley, The Chancellor Seguier on Horseback *(2005), oil on canvas,*
108 × 144 in. © Kehinde Wiley Studio.

One

---*---

The Injury of Isolation

OR,

How to Dream Like a Renegade

Justin Cone tilted in his wheelchair. He executed this delicate balancing act effortlessly, while simultaneously craning his head to take in the audience behind him. His neck muscles began to bulge as he surveyed the teenagers. He was perched in the front row of a high school assembly on gang violence in Chicago. It was the winter of 2008; twenty-seven public school students had been killed since September. This was an unprecedented number at the time. Little did Justin and I know that the bloodshed would only increase. The ignoble number of deaths in 2008 would be surpassed year after year after year. By the end of 2011, three years later, 260 would be dead.[1]

Justin had been to many such assemblies, but this time he encouraged me to come with him. There was something remarkable about these particular speakers, he promised—something that a gang researcher just had to see for himself. I soon found out what Justin deemed extraordinary: the young men onstage looked like him. They, too, used to belong to a gang and had been disabled by a gunshot; now they were onstage, calling attention to their wounds.

"Watch this," Justin said, directing my attention to the stage. (I had been looking down, fiddling with my recorder—making sure the device had enough digital space to capture what the speakers were about to discuss.)

"They're gonna make folks really uncomfortable now," he said.

As my eyes focused on the stage, I saw that the disabled ex-gang members were holding plastic bags and medical tubing in outstretched arms, explaining in precise and graphic detail the daily realities of life in a wheelchair. The teenagers squirmed as they realized that the men were holding catheters and enema bottles. Justin gave me an I-told-you-so look. The men onstage calmly segued from medical necessities to larger truths; their bodies now bear witness to violence—violence that can and should be prevented.

"They say when you gang bang, when you drug deal, the outcomes are either death or jail," Tony Akpan, one of the disabled speakers announced from the stage. "You never hear about the wheelchair. I didn't know this was an option. And if you think about it, it's a little bit of both worlds 'cause half of my body's dead. Literally. From the waist down, I can't feel it. I can't move it. I can't do nothing with it. The rest of it's confined to this wheelchair. This is my prison for the choices I've made."

After listening to members of the Crippled Footprint Collective, I began to see the novelty of what disabled ex-gang members were doing in Chicago. I started to realize that in Chicago, the disabled gang member emerges as a prominent figure—one who highlights the sobering realities of coming of age in a poor community under a persistent cloud of violence. Anti-violence forums like the one that Justin and I attended, and others that I would help organize, revealed aspects of the gang experience scarcely mentioned in ethnographic studies of street gangs. Contemporary scholarship fails to acknowledge that victims of gun violence are much more likely to be disabled than killed.[2] Chicago is a prime example of this trend: over the past fifteen years, more than 8,000 people have been killed, while an estimated 36,000 have been debilitated.[3]

When I sat next to Justin at that high school assembly, I wasn't aware of these statistics; nor did I know that the former gang affiliates onstage would inspire him to pursue a new career path. Soon after the talk, Justin proclaimed that he wanted to be an anti-violence activist.

"If the killings won't stop," he explained, "then we're gonna need more hands on deck."

Justin already worked at a violence prevention agency, Safe Futures; but he was now motivated to learn the craft of public speaking. He wanted to tell his story to gang-affiliated youth in Chicago and eventually start a violence prevention organization of his own. After watching the Crippled Footprint Collective, he had a new mission. "I've never been more sure about anything in my life," he said a few weeks after the assembly.

That conversation came at the beginning of what would be three years of ethnographic fieldwork in Eastwood. I had come to Eastwood to study gang violence. But I soon started realizing something else: Justin's disability was obvious because of his wheelchair. But in Eastwood, injury was everywhere. And injury took many different forms. There, people did not merely speak of injury in terms of gunshot wounds. Longtime residents saw injury in the dilapidated houses that signaled a neighborhood in disrepair; gang leaders saw injury in the "uncontrollable" young affiliates who, according to them, symbolized a gang in crisis; disillusioned drug dealers saw injury in the tired eyes of their peers who imagined a future beyond selling heroin; and health workers saw injury in diseases like HIV and the daily rigors of pain and pill management that the disease required. "These pills," an HIV patient, Amy O'Neal, told me, "they teach me that every day's a battle between life and death."

As I spent more time with Eastwoodians like Amy, I witnessed how injury invaded people's lives. People in Eastwood interpreted injury on a vast spectrum; they forced me to stop thinking of this concept as an objective condition, something that a doctor could identify or diagnose. Instead, I began to think of the myriad injuries that Eastwoodians described as encumbrances that followed them through life, weighed them down, and affected their future prospects. Even further, I saw that injury wasn't just physical. I learned that community redevelopment projects of the local government—despite its good intentions—also injured Eastwoodians; so, too, did historical emotions like nostalgia and philosophical sentiments like authenticity. Over time, this range of injurious possibilities started to inform the way I thought about the diseases and disabilities (and other kinds of physical harm, like addiction) that disproportionately impacted poor black communities like Eastwood. And I realized the limits of how scholars and experts have been talking about violence and injury, even when they are trying to help places like Eastwood.

What really struck me was this: each time that I sat in a teenager's house and listened to him tell me about the pressures to seek retribution after a close friend was killed or I heard former gang members recounting stories about being gunned down and left for dead, I immediately noticed the evidence of injury. Bodies that were partially immobilized, futures that seemed destined for pain and disappointment. Then I noticed the bulging necks and fierce eyes of Eastwoodians as they told me their stories. Bodies that despite their injuries weren't slunk or broken, but upright and inspired. Minds that weren't consigned to a life of drudgery, despite terrible odds, but were busy planning for the future. Eastwoodians weren't afraid to dream of a better life. Whether dreaming meant pursuing a new career path, imagining a different kind of gang—or both—in Eastwood, injury was intimately tied to dreaming. But how can we understand this kind of inheritance?

There are so many kinds of dreams.[4] But in the long tradition of African American activism, dreams have typically been linked to concrete aspirations for social reform. In his 1951 poem "Harlem," Langston Hughes, writer and social activist, famously questioned the outcome of a "dream deferred." Does such a dream dry up, fester, stink, crust and sugar over, or sag like a heavy load, he pondered. Then, foreshadowing the hundreds of race riots that would take place in the 1960s and 1970s, he ends his poem with an emphatic query: Or does it explode?

It wasn't Hughes, of course, but Martin Luther King Jr. who delivered perhaps the most well-known reference to dreaming, on August 28, 1963, during the March on Washington for Jobs and Freedom. Prompted by the gospel singer Mahalia Jackson, who from the crowd exhorted King to "Tell them about the dream," King departed from his prepared text and sermonized on his aspirations of freedom and equality, and how that dream would rise from the deleterious social conditions of slavery and segregation.[5] From where King stood, on the steps of the Lincoln Memorial, a black president might well have embodied the integrated society King longed to see. Perhaps this is why, as I began my field research, Barack Obama (the embodiment of an integrationist's "dream deferred") was the latest aspirant to capture the imagination of black America.

Obama's memoir *Dreams of My Father* was written just before he launched his political career and draws on his personal experiences of race relations in the United States. Determined to graduate from Harvard University (the school where his immigrant black father began his studies but couldn't afford to finish), Obama initially pursued his father's goal, but eventually came into his own by developing his potential to lead. Inner-city Chicago figures prominently in Obama's story, as he moves to the South Side after finishing law school and works for a nonprofit agency as a community organizer. From the difficulties of those Chicago days, as his program battled with entrenched community leaders and local government apathy, a politician was born.[6]

The Eastwoodians with whom I spent my days and nights over the course of three years were intimately linked to dreamers like Obama. This was not merely because he eventually became their senator and then their president, but because he learned his first political lessons in Altgeld Gardens, an inner-city neighborhood like their own. They were also linked to dreamers like Hughes, through the tortured history that led African Americans to migrate from the South and settle in northern outposts like Harlem and Chicago; they were linked to dreamers like King through civil rights organizations, such as the Southern Christian Leadership Conference (SCLC), that met and strategized in churches and parks and run-down houses all over the West Side of Chicago. Yet their Eastwood dreams were not tied to a particular social movement like the Harlem Renaissance or the civil rights crusade. No charismatic figure vocalized their aspirations for them. Quite the opposite, in fact, particularly for the young black men at the heart of this story. Local leaders often articulated the problems of their community in terms of the "crisis of the young black male."[7]

The people I lived with did not speak from a position of institutional authority; they knew that no one, except maybe green graduate students, cared much about their dreams. Nevertheless, Eastwoodians—

young and old, male and female alike—dreamed in ways that expressed desires for a different world. Now lest I be accused of suggesting too rosy a picture, I should say that these dreams were not grandiose. These were not the genre of dreams that have been Disney-fied and squashed into the storybook realm. In fact, when I first moved into Eastwood, I did not recognize residents' struggles as dreams because they were often quite banal. Safe passage to school became something to dream for, as did a stable job and affordable, livable housing. These dreams, it is critical to note, didn't always come true: Children were gunned down on the way to school; adults searched for work to no avail; the threat of displacement haunted residents daily. In the face of these hardships, the scant resources that Eastwoodians did obtain barely scratched the surface of actual need. The brutal honesty with which they acknowledged the difficulty of real change suggested that the power of such dreams is in having them and working toward them, regardless of whether or not they come to fruition.[8]

Another remarkable thing was this: Eastwoodians' dreams were tied to overcoming the very obstacles—mass incarceration, HIV, gun violence—that are often discussed by reporters, government officials, and scholars in terms of the ways they incapacitate people. Slowly, I began to realize, if injury immobilizes people, like that fatal bullet that fractures the spine, then dreams keep people moving in spite of paralysis. Everywhere I went—high schools, detention centers, churches, and barbershops—I witnessed people exerting tremendous effort in a desperate attempt to pursue their passions. The more time I spent with residents like Justin and Amy, the more I began to understand: In Eastwood, injury endows dreams with a renegade quality.[9]

Justin's goal to become an anti-violence activist was a prime example of the renegade spirit that dreaming in Eastwood required. He and I bonded during the many afternoons I spent volunteering at Safe Futures. The more we talked about the gang, the more I realized that this organization couldn't be understood outside of the community that gave birth to it. I learned that to be an anti-violence activist (or an ethnographer) in Eastwood, you had to position yourself within a community rife with social problems. This positioning entailed learning about the problems specific to Eastwood.

Redevelopment, for instance, was a hot-button issue when I was conducting research. I moved to Eastwood in 2007 as a graduate student to learn everything I could about gangs. But I soon found out that if I wanted to accomplish this goal, then I also had to learn about the ways in which Eastwoodians were grappling with the threat of gentrification. (It turned out that gang members *did* want to talk about territory and turf, but not in the ways I expected.)[10] My first task was to figure out which organizations the local gang aligned themselves with to voice their concerns about housing, and which organizations held opposing views and an alternate vision for the community; I had to recognize how the gang could sometimes symbolize all the ills of the community, but how at other times a person's gang affiliation became submerged within the larger issue of dislocation; and I had to distinguish between the times when everything I read about poor black communities like Eastwood enhanced my perspective, and the times when everything I read prevented me from seeing what was right before my eyes. This was no easy task, in large measure due to the avalanche of books and articles—on Chicago's gangs, its crumbling housing market, its impoverished and underperforming schools—that is published every year.[11]

In part because of the attention of scholars and journalists, Eastwood and communities like it attract a lot of "help." Although the neighborhood is only about two miles wide and a mile and a half in length, Eastwood has nearly 180 nonprofit organizations. There are even more churches—187—on record, many of which are committed to social reform. And these figures don't include the efforts of informal groups, schools, ministries, and block clubs. Additionally, in recent years select institutions that host a number of social welfare programs have teamed up with the city government to redevelop the community. In other words, Eastwood is awash with help, and yet it is not clear if all these efforts are really helping.

In 2007, not long after I began volunteering at Safe Futures, I met Aaron Smalls. He worked for the city's Department of Planning, and he was visiting local nonprofits as part of what he called a "scouting trip." Shortly after his visit, I scheduled a meeting with the commissioner at his office in City Hall, where he explained the local government's interest in redeveloping Eastwood. The first thing he mentioned was that this area was "doomed for failure" because residents lacked the basic skills and qualifications to secure livable wages. Though I didn't agree with his interpretation of "doom," it was certainly true that of the 41,768 residents living in Eastwood, nearly half (42 percent) were below the poverty line.

"Those who are employed," Mr. Smalls said, "often find themselves in repetitive, low-wage jobs—or without jobs altogether." I paused for a moment to scribble down his observation. This was also true; at nearly 51 percent, Eastwood's unemployment rate was three times as much as the rest of Chicago, and five times higher than the national average.[12]

"Additionally," Mr. Smalls said, waiting for me to look up from my legal pad, "with the large population of ex-offenders—who often struggle with drug addiction, poverty, low rates of education, unemployment, and unstable housing—Eastwoodians simply don't have the necessary resources to improve their community." In my notebook I drew a sharp black line beneath this statement. Here, it seemed, was where Mr. Smalls's perspective on the community diverged from the beliefs of the community itself.

The facts about Eastwood were not under dispute: 34 percent of residents between eighteen and twenty-four years of age lacked a high school diploma; and 57 percent of all Eastwoodians were in some way involved in the criminal justice system—in jail, on parole, on house arrest. It wasn't the statistics themselves but the *interpretation* that was the basis of disagreement. By the time I interviewed Mr. Smalls, I had logged many hours in Eastwood, watching residents pursue the future lives they imagined for themselves. I noticed that these residents did not deny being injured by a host of social forces (from redevelopment to the heroin trade to jail). Rather, they considered their experience of injury to be foundational to their worldview. The gaping statistical deficits were part (but only a small part) of who they were. Indeed, as these men and women vocalized their daily struggle with a myriad set of injuries, I saw that the statistical snapshots that government officials used to make sense of the inner city did more to occlude my understanding of Eastwood than enhance it.

After my meeting with Mr. Smalls, and many other similar meetings, I grew increasingly frustrated. Government officials and the residents I came to know seemed to be talking past one another. That is, the former didn't seem to comprehend what the latter demonstrated every day: in Eastwood, dreaming seemingly ordinary dreams (of being a home owner, or living in a safe and healthy environment, or even becoming an anti-violence activist) was more than an uphill battle. It was an act of defiance.

Less than a month after Justin took me to see the Crippled Footprint Collective, he began to hone his public-speaking skills. We would meet once a week in his living room—most often on Thursdays in the late afternoon. I watched as Justin tenuously gathered together details about his upbringing and folded them into a narrative about the fatal night in which he was shot and paralyzed. Week after week, he would memorize and then recite his journey about living in Eastwood and growing up in a gang.

"I joined up, and never really thought twice about it," Justin said, practicing his speech one evening in February. "It seemed like I was where I should be because a lot of my friends and family, they were all involved in the gang. So it wasn't anything new to me. But after a while, when my friends started to die, I noticed that I was surrounded by violence more and more."

I already knew the biographical details of his life. How his cousins and uncles, father and grandfather, all belonged to the "Divine Knights," the street gang that has controlled Chicago's West Side for over a half century. Yet I was in awe sitting in his living room, listening to him articulate the meaning of belonging and loss, and how the prevalence of violence altered the person he would become—that is, after his social ties to the gang started to perish, person by person. As Justin funneled a history of gang involvement into a narrative about a single violent event, he transformed the way I thought about the community and how Eastwoodians refashioned themselves through the most intimate of injuries.

Soon after I started listening to Justin, he began offering advice about the research I was conducting in Eastwood. There, in the living room of his greystone apartment, we forged a reciprocal bond. Not only were our sessions a chance for Justin to practice for the day when he, too, might speak to a crowd of high-schoolers; they became an invaluable opportunity for me to get another perspective on my field notes. Justin had lived in Eastwood for his entire life and had belonged to the gang since he was fourteen years old, so he was well positioned to counsel me on the accuracy of my initial observations about the gang and the community.

By the spring of 2008, Justin and I were so pleased with the progress we were making on our respective projects that we told other long-time residents about our Thursday-afternoon sessions. Over the next two years, a number of different Eastwoodians visited Justin's house: Mrs. Margaret Dickerson and Mrs. Francine Pearl stopped by when they wanted to strategize the most effective way to protest the city's plan for redevelopment; Tamara Anderson and Mr. Otis Ball (who is called Mr. Otis) came over when they wanted to brainstorm ideas for building a museum that showcased the Divine Knights' civil rights roots; and Amy O'Neal appeared on several occasions to practice delivering her own narrative about living with HIV. I learned a great deal about the everyday struggles of my neighbors, but just as important, I witnessed the openness and support of a community that was battered but far from beaten.

The array of Eastwoodians who came to our Thursday-afternoon sessions helped Justin craft his message. His evolving narrative taught each of us about our own projects. Listening to Justin talk about the inextricable ties between the Divine Knights and his family made Mrs. Pearl think about how the language of gang violence was employed by city planners to justify redevelopment—language that disregarded bonds of kinship. For Mr. Otis, the focus on disability triggered nostalgia for a time when the Divine Knights were more politically, and less violently, inclined. Though Justin's speeches were primarily about his upbringing and the injuries he had suffered, thanks to this kind of collaboration, he began to layer his biographical account with a broader politics about how the allure of the drug economy transformed the gang's outlook away from collective social action and toward profit making. He began to understand why gang elders like Mr. Otis held out hope that a political gang, one that had once played a constructive role in the community, could still emerge. For both Mr. Otis and Justin, the gang wasn't something that could realistically be eradicated. Therefore, they were interested in harnessing its potential toward a political end. I soon realized that their orientation toward the inner city's social problems differed from that of many local experts and from scholars around the country who came to Eastwood to understand urban poverty.[13]

When it comes to gang research, sociologists and anthropologists alike have long examined the factors that have prevented inner cities from developing sustainable institutions. In the second half of the twentieth century, when poverty, unemployment, business failure, and crime swept through larger swaths of America's cities, the urban black neighborhood—otherwise known as "the ghetto"—became the quintessential "disorganized society."[14] That is, based on the contention that social relations within a neighborhood are supposed to be orderly and recurrent, scholars regarded the inner city as deprived (or "disorganized") because it was deemed to lack the common networks and norms essential for a community to flourish.[15]

Scholars of black Chicago now tried to understand the inner city's separation from "mainstream" America. In *The Truly Disadvantaged*, William Julius Wilson gave us new insight into the social and historical circumstances of a subclass of black Americans, revealing them as living in relative remoteness from the surrounding city.[16] He characterized them as "socially isolated" because residents of urban Chicago were unable to find work and suffered from inadequate integration into the typical urban institutions.

Wilson's work helped dismantle the racist presuppositions that were still embedded in mainstream sociological scholarship of the 1970s and 1980s, which suggested that African Americans were predisposed to delinquency and violence, and which relied too heavily on notions of pathology as determinants for urban decay.[17] The causes of skyrocketing unemployment rates among urban blacks in the 1980s, he argued, had less to do with their cultural proclivities and more to do with structural factors, such as the profound shift in the economy from manufacturing to service industries. But despite Wilson's astute critique concerning strict cultural explanations for urban poverty, the way in which scholars and experts have employed his work often places the causes of disorder squarely at the feet of "the family" and "the community."[18]

As I scavenged for responses to these "culture of poverty" approaches, I was heartened by those scholars who, like Wilson, offer a different perspective on the enduring sociological concern with the ways that urban communities are organized. Philippe Bourgois, for example, has studied drug dealers in the pursuit of a difficult kind of dignity, sandwiched between the criminal justice system that targets them for detention and employers who regard them as bereft of moral virtue. These urbanites dwell in troubled, often forgotten outposts, where the 1950s promise of industrialization became a 1980s "junkyard of dreams," as Mike Davis calls it. In this wasteland, gangs package narcotics to stimulate the local economy, Sudhir Venkatesh has shown, taking it on themselves to bear the responsibility for job growth in government-neglected streets.[19]

These innovative scholars have brought to life what researchers who highlighted the distinction between the inner city and "mainstream" America have missed: the mutually reinforced tensions between local communities and their broader social and historical contexts.[20] Building on Wilson's frame of "social isolation," they emphasize the many factors, big and small, that make certain areas marginal, and by doing so, they offer a more accurate accounting of the complex mix of both causes and symptoms that constitute the inner city's ills.[21]

Like Justin, I began to hone my own approach, my own narrative of broad social historical transformations and then the daily manifestations of those decades-long changes. I noticed that when most scholars spoke about the inner city's social and economic isolation, they were referring to urban residents disconnected from neighborhood institutions and opportunities in the legal labor market. But I began to see that I couldn't understand Eastwood through the frame of isolation alone. This was because in Eastwood the wider world is perpetually present. Gang members weave in and out of community institutions like juvenile detention centers; HIV-positive teenagers and drug addicts are connected to government-sponsored churches; and dilapidated houses trigger tax incentives that spark citywide economic investment. I began to see that the very same historical factors that have spawned a theory of isolation—everything from high unemployment and crime, to the loss of manufacturing jobs in the inner city, to the evacuation of the middle class—now are a reminder that the ills of the inner city are inextricably linked to the ills of a globalizing world. The prevalence of government-sponsored anti-poverty programs, the drug trade, mass incarceration, and the growing tide of gentrification are all signs that life in Eastwood is both isolated from and burdened by the rest of the country.[22]

I wondered if I could supplement a theory of isolation with other, more fluid concepts. I was initially enamored with the anthropological approaches to governance and violence. I found them to be vital assets in my attempt to illuminate large-scale phenomena. With a focus on the practices of government, I could see Eastwood as a community that was in political and cultural transition. When development seemed a profit-able possibility, government officials brought to life a legislative lan-guage that emphasized social reform. This legislation made the uncriti-cal socioeconomic label of "the urban poor" seem normal in the eyes of local experts, who mobilized government-sponsored institutional mis-sions to measure, diagnose, count, and contain gang members, drug ad-dicts, and disease-infected residents—all in the name of uplifting the community.[23]

In a similar fashion, a focus on those social forces that normalize dis-ease, disability, and "premature death" for urban residents placed East-wood's drug problem on a macro scale. Examining the mass incarcera-tion of drug dealers and users, I could see that the 1980s "war on drugs" was directly influenced by a bankrupt local economy and a failing public school system that together funneled risk for incarceration and infec-tious disease into Eastwood. Over time, instead of examining the ways that broader social forces constricted the life choices of Eastwoodians, many community leaders came to see these inequitable social conditions as inevitable.[24]

Were I content with painting a picture of Eastwood with broad brushstrokes, these theories would have more than sufficed. They proved indispensable in helping me to see general patterns for comprehend-ing the social problems of urban poverty. But it wasn't the general I was after. The general, I felt, didn't do justice to the relationships I was forging on the ground. To honestly articulate the experiences that my neighbors were offering me, I realized that I needed to enhance these larger structural and institutional processes with a more nuanced account of the ways in which Eastwoodians moved through and made sense of their lives.[25]

After years of grappling with the sociology and anthropology literature on gang and community life, I decided that the most tenable approach was a concept of the past as an ambiguous space, as somewhere between *history-as-registered* and *history-as-lived*. In this concept, the past is both "what happened" and "that which is said to have happened."[26] Anthropologist Michel-Rolph Trouillout describes the difference: The first term emphasizes a certain large-scale social or historical process, like mass incarceration; the second term highlights the ways that these processes are understood on the ground, by the people involved in them. Of course, people always register historical events in some form or fashion. But who decides which version of history will be told? This is the critical question. Trouillot teaches us that local understandings of history are effectively "silenced" if not unearthed through ethnography, by walking the streets and talking to people, by combing through historical archives with these local interpretations in mind.[27]

Though I found Trouillout's binary invaluable, soon after my research began I started to see a third side of this ambiguous space: *history-as-emergent*. I started to see this emergent history everywhere; Eastwoodians congealed the past into communal projects that they deployed as a means to assuage their myriad injuries. I noticed that the representations of the past felt palpable, alive, not merely the backward-looking forms of history in Trouillout's distinction between what happened and that which is said to have happened. This emergent history was, more accurately, a contemplative juxtaposition between how life was, how life is, and how life could be. This comparison was forward-looking and future-oriented; and it allowed Eastwoodians to reimagine alternative pathways for themselves and their community, no matter the many obstacles between the *is* and the *could be*.

The way Justin deployed his life story to address different implications about what living with a disability means was a prime example of an alternate interpretation of how life could be. Indeed, his method of exploring the social costs of gang involvement set him apart from a number of gunshot survivors that I met in Chicago, who hoped to transcend the designation of "disabled" so that others would think of them as "normal." Justin didn't try to attain some elusive conventional standard. He didn't want to leave his past behind. He dwelled in a space between life and injury, and didn't attempt to escape.

Eventually, I realized that I had to get comfortable in this ambiguous space myself. I wanted my work to grapple with what Eastwoodians already knew; I wanted to conduct the kind of research that did not exclude ambivalence and historical indeterminacy, and in doing so found a point of departure precisely in the murkiness of everyday life. Given that meaning is always to some extent arbitrary, that social life rests on ambiguities that cannot easily be excised, I came to understand that each of our many collective worlds, in Eastwood and everywhere else, are made via the dynamic unfolding of "contestable messages, actions, and images."[28]

As I worked diligently to understand the broad picture of everyday life in Eastwood without dissolving the fine articulations of daily struggle, as I accounted for the material effect of governmental expertise and structural forces, and as I attempted to shed light on the ways that Eastwoodians envisioned alternative forms of existence, I began to see the consequences of injury more clearly. Through the eyes of Eastwoodians, I saw how injury could be crippling, but could also become a potential, an engine, a generative force that propelled new trajectories.

In the end, I came to realize that Eastwoodians are constantly plotting futures for themselves in ways that demonstrate the inner city's interconnections with broader social worlds. Seen bottom-up, the hustling and dancing, the occupying of street corners, fighting and urban strife—all the details of urban life that are often viewed in terms of death or paralysis (sometimes physical, sometimes social or spatial)—can instead be seen in terms of collective and individual striving. From the bottom up, in other words, the underside of injury is revealed.

My years in Chicago gave me access to gang leaders and grandmothers, pastors and HIV patients, drug addicts and school administrators, inmates and scholars. Hearing their perspectives helped me connect to an ambiguous space, a past retold in the present, which shapes possible futures. And the most tremendous aspect of this emergent history is what it creates: a radical refraction, illuminating the ways in which Eastwoodians shift their bodies, crane their necks, and transform injury into another way to dream.

Late Death

Eric just called to tell me that she died. He didn't say hello or what's up. Just: "She's gone." The conversation only lasted about two minutes. I had four thoughts:

My first thought was, who is "she"? My mind went to Shawn, Monica, Amy, Susan, and all the other young women I know in Eastwood. Then Eric said, "Mrs. Dickerson."

My second thought: I expected all those other women to die before Mrs. Dickerson, a grandmother who had a late death, who lived a full life. Why did the deaths of teenagers and twenty-somethings come to mind so easily?

My third thought was of her smile. Her gold-toothed smile, I should say. I thought about the time I was in the backseat of her car, and when Mrs. Dickerson turned on the ignition, a rap song blared from the speakers. She was smiling and singing along with T-Pain. I couldn't believe she knew the words. And I'm laughing—like, really laughing. It's uncontrollable at this point. And just as I'm about to get myself together, Christina tells Mrs. Dickerson that her gold tooth looks just like T-Pain's in the video. *That moment*—in a car with a seventy-four-year-old woman, listening to gangsta rap, laughing hysterically—makes me

want to understand the relationship between grandmothers and their grand-
children in the gang.

And so my last thought was how I
never thanked Mrs. Dickerson for that.

—11/26/10, 10:30 PM

CHAPTER ONE

𝔇𝔢𝔳𝔢𝔩𝔬𝔭𝔪𝔢𝔫𝔱

———✳———

OR,

Why Grandmothers Ally with the Gang

Just before noon on February 19, 2009, one dozen members of the Divine Knights Gang, all wearing red bandannas and red scarves, are waiting outside one of Chicago City Hall's many courtrooms. Today the Divine Knights have come to City Hall to oppose a redevelopment plan targeting their community. The Knights are joined by older Eastwood-ians, many of whom are part of the Neighborhood Coalition, the area's most influential political action group. Like the gang affiliates, members of the Neighborhood Coalition are wearing red — red T-shirts, red hats, red pants, and red scarves. Inside the courtroom, government officials are preparing to debate the merits of the Eastwood Plan, which calls for the redevelopment of 652 properties within the Eastwood neigh-borhood limits. Most of these properties are abandoned commercial structures, vacant residential buildings, or empty lots, all of which the Divine Knights and the Neighborhood Coalition are happy to have re-developed. What they're fighting to keep out of the Eastwood Plan are residential units that the local government has deemed "unfit for living."

Of the thirty-seven units designated as unlivable, thirty-three are occupied. Under the legislation, these thirty-three units could be acquired by the city. Once acquired, the current residents would likely be forced from their homes and into a housing market where it's doubtful they would find affordable shelter.

At the sound of clicking heels, the red-clad group turns and sees their opposition approaching. This is the Delivery Development Corporation, represented by fifteen professional-looking men and women wearing business suits and carrying briefcases. Known as "Delivery," the corporation builds and rehabilitates housing units in Eastwood. The representatives are accompanied by a group of freshly shaven black men dressed in khakis and polo shirts that don't quite fit. The men appear both uncomfortable and proud. Their powder-blue polos, emblazoned with the Eastwood Community Church's insignia, are the daily uniform of the neighborhood's recovering addicts. The men live in a rehabilitation center that, like the Delivery Development Corporation, is owned by Eastwood Community Church. Made to attend by the center's administration, they are positioned as supporters of the Eastwood Plan.

As they move closer to the group in red, the men in blue polos visibly relax their postures. They recognize the older men and women from the Neighborhood Coalition and members of the Divine Knights. Eric Childs, a former gang member, is the first to say what everyone already knows. "Look at this shit," he exclaims, pointing to the urban professionals. "They've got the grandmothers over here fighting against their own grandsons!"

In the pages to come, I will explore how, in the struggle over Eastwood's future, the community's "grandmothers" and their "grandsons" came to align themselves on opposite sides. Here, the notion of a "disreputable" gang member is linked to the conception of an "undesirable" neighborhood. When taken up by powerful institutions, such impressions can lead to a dangerously delimited logic, which goes like this: Some homes in Eastwood are dilapidated, and therefore an infusion of people and resources from outside the community must help transform it. The religious, political, and economic institutions that serve as gatekeepers for urban renewal are the ones that take this idealistic tact. They presume that longtime residents are disconnected from neighborhood institutions and devoid of resources, and therefore have little to contribute to the process of community development. Longtime Eastwoodians, in turn, experience this lack of inclusion as an affront. For them, contributing to redevelopment entails refiguring idealistic ideologies of local institutions through a pragmatic approach that seeks to render their institutional connections visible—that is, before the history they hope to preserve turns to rubble and ash.

Tamara Anderson wants to build a museum. A forty-something, second-generation Eastwoodian, Tamara is a leader of the Neighborhood Coalition, one of the most influential political action groups in the area. On the floor above her jewelry shop, located in the heart of Eastwood, Tamara wants to display a history of her hometown that includes everything from clippings and photographs of the riots that took place in the 1960s to the marches and the parades that occurred in the 1970s, to a symbolic cane signed by members of the Divine Knights. In erecting a monument to Eastwood, Tamara seeks to overcome the local media's tendency to negatively define her neighborhood for her. She hopes to make the argument that Eastwood is a historic section of Chicago and that it has the right to be preserved. This is a strategic move. A steady stream of criminal activity in Eastwood continues to make the community synonymous with violence and gangs. By calling attention to the neighborhood's non-violent past, Tamara hopes to make an overhaul of her entire neighborhood less appealing.[1]

In her efforts, Tamara collaborates with Mr. Otis, one of the oldest living members of the Divine Knights. That she is joining forces with a gang in order to save a "gang-infested" neighborhood is an irony that doesn't go unnoticed. But for Tamara, this apparent conflict of interest seems less so after she learns of the Divine Knights' politicized past— a past that, in her newfound understanding, complicates the Knights' present criminal characterization. What's more, Mr. Otis is essential to her museum project. He and his wife have maintained an archive of community life in Eastwood that dates back more than a half century. A person could get lost in all the history contained in Otis and Emma Ball's basement.

In November 2007, a little over a year before the merits of the East-wood Plan are to be discussed at a City Hall hearing, Mr. Otis, Tamara Anderson, and I are in this basement digging among the transcribed doctrines, creeds, and philosophies that form the Divine Knights' can-non of regulatory procedure. Artifacts evidencing the gang's political contributions to Eastwood are covered with dust. Tamara is looking for evidence of how glorious Eastwood was once, while Mr. Otis couples newspaper articles about the Divine Knights' community-service ini-tiatives with selections from the gang's official writings.

"There is no good reason why gang literature has to justify violence," Mr. Otis says as he sifts, knee-deep, through his homemade archive.

Days later Mr. Otis and I visit the space that Tamara hopes will be the Eastwood Museum. "I know it's not much," she says, "but it's some-thing." We walk through an empty gallery space with hardwood floors and plenty of natural light, stopping before a slender eight-foot wall roughly the size of a Chinese partition. "I was thinking we could have a section about youth here," Tamara says. "Maybe something about the programs that the Divine Knights used to have."

"I can see it," Mr. Otis says. "I have a video that I like to show. It's from the nineteen seventies. Some of the leaders are being interviewed, talking about the true meaning of the gang. We can play that." Imagin-ing the Knights' altar, he adds, "Of course, we could have some photo-graphs and newspaper articles too, and there's a cane that we used to have at the old reform school. All of the students signed it. I could also bring that in. Yeah, I'll bring in the cane."

Mr. Otis's notion of the Divine Knights, needless to say, is quite different from that of a lot of Chicago's community leaders. They see a dangerous group of thugs. He sees a constructive institution—an insti-tution that could cleanse its reputation by mobilizing around the tradi-tions he holds dear. Only the gang, from his perspective, has lost its way.

At the gang's headquarters, on a day when a fight breaks out, I am reminded of these competing conceptions of the Divine Knights. By the time I am able to reach the huddle, the fight is over. Tiko Hunt, a boisterous fifteen-year-old, fills me in. "There was some guys out here, from Canton, Ohio, I think," he says. "They came around here a couple of days ago and said they were our fam," meaning that these out-of-towners alleged to be members of the international "Family Alliance" of street gangs to which the Divine Knights belong.[2] "They said they came to see Eastwood, to visit the headquarters. But they were out here acting suspicious. These fools were taking pictures and telling people on the street that they wanted to meet with gang leaders. Colt made some calls. But ain't nobody in Ohio ever heard of these guys.

"So yesterday," Tiko continues, "Colt said if they come back, they might have a problem. And they definitely did—as you can see."

According to the Divine Knights, Eastwood, in terms of gang legend, has long been considered a Mecca. The Knights are proud of their many visitors. "Isn't it common for affiliates from other states to stop by?" I ask.

"Yeah, that's true," Tiko says. "But usually when out-of-towners come around, they're with somebody. They know somebody. They're someone's cousin or friend. These clowns tried to prove they were our fam by saying some backwards gang constitution, so Colt gave the signal and all the Knights beat them down."

Over Tiko's shoulder, Colt Pratt, in the midst of telling the beat-down story, is swinging his arms in simulation. A freshly assembled crowd of gang members listens intently. Someone asks if the visitors might have been undercover agents from a law enforcement agency— CIA, DEA, FBI—or one of the many special gang taskforce units. With each new scandal, it seems, a new taskforce—and acronym—is born.[3]

"Nah, they're too dumb to be them alphabet boys," Colt says with a smile. "The Feds would've at least done their homework. I mean, they ain't even know simple shit. Watch this." He calls on Tiko to display what, in his estimation, any respectable gang member should know. "Gang symbols. Begin," Colt orders.

Tiko strikes a military pose. Then, carefully measuring each word as if onstage at a spelling bee, the ninth-grade dropout recites from memory this paragraph found in the Divine Knights handbook:

"Cane. The cane represents strength. Symbolically, the strength the cane represents comes from our elders, who use it for physical support. The knowledge that we obtain, the wisdom that we obtain, and the understanding that we obtain is the strength that our elders have given us. The cane also represents the need for all Knights to support one another in these trying times. This symbol means: 'I'm Conscious.'"

To signal that Tiko has performed sufficiently, Colt taps him on his head. The youngster then retreats to the gang's headquarters.[4] Though the cane invokes a sense of shared consciousness in official gang discourse, for the rest of Eastwood it is a controversial symbol of ownership. When scribbled on a street sign, a school desk, or the wooden boards that shield the windows of an abandoned building, canes are an assertion that Divine Knights control the area. In Eastwood, the way in which gang members exercise this "control" might range from violent feuds over drug territories to harassing teenagers who find themselves in the "wrong" section of town.[5]

Because of a recent school closing, Tamara Anderson's niece, Patrice Anderson, has recently been the victim of such territorial harassment. One year ago, her former school chained its doors and boarded its windows. Ever since, Patrice and her friends have had to cross a rival gang's territory—the Bandits—in order to get to their new school, Brown High. Often, belligerent gang members chase them home from school. The harassment started with simple questions, Patrice tells me: *Where were they from? Were they visiting someone? Did they plan to walk through their territory every day? Did they know these streets belonged to the Bandits?*

Answers to these questions only emboldened the gang. Now that the Bandits know students like Patrice are headed from Brown High to the northernmost section of Eastwood, where the Anonymous Knights reside, they have made a habit of tormenting harmless high-schoolers for sport. Today, standing in Tamara's jewelry store, Patrice mocks the Bandits' taunts. Despite being out of breath from having just fled the rival gang, she deepens her voice into a false bluster. "This is our section of Eastwood!" she shouts. "You better run."

Tamara, though sympathetic to her niece's predicament, does not unequivocally condemn the Bandits' behavior. Her refusal to do so inspires in Patrice a harsh assessment of her aunt's newfound collaboration with the Divine Knights. "The museum project is unnecessary at best, and likely dangerous—especially if it runs the risk of glorifying these thugs," she says, her lip curled precociously. "You're just giving them another reason to think that joining a gang is cool. They already think they run this neighborhood. See"—Patrice points to a huddle of gang members near Tamara's store—"they're everywhere you look."

"I wish the world was as simple as you see it, Pat," Tamara says. "I wish things were so black-and-white. But we have to face the fact that many young people in this community are in gangs. And some of them will never quit. Over the years, I've come to realize that we've got to meet people where they're at—not where we want them to be.

"What do I say to your cousin, Christopher," Tamara continues, "when he says that he's gonna be a Divine Knight for the rest of his life? Well, I'll tell you. I say, 'You can be a different *kind* of gang member. Not one that kills people, but one that has a positive effect on your peers and on your community.'"

"I gave up on Christopher a long time ago," Patrice says. "But good luck dealing with the Knights. And good luck getting customers when you got gangbangers slinging God-knows-what in front of your shop."

At its core, Tamara and Patrice's debate is about how best to deal with gangs. Tamara has adopted a pragmatic approach. She believes it is imperative, sometimes, to strategically align herself with certain gang members. Within the Eastwood community, gang members can have different roles, and those roles are not reducible to gang affiliation alone. Some are family, like her nephew, Christopher Anderson. Others are political allies, like Mr. Otis. Others still are unavoidable presences, like Reginald "Red" Walker, a Divine Knights chief who benefits Tamara by shepherding gang members away from her store so that non-affiliated patrons feel welcome.

Meanwhile, Patrice has taken an idealistic stance. Her perspective refuses to entertain the hard-edged reality of street life, and she is fearful that empathy will ultimately morph into an excuse for criminality. In Patrice's view, her aunt's pragmatism is misguided and potentially hazardous. The "wrong" kinds of values are being rewarded. Even if the community is made a little safer in the short run, without large-scale moral transformation—a precondition, in the idealist camp, for collaborating with gangs—community leaders like Tamara are, in Patrice's estimation, aiding and abetting the activities of "disreputable" residents.

But for Tamara, and those like her who are trying to stem the daily tide of violence in Eastwood, shunning the gang altogether is unrealistic. Far beyond the walls of her jewelry shop, pragmatic urban residents remain stalwart in their determination to work with "troublesome" neighbors, including members of the Divine Knights.

With Patrice comfortably in the back of the jewelry shop, Tamara steps outside and confronts the group of Knights. Red Walker, the chief, is the first to speak up. "Hey. How you doing, Mrs. Anderson?" he says with a smile.

"I hate to disturb you boys," Tamara says. "But, Reginald, I believe we had an agreement. Did we not?"

"Oh yeah. We sure do," Red says. "We sure do, Mrs. Anderson. We were just leaving."

Four months ago, Tamara was elected president of her block club. As president, she is charged with monitoring a narrow strip of Eastwood. The position affords her political capital, some of which she has spent on forming a pact with Red: during the hours when the store is open, the Knights will find a different place to congregate. Honoring his end of the bargain for the sake of keeping his relationship with the block club peaceable, Red leads the group to an empty lot, adjacent to the building where I live.

Middle-class idealism plays a key role in how scholars and institutional leaders currently understand redevelopment. Mary Pattillo's heralded book *Black on the Block*, for example, centers on conflicted middle-class blacks who aspire to live in a historically African American neighborhood on Chicago's South Side, North Kenwood-Oakland. As they negotiate with the city's economic and political elite, the middle-class protagonists of Pattillo's study remain admirably attentive to the needs of longtime North Kenwood-Oakland residents, who, by comparison, aren't as financially stable. Alongside a number of recent books on gentrification, Pattillo argues against a simple rendering of redevelopment.[6] The standard version is this: A new class of resident sweeps into a decaying neighborhood, gives it a facelift, and harbors little regard for the people they displace in the process. But the middle-class blacks in Pattillo's story think and care deeply about processes of gentrification.

They strive to minimize the harm their presence brings to the poverty-stricken residents who have lived on the South Side for generations. In fact, they feel an ethical imperative to advocate on behalf of poor blacks, especially those who may be displaced if redevelopment proceeds unchecked.[7]

Pattillo's book—specifically the intimate portrait of privileged blacks and their motivations—has helped reorient the scholarly understanding of contemporary redevelopment. Yet her work and others in its mold are centered on the population that enters a "blighted" community from outside of it. In the community Pattillo describes, it is the middle class that often speaks on behalf of their poorer counterparts. Taking this perspective as a point of departure, I show that in Eastwood, it's not that longtime residents are disconnected from neighborhood institutions or unable to contribute to redevelopment. Rather, the local government doesn't regard their institutional connections as legitimate.

In Eastwood, many institutional leaders are similarly oriented to the middle-class residents in Pattillo's study—only with a caveat. In these leaders' eyes, the legitimacy of community contributions from poor residents is contingent upon those residents demonstrating moral transformation. Just as an attendee at an Alcoholics Anonymous meeting must begin by admitting she is an addict, longtime Eastwoodians (especially those who discredit themselves by working with and harboring sympathy for gangs) must admit they are, or have been, disreputable urban presences who now aspire to middle-class standing. Such admissions are a condition of institutional legitimacy: they are a prerequisite for gaining entry into the powerful religious-political-economic nexus that determines the scope of redevelopment projects citywide.

Most prominent among the institutions allied with the idealistic vision of redevelopment is the Eastwood Community Church. This church insists on having a central role in shaping Eastwood's future. Founded in 1978, Eastwood Community Church now administrates more government-sponsored programs than any other nonprofit in the neighborhood. Over the past thirty years, it has been at the fore of numerous community-development initiatives and social welfare programs, including the Rebirth Rehabilitation Center and Delivery Development Corporation. The Rebirth Center, responsible for bringing the men in blue polos to City Hall, is a residential program designed to equip and encourage men to reenter society after prison and/or recovery from substance abuse. The Delivery Development Corporation builds and rehabilitates housing units in Eastwood.

Eastwood Community Church's pastor, a middle-aged white man named Tim Montgomery, is the CEO and founding president of Rebirth and Delivery, respectively. Under Pastor Tim's leadership, more than four hundred men (and four hundred housing units) have been "rehabilitated." "It is no mistake that when people speak of the church, they often mention Rebirth and Delivery in the same breath," Pastor Tim has said.

The same pride and effort with which the church attempts to rehabilitate the "misguided" men of Eastwood are also directed toward changing the landscape of the community itself. But as the church tries to heal physical and emotional injuries, many residents claim its development projects inflict a form of social injury through the threat of dislocation. Longtime residents most often make this argument—namely, that the church's ability to impose a middle-class identity on Eastwood residents helps to explain its considerable influence in the eyes of the local government. Pastor Tim, a white man, has been extremely successful at advancing the notion of moral transformation as a precondition for governmental investment.[8] That a church would seize upon moral transformation should not surprise us. But perhaps this question should: In an urban landscape featuring 187 churches—all of which are vying for governmental support and most of which are led by blacks from Eastwood—how does a middle-class white man from Colorado wind up with the majority of grants earmarked for improving a "blighted" area? Many residents believe that Pastor Tim's outsider status is an asset. By inflicting a middle-class mind-set on how to transform longtime inner-city residents, Pastor Tim's church consistently narrows the lived realities of the neighborhood—and gets rich in the process.[9]

December 2008 marks the thirtieth anniversary of the Delivery Development Corporation's founding. Eastwood Community Church celebrates with a black-tie affair that takes place in the DuSable Museum of

African American History. The museum is only a few miles from East-wood, though for many in the community it seems a universe away.[10]

Prior to a formal presentation that outlines the prestigious non-profit's accomplishments, a silent auction is held. Successful business-men and -women—politicians, lawyers, doctors—write down num-bers on scrap pieces of paper, bidding on historic items. The sale of these items will help fund Delivery's agenda. Hors d'oeuvres are served: turkey soufflé in martini glasses, chocolate-covered strawberries. The guests mingle, gliding between marble statues, crystal figurines, glass-encased artifacts, and oil paintings of prominent blacks.

Following appetizers, the guests migrate to the main assembly hall. There they listen to a cappella gospel sung by two men from the Re-birth Center, Jeremy Woodall and Micah Nobel. Both men are former members of the Divine Knights; now they're stars of Rebirth's choir, which sings songs of redemption across Chicago. Those familiar with the Rebirth Center know that Jeremy and Micah are no longer par-ticipants of the program but have graduated. They are not wearing the powder-blue polos that bear the Eastwood Community Church insig-nia across the heart. Jeremy and Micah wear crisp dress shirts. In their proper church attire, these born-again singers rejoice the ways in which, through Christ, they have successfully turned their lives around. Jeremy and Micah are inspirations for the blue-shirted men in the midst of this transformative process, some of whom are in attendance. Their presence is proof of positive change that the church's programs have brought to the community.

After the performance from the Rebirth Center alums, elementary and middle school students from Heavenly Sounds, the church's gos-pel marching band, approach the stage. In the front of the band, the boys and girls are harnessed with snare drums; in back, they're strapped down with bass drums. The students call the ceremony to attention with a percussive *boom-tap-tap*, a drum roll that introduces Pastor Tim.

"As everyone knows," the pastor begins, "the first commandment teaches us to love God. But let us be reminded today that another im-portant commandment is to love thy neighbor.

"Eastwood Community Church," he continues, "started as a Bible study with a group of football players I used to coach at Brown High School. Now, when I was a teacher, let me tell you, I learned much more from the kids than they ever did from me. As a white man from a farm town in Colorado, there were many times that I felt out of place and insecure moving into an African American community in the heart of Chicago. But those players convinced me to get my master's and then my PhD. They convinced me to become their pastor.

"But before all that, in the basement of the dilapidated building which is now Eastwood Community Church, one of those kids asked me a question that none of my professors and to this day none of the renowned theologians I've met have ever asked. We were talking about how rough-and-tumble Eastwood is—the gangs and the guns—and George Saratoga asked, 'If God says love your neighbor, then shouldn't you love your neighborhood?' I was taken aback, needless to say. This question was the inspiration for the Delivery Development Corporation. And it's the inspiration for tonight's program, one that honors those who continue to love their neighborhood."

With this, the lights in the assembly hall are dimmed, and a documentary begins to play. In the film Paul Barnett, an Illinois state representative, offers testimonial on behalf of Pastor Tim and Delivery. "I told Pastor Tim," Barnett explains, "I said, 'Do your work on the spiritual end, I'll do my work on the political end, and we can transform this neighborhood.'"

Here, the presence of a prominent elected official is critical in affirming Eastwood Community Church as a notable organization deserving of government investment. What's more, the church's association with a reputable politician also works to juxtapose the image of the well-connected and "productive" resident who contributes to the community against the image of the discounted and "dangerous" urban inhabitant who invokes fear.

This point is exemplified when Barnett recalls an encounter with then-mayor of Atlanta, Andrew Young. Young lived on the West Side of Chicago in the 1960s, prior to becoming a top representative in the Southern Christian Leadership Conference, a civil rights organization. Barnett approached Young and asked about his experiences in communities like Eastwood. "And Andrew Young, he says, 'Eastwood, Chicago?' I could tell he was puzzled," Barnett explains. "He was asking himself, 'Why in the world would someone ask me about Eastwood?'"

The representative continues, "Then Young said, 'If I had died in Montgomery, Alabama, it would've been for a cause: because a racist policeman or a white southerner couldn't cope with changing times. But if I had died in Eastwood, Chicago, it would've been 'cause a drunkard had a little too much that night, for no reason at all.' This was how he remembered Eastwood. Eastwoodians shouldn't be looking up to people who resent their neighborhood, people who don't even want to be here. We should look up to the people who walk around here every day. That's the concept of Eastwood Legacies. That's what a legacy is."

The rest of the Eastwood Legacy Program is dedicated to people who grew up in Eastwood and live there still. Brian Smith went to college but came back. He now works as a business consultant for Delivery. The film highlights the basketball tournaments that Brian hosts in the summer and the web design course he teaches in the church's computer lab. Brian lives only a couple of streets away from the house he grew up in, we learn. In the documentary, he greets a postal worker standing in front of his new home, which was built by Delivery. In addition to Brian, Travis Jackson, who works for Microsoft, and Taneesha Scott, Pastor Tim's personal assistant, are also honored as "future legacies." These young black professionals were raised in Eastwood, and they all continue to sacrifice, to "give back."

Next, "present legacies" are acknowledged. The documentary bestows Margaret Dickerson and Alderman Debra Peele with this honor. Mrs. Dickerson, though well into her seventies, remains active in the community. We learn of her long-suffering: her migration from Alabama to Illinois as a young girl, and later the riots she lived through in the 1960s, the shoot-outs in the 1980s. Through all of it, her commitment to the community never wavered.

Then Alderwoman Peele discusses growing up in Eastwood. She argues that the community has taken a turn for the worse since her childhood. There is hope, however. "Through hard work, we can all make Eastwood a glorious neighborhood again," Peele says, fully inhabiting her role as a community leader.

The documentary ends with a sampling of Eastwood residents living in houses built by Delivery. One woman, Joan Stewart, is brought to tears by the memory of showing to her children the rehabilitated playground she used to frequent as a child. The building Joan is currently living in—one of the nearly four hundred that Delivery has rehabilitated—lay vacant for fifteen years, she says. A before-and-after visual of the boarded-up building turned comfortable residential home confirms Joan's story. "When I see people from Delivery on the street," she says, "I stop and thank them for doing something. God used them to do something that needed to be done."

And yet, lurking behind the professionally edited documentary, the tears and moving speeches, the hors d'oeuvres, and the silent auction is the primary purpose of this evening: Eastwood Community Church's continuing campaign to transform Eastwood into a middle-class neighborhood. Conveniently, Hyde Park, the now middle-class neighborhood to which everyone has driven for this formal affair, serves as a model.

Reformed gang members and drug addicts singing songs of redemption, young boys and girls happily taking part in the church's social programs, professionals who continue to contribute to their neighborhood through sacrifice—such displays are evidence of what the religious-political-economic nexus has already accomplished. It has provided resources in the church's effort to groom a class of residents as the soon-to-be saviors of the community.

For Eastwood Community Church, love for your neighbor and love for your neighborhood are inextricably linked. The church's passion and the sincerity of its dedication are obvious. Less obvious to many of Eastwood's longtime residents, however, is which neighbors, exactly, will receive this love. Furthermore, who will benefit from a revived neighborhood after the inevitable injuries of development—the demolition of existing houses, the increase in property taxes, among others—occur?

Delivery, the most prominent development company in the area, is naturally at the center of many residents' concerns. Sure, the church's development arm has rehabilitated homes in the past, but up until now its efforts have been relatively modest. Four hundred houses over a thirty-year period is a minuscule figure compared to the large-scale change that city planners are promising. The fear now is that new legislation will provide tax incentives for institutions like Delivery to remodel the neighborhood full stop. Consequently, a sizable segment of the population will have to relocate.

It is important to note that Eastwood's longtime residents are all too aware that when legislation similar to the Eastwood Plan was enacted in other poor areas of Chicago, many of the folks who used to live in those low-income pockets were transplanted. They—longtime residents—are at odds with institutions that they view as having an idealistic orientation; they see institutions like Eastwood Community Church and its government-supported development arm as wielders of a limited kind of moralism.

In response to the church's brand of idealism, which promotes a privileged few to leadership roles and then tasks these leaders with transforming the community (as was apparent in the celebration of Eastwood's Legacies), the Neighborhood Coalition is fighting the threat of redevelopment pragmatically. Their approach, considered more controversial than the church's, involves making their hidden connections to America's most prominent institutions visible and thus legitimate in the eyes of the local government.

Founded by Eastwood residents in 2007, the Neighborhood Coalition formed in response to a rumor that the local government was going to categorize Eastwood as a Tax Increment Financing, or TIF, district. Simply stated, TIF channels funding toward improvement projects in distressed or underdeveloped areas by using future tax gains to finance those improvements. When a road or school is built, often there is an increase in the value of surrounding real estate; this will lead, the government hopes, to new investment. The increased property value in the area generates new tax revenues. This "tax increment" is a bet on a more lucrative future and is a way to create funding for current public projects that might otherwise be unaffordable.

Many question whether TIF districts actually serve the people who live within them. Oftentimes, as investment in certain areas increases, real estate values rise and the stage is set for gentrification. The Neigh-

borhood Coalition, in particular, wants to make sure that current Eastwood residents will be able to take advantage of the "new Eastwood"
that has started to appear on billboard advertisements.[11]

Throughout the spring and summer of 2007, Tamara Anderson convenes meetings with home and business owners, leaders of nonprofit organizations, and other Eastwood residents concerned about the implications of redevelopment. On November 11, at a meeting in the House
of Worship, on Murphy Road, Tamara has promised the audience—
almost eighty Eastwoodians—that the TIF Advisory Council will be
discussed. The district's alderwoman (and present legacy), Debra Peele,
is taking applications for the council, which will advise her on what
businesses are to be constructed in Eastwood. Many in the community,
however, are skeptical about Peele's role. They are aware that religious
institutions help elect politicians and that politicians, in turn, funnel resources back to those institutions. Peele, they claim, is beholden to the
whims of the very organizations threatening to displace them.

A spot on the TIF Advisory Council is precisely the kind of involvement the Neighborhood Coalition covets. But since the committee will
be handpicked by Alderwoman Peele, and given that the application
process is so vague (only one's name, address, institutional affiliation,
and reason for wanting to be on the council are asked for), it is thought
that the alderwoman will simply choose her political allies or community elites. "Don't feel discouraged," Tamara tells the crowd. "Everyone here should apply. But when you do, make sure you do not say
you're from the Neighborhood Coalition. That might seriously hurt
your chances."

For months now, Tamara has been educating Eastwoodians on TIF.
This meeting, like the ones before it, is heavy with discussion about what
the city has done to poor communities of color in Chicago under the
guise of redevelopment. The attendees grouse about housing projects on
the North Side of the city that were dismantled and then replaced with
sleek, modern condos. "Everyone who used to live there cannot afford
to anymore," Tamara says. "And all because politicians think it is more
profitable to have a Starbucks than a poor family in their district."

At this statement, an old man stands up to challenge some of
Tamara's assumptions. By his tone I can tell that, in his view, Tamara

is falsely portraying TIF as a conspiracy theory. As would a lawyer engaged in cross-examining, the old man attempts to pin down her faulty reasoning. "You really think the government officials want to take our property? Why would they want to do that? What makes you think they will develop for-profit businesses rather than something that will benefit the entire community? I think Debra Peele is a fair woman. She's from Eastwood. Why wouldn't she give residents input?"

Eric Childs, a thirty-year-old community activist and former leader of the Divine Knights, enters the debate. "Listen, man, everyone knows this TIF business—and that's just what it is, a business—leads to favoritism for the well-connected. And in Eastwood that's Delivery. Even without the TIF, for years now Delivery has worked with national organizations like the Linder Association and the Neumann Foundation (where, by the way, the mayor's ex–chief of staff is the director) to steal people's homes. All you have to do is look on the Internet for the 'Future City's Project.' They tell you how they're going to take your land in the next couple of years." For emphasis, Eric adds, "These are the organizations that the mayor uses to kick black people out of Eastwood."

Eric is the founder and president of his own nonprofit organization, which he describes as an "applied research firm." Each morning at seven A.M. in the House of Worship parking lot, Eric assembles a group of young people in search of work, many of whom have recently been incarcerated. From there, Eric and his almost entirely black crew travel to construction sites in poor neighborhoods all around Chicago. At the sites, he causes a stir until someone from management agrees to talk to him. Eric knows that at least 15 percent of the labor force at a construction site must come from local neighborhoods, and after pulling the site's government contract from the archive at City Hall and combing over it, he's able, usually, to pressure management into hiring from his crew. If management refuses, Eric threatens to alert the proper authorities that the site in question is under the 15 percent threshold. Additionally, he often has his crew stand in front of the site's tractors. Employing this approach, Eric has gotten work for many Divine Knights.[12]

Back in the House of Worship meeting, Tamara agrees with Eric's assessment of TIF while also delicately qualifying his racially charged statement. "I don't want anyone to think that we're being biased," she says. "We're just being cautious. What we want is dialogue and transparency. We are willing to listen to anyone, which is why we've invited Delivery's board of directors."

"We got a member from Delivery's board here," Eric says. "If he wants to refute anything I've said, let him speak up."

Dennis Abner stands and clears his throat. He begins, "Well, first let me say, no, Eric—I actually don't want to refute anything you've said. I'm not here for that. And I'll be the first to admit that, over the past thirty years, Delivery hasn't always included the perspectives of community residents before starting their development projects. But they, I mean we—*we* are trying to change. That's one of the reasons why I'm on their board of directors. That's one of the reasons why I'm here tonight. I want to open my arms to the community, on behalf of the Delivery Development Corporation."

As Abner expresses his desire to fold the Neighborhood Coalition into the city's systematic plan for redevelopment, I allow myself to imagine that collaboration between two groups that care deeply for their community is possible. But, as suddenly as the prospect comes to my mind, I witness a conversation that illustrates the unlikelihood of Delivery and the Neighborhood Coalition ever banding together. It begins after the meeting when Abner joins a group of concerned residents huddled around Eric. One is a member of the Divine Knights named Sterling Johnston, who asks Eric for help finding work.

"I'm here every morning," Eric says, meaning the House of Worship. "I can make sure you get work."

Sterling, though, is anxious to get a job, and he doesn't know the full extent of Eric's tactics; he seeks reassurance. "You know I don't have any qualifications for construction work, right?" Sterling says.

"No qualifications necessary."

"That's where me and him disagree," Abner interjects. "I know all about your *organization*, and I respect what you are trying to do. But I think you should try to get these guys qualified, to be journeymen or what-have-you. They need a secure job, a piece of paper so that they can show future employers that they have some tangible experience." He adds, "The Eastwood Community Church has the 'Stable Work' program where we teach people the process of how to get a job and what to do after they get it. Eric, you may get somebody a job today, and it may be a different one tomorrow. Young man," Abner says, "I'm not going to advise you not to get a job if you need one. But Eric's plan should be a last resort."

"Tomorrow," Eric says, "your last resort will be his first paycheck."

Neighborhood Coalition meetings are comprised of residents who, like Eric, are critical of conventional routes to social mobility. For them, an unbridled faith in the principles of meritocracy is fanciful. Regarding employment for ex-felons like Sterling, such skepticism seems warranted. Eric's nonprofit is effective, in part, because construction companies would rather hire illegal immigrants than young men like Sterling, who must go on the books. To save money, they're willing to break the terms outlined in their government grant. Likewise, many Eastwoodians believe that, if given the opportunity, city officials, politicians, and developers will act in their own best financial interests and work to replace the longtime, often poorer, residents with more wealthy taxpayers. Despite the high-minded ideals that Delivery and the like espouse about maintaining a place in the community for longtime residents, those longtime residents fear the local government will flush them out, only to welcome middle-class professionals in. That is, unless they willfully inhabit the role of morally transformed resident, which most refuse to do.

Though poor by economic standards, Eastwood is celebrated for its unique residential architecture, especially its abundance of greystones. Known as "brownstones" in other parts of the country, in Chicago these limestone structures typically refer to the freestanding houses originally built between 1895 and 1920. The stone came from East Coast and Midwest quarries, and the houses were initially built with single families in mind. Eastwood has the largest concentration of greystones in Illinois, enough to have prompted the city of Chicago to enact the Greystone Project in 2004. The project's stated goals are to "estimate the number of greystones and understand the characteristics of greystone occupants." Understandably, many Eastwood residents are suspicious. For the most part, they've been excluded from any of the "assessment" processes sponsored by the city and therefore tend to view the Greystone

Project as another government-sponsored initiative that threatens to displace them under the auspices of "rehabilitation." This is why, when it comes to issues concerning redevelopment, some longtime residents have decided to take their fate in their own hands.[13]

A few days after the Neighborhood Coalition meeting, the archivist of Eastwood's past calls to ask if I would be free to come to the men's shelter at the House of Worship. I arrive there in the early afternoon, and Mr. Otis meets me in the lobby. He doesn't say anything. The old man nods slightly to indicate that he sees me and then turns his attention to a large glass windowpane. Outside, I watch people on their way to Chilly's Liquors stumbling on broken concrete. This is Murphy Road, which used to be Eastwood's main thoroughfare. It is the same road that was devastated during the riots of the 1960s when many of Eastwood's streets, along with its economy, went up in flames.

Murphy Road is parallel to James Street, where, not two miles away, Eastwood Community Church is located. The contrast is striking. Next to the church are a development corporation, a health care facility, a learning center, and a state representative's office. Next to the House of Worship reside a liquor store, vacant lots, and a dusky gas station at which homeless men hustle approaching cars, hoping to pump fuel for some pocket change.

"Some really important things—some political things—are about to happen with this church," Mr. Otis says as we enter a conference room. "See, the governor and the speaker of the Illinois House have a growing conflict. The speaker just sued the governor and won. On top of that, the speaker wants his daughter, who is now a district attorney, to run against the governor in the next election."

In his taxonomy of Illinois politics, Mr. Otis divides those who have incentive to support redevelopment from those who do not. From my understanding, his classification of political allies breaks down like this: Eastwood Community Church, the speaker of the House, and Paul Barnett (the state representative featured in Delivery's documentary) are on one side of the fence; the governor and the House of Worship are on the other. "The governor is looking for a different section of the city to support," Mr. Otis says. "Tomorrow he's having a press conference to announce a new plan for community redevelopment. At that press conference, Pastor Ray Stephens, the leader of this church, is going to stand beside him. With Pastor Ray being beside him like that, the governor is saying that he's going to support *this* church and investment on *this* street."

Just then, Eric Childs joins the group in the conference room, along with Henry Todd, a twenty-four-year-old member of the Divine Knights who has recently returned from an army tour in Iraq. "So," Mr. Otis says, "the reason why I brought you all here is because tomorrow, when Pastor Ray goes to the press conference, we have to be his security. We have to be his *foot soldiers*."

For the Divine Knights, "foot soldier" denotes a specific rank in the gang. Today many foot soldiers are street-level drug dealers. But they are also the population that Eric pulls from when a large mass of people for a political demonstration is needed. As a group, foot soldiers have historically been regarded as a loyal constituency. Unlike the young affiliates that gang leaders call "renegades," foot soldiers are both reliable and flexible enough to engage in a number of divergent missions.[14]

"Pretend this is the car," Mr. Otis says, pausing to move a chair to the center of the room. "The car is Post One. So what will happen is this"—he gestures for Henry and Eric to come forward and join him in the scenario. "Two men will get out of the car. One person opens the door for Pastor Ray. And one man stands on the other side of it. The other two fall behind like secret service agents, or bodyguards. Post Two is the door of the high school gymnasium where the press conference will take place. The two bodyguards in front get to the door first—before the pastor. One of them will open the door. The other man will follow Pastor Ray and then escort him to the podium."

Mr. Otis's strategy is a surprisingly blatant imitation of Eastwood Community Church's. Even though neither Tim Montgomery nor his church has ever had military-like security at their numerous press conferences, they've been able to secure political sponsorship by projecting the semblance of order. The church's army of programs (like the Rebirth Center and Delivery Development Corporation) and their sponsors (like Representative Paul Barnett) fortify the institutional nexus that affirms Eastwood Community Church as an organization worthy of government investment.

"We have to make sure we all look sharp," Mr. Otis says. "Haircuts and clean shaved. Black suits. Dark ties. We have to make Pastor Ray look important, so we can make Murphy Road look like James Street. We can have our own version of everything that Tim Montgomery has over there."

Compared to Tim Montgomery, Pastor Ray and the House of Worship are lacking in notable outreach programs and meaningful political sponsorship. The protection offered by sharply dressed, freshly shaven foot soldiers might make the House of Worship appear to be a top-flight institution that merits the governor's support—that's Mr. Otis's hope, at least. But just as I begin to think that this operational dry run is all about political rivalries—that Mr. Otis is merely envious of Pastor Tim because of the resources his church has been able to accumulate—he reveals something else he wants to understand: the institutional rationalities that underlie how redevelopment is imagined.

"You all have spent time in America's institutions," he says, addressing Henry, Eric, and me. "And that shapes the way you see things. Eric did five years in the penitentiary; Henry is doing his time in the military; and you're doing yours at the university. Them boys on the block already taught you that a PhD don't mean nothing out here. You wave your degree around them, and they'll rip it up and leave it in the gutter. Eric's credentials mean more than yours around here. But outside of Eastwood, they don't.

"All these years that *we've* been in *their* institutions," Mr. Otis continues, now pacing in front of me. "We've been programmed to see the world in the way other people want us to see it." At Mr. Otis's use the collective "we," which effectively recruits me to his cause, I cannot help but reflect on my own education, the project that brought me to Eastwood, and the fact that as a student from the University of Chicago, I am a representative of a powerful institution—one that, as some locals see it, imposes rules and standards on the community. My age, race, and gender intersect such that I am a prime candidate for ideological rebirth, and for embracing and advocating for Mr. Otis's vision of redevelopment.

Like Eric, who exploits the contradictions he finds within the city's legal ordinances, Mr. Otis also finds governmental classifications lacking. Still, from his perspective, being a product of America's institutions enables you to master the rationalities upon which these institutions are based. Prior to his post at the House of Worship, Mr. Otis mastered the logic entailed in a city government job, where he learned that there was more to the designation of a "dilapidated" house than merely its physical appearance. "Before I started running this shelter," Mr. Otis says, "I was working for the government. I was writing code violations on people's property on the North Side of Chicago. Then they transferred me to the West Side, where black folks live. All of a sudden, my job changed: I had a quota—had to write up a hundred violations a month. I was making money, but I wasn't happy. How *could* I be? I was putting my own people out of their houses—houses they had saved their whole lives to buy; houses their grandparents left them. I was helping to destroy my own people, and I was miserable. Finally, I had to quit. I had to come work with these men at the shelter. It's not a luxurious life. But, you know what? I'm happy. For the first time in my life, I'm happy."

This story suggests that governmental categories are not objectively precise; rather, they project precision in particular contexts and in particular moments, such as when a local government wants to acquire land in a certain area of Chicago. Like this, institutional racism becomes opportunistic as well, and the illusion of neat legal categories masks the injustice of their underlying ideologies.

The black utopia Mr. Otis envisions—a racialized imaginary, couched in masculine ideals of leadership, wherein the Divine Knights replace the Eastwood Community Church as the dominant community institution—is a conception of community that thrives in Eastwood but is never recognized in the government's articulations of what Eastwood should be. As far as Mr. Otis is concerned, Henry, Eric, and I have a duty to direct our respective understanding of the American institutions we've inhabited toward serving our community in a way that primarily benefits black people. After all, we've mastered the "habitus"—the schemata, the dispositions, the tastes—characteristic of our respective institutions, whether we realize it or not.[15]

The next day Mr. Otis informs me that the press conference is canceled on account of yet another scandal in which the governor is embroiled. I feel a sense of relief, as I am not ready to perform the role of bodyguard. But there is more to it. After our meeting at the House of Worship, I realize that Mr. Otis's concept of community would likely exclude those residents who do not buy into his idea of a black utopia.

Weeks later I am once again waiting in the House of Worship parking lot, this time at the behest of members of the Neighborhood Coalition. For weeks the coalition has attempted to schedule a meeting with the head commissioner of Chicago's Department of Planning, and thus far no one has returned their calls. Today the coalition plans to confront the commissioner, Aaron Smalls, in person, on his lunch break. Tamara Anderson, Mrs. Dickerson (another long-term resident, who received Eastwood Community Church's legacy award back in December), Eric Childs, and three members of the Divine Knights have all ridden the El together to the Department of Planning; several coalition members pick me up at the House of Worship, and we drive downtown to join them.

It is early December. In the department's lobby, children from a consortium of Chicago elementary schools are singing Christmas carols. A large group of government workers assembles to watch. Soon Mr. Smalls arrives. Tamara approaches him without hesitation, introduces herself, and hands the commissioner a package outlining the Neighborhood Coalition's concerns with the city's redevelopment plan. Mr. Smalls, visibly distracted by the carolers, takes the package and then brushes past Tamara. With three gang members standing close by, Eric steps in front of the commissioner and takes hold of his lapels. "It's very important that you take what we have to say seriously," Eric says. "You're not gonna ignore *me* like you did *her.*"

"You must have misunderstood," Mr. Smalls says. "I wasn't trying to ignore her."

"*Look*, nigger, you think this is a game?"

"Oh, you want to go there? You want to call me a nigger?"

"I'm sorry," Eric says. "You're right. You're not a nigger. You're a *mother-fucking* nigger." Jabbing an index finger into Mr. Smalls's chest, he adds, "You're the *worst* kind a nigger: A *half*-white *house* nigger who thinks he's better than *me.*"[16]

"What is it that you want?" Mr. Smalls says.

"We want you to stop trying to kick us out of our homes. Our message is clear: You keep coming after us, and somebody might come after you." On cue, the gang members standing behind Eric step forward.

Mr. Smalls says, "Wait a second. Are you *threatening* me? Should I ask one of these police officers to sit in on our conversation?"

"To answer your first question: Yes, I'm threatening you. To answer your second, I'll get the police for you." Eric approaches the building's security guard and asks him to join the huddle, explaining that he's about to "kick Mr. Smalls's ass."

Quickly, a group of police officers surrounds Eric and the gang members, and one of the officers tells them to leave. Eric obliges, hurling insults at Mr. Smalls as he exits.

Outside, he and the other Divine Knights lean against the building. "We thought you might've been arrested," I say.

"Aw, man, we're straight," Eric says. "They didn't kick us out. We *got* kicked out."

I ask him to explain the difference.

"You're a scholar, so I know you appreciate the Martin and Malcolm thing me and Tamara got going on. Now, she's the lesser of two evils. All I did was ensure that Tamara gets a meeting. Smalls was never gonna talk to her otherwise. I did what I came to do. Go back inside. You can tell them we're okay."

Back inside, the rest of the Neighborhood Coalition waits patiently. Mr. Smalls approaches the group, scanning faces. "I've just reviewed some of the points you outline here," he says, holding up Tamara's packet. "I think I understand what you all are concerned about a lot better now. Listen, I can meet with you guys today, if your schedule permits."

The Neighborhood Coalition is playing a game of urban chess. They are attempting to counter the assumption that gangs are always dangerous and, at the same time, strategically deploying the popular image of the "threatening" gang to advance their agenda. At the Department of Planning, Eric Childs and the Divine Knights showed that they were willful pawns capable of intimidating a civil servant. Once removed, the women of the coalition were granted an audience with the commissioner—pragmatic tactics in action.

Compared to the ideals of uplift that Eastwood Community Church espouses, in other words, the Neighborhood Coalition views pragmatism as a more immediate way to solve community problems. The distinction proves instructive because it allows us to understand how these disparate perspectives map on to class-based aspirations. That said, the danger in starkly contrasting idealism and urban pragmatism is that this dichotomy could be mistaken as an assertion that the Neighborhood Coalition is devoid of ideals. Such an assertion could not be further from the truth. Pragmatism is not antithetical to idealism for the coalition; rather, it is the ideal they cherish most.

Members of the Neighborhood Coalition believe that any effort to solve community problems should include the "common herd"—poor residents who, the church would say, are in need of shepherding. The coalition depends on the "lower ranks." Indeed, they make use of their intimate knowledge of institutions to expose the fact that the city government buys into a problematic rendering of Eastwood, simultaneously as internally homogeneous and externally distinctive.[17] This simple bifurcation assumes that the neighborhood is abandoned and devoid of resources necessary for it to flourish. And yet, despite the fact that gang members are threatening in the eyes of Mr. Smalls and others who serve as gatekeepers for the religious-political-economic nexus, they are vital resources for the Neighborhood Coalition. They help to convey all the ways in which government officials fail to appreciate the nuance of urban residents' own analyses of their community and, by so failing, produce injury in the process of redevelopment.

The Eastwood Plan—which focuses on the 652 properties in Eastwood that have been designated, by an independent research firm, as "unfit for living"—is part of a larger proposal to make Eastwood a TIF district. If Eastwood becomes a TIF district, these residential units may be removed or otherwise impacted. Accordingly, members of the Neighborhood Coalition have decided that a focus on housing is the best way to voice their concerns. Their goal is to prove that terms like "blighted" and "dilapidated" that the government reads as absolute are, in fact, quite subjective.

On a Tuesday in January, I meet with the same members of the Neighborhood Coalition who escorted me to City Hall in order to discuss the thirty-three occupied homes on the Eastwood Plan acquisition list. I arrive at a coffee shop at 9 AM and greet the ladies of the coalition—Mrs. Pearl, Mrs. Dickerson, and Tamara Anderson. Yet to show is Christina Hall, a young woman from the Justice Institute, a nonprofit organization that helps communities like Eastwood fight dislocation. The Justice Institute has advised other neighborhoods in Chicago battling gentrification, most recently the Mexican neighborhood of Little Village and, before that, the primarily Puerto Rican Humboldt Park.

"I've been meaning to ask you," Mrs. Pearl says. "How'd you get interested in the Neighborhood Coalition?"

"I'm trying to understand how redevelopment affects gang members," I say. "Tiko was supposed to take pictures of the dilapidated houses, and I was going to help by handing out flyers, but we decided to switch places." When it came to redevelopment, Tiko and other young gang members were initially indifferent. After working with the coalition, though, they began to care deeply about the matter.

"Well, I know you're at the university and all," Mrs. Pearl says. "And I think it's good that you're getting an education. But those boys you '*study*'—those boys ain't gang members to us. They're our grandbabies. If one of them was at this table, that's the capacity he would be serving in."

Mrs. Dickerson nods in agreement. "Mmm-hmm."

During the drug boom of the 1970s and '80s, when significant numbers of Eastwoodians were either incarcerated for drug trafficking or struggling with addiction, grandparents fulfilled a vital parental role in the community. Owing to community ruptures, grandmothers in particular were often responsible for raising or helping to raise a generation ravaged by the "war on drugs." These grandsons *should* be the heads of their households and *should* be future leaders of Eastwood—this is the popular, and often uncritical, sentiment within the community.[18] Still, from the grandmothers' perspective, turning your back on urban residents merely because they have not lived up to the expectations that society has placed on them damages the community as a whole. This perspective helps explain why the women of the Neighborhood Coalition take accountability for—and ownership over—the gang's image of violence. Gang members, they might say, are like those sturdy, boarded-up greystones: rugged and frayed on the exterior, but valuable assets at their core.

Christina, when she arrives, compliments the neighborhood. "I didn't get to see it last night because it was dark, but it's really beautiful," she says.[19]

"Yes, it is," Tamara says. "It's beautiful. But it's changing. This is the first Starbucks in Eastwood. It opened up a couple of months ago."

"Hopefully we can stop the TIF before there's one on every corner," Christina jokes.

I notice Pastor Tim in the back of the shop. As he walks over, Tamara explains to Christina that he's the leader of the Eastwood Community Church. "You ladies look so gorgeous today," he says. He hugs his three neighbors, introduces himself to Christina, and then asks me how I'm doing. The question, though, seems to be *what* am I doing. Pastor Tim is familiar with my research. He has driven by street corners and seen me congregating with gang members. But today he seems surprised that I am with three older women—his opponents—and a young white lady. After a brief chat, he mentions another obligation and leaves. Christina, aware that Pastor Tim is for TIF, questions his cordialness.

"Well, part of it is his personality," Tamara says. "He's a nice guy. A lot of good people think that the TIF is a positive thing. He's one of them. But also, he's not from here. About thirty years ago, he recruited people to join his church, to come to Eastwood, and to help uplift the community. The problem with the church's philosophy is that they think you have to kick some people out in order to uplift it—you know, get rid of the riffraff. They see some of us as problems. We see them as relatives."

First on Christina's to-do list is outreach. She wants the women thinking about ways to involve more organizations with the Neighborhood Coalition. Mrs. Pearl offers to contact the NAACP; Mrs. Dickerson, the Urban League. Tamara shoots them down, however, claiming that both organizations are "co-opted" and therefore unwilling to work with the coalition.

"Even so," Christina says, "Make them declare themselves publicly. Make them pick a side. We can even start thinking about conservative organizations as well. That's the beauty of framing it as an issue of displacement. You get the organizations on the left interested in civil rights, and the organizations on the right interested in property rights."

Tamara takes heed and begins to list a number of groups with various political orientations—the AARP, an organization for home owners, the National Council for Churches, and the United Block Club Council. The breadth of her political network—and, by extension, the coalition's—is staggering. Because poor urban residents are often thought to be isolated from mainstream political institutions, it is especially encouraging to see the Neighborhood Coalition's ethos of collaboration emerge.[20] Although these women are often suspicious of outsiders' motives when it comes to Eastwood, they don't isolate themselves from all forms of government and institutional authority. Nor are they strictly opposed to development. The coalition might be weary of institutional influence, but its members nevertheless maintain complexly braided relationships with institutions that do not share their outlook on the inner city.[21]

The strategy session over, we pile in Mrs. Dickerson's Cadillac to begin the coalition's version of a reconnaissance mission. The objective is to contest local government efforts to categorize certain homes as undesirable. This neighborhood, the grandmothers argue, cannot be wholly categorized as blighted. The Eastwood Plan omits the neighborhood's abundance of life. In addition to inverting governmental rationalities based on their comprehensive understanding of them, the members of the coalition mobilize the most "disreputable" among them to contest the influential nexus and to display the vast reach of their social network. We witnessed this when they exhibited the gang's political contributions in their museum; when they enlisted gang members to attend their meetings; when they made it clear that ex-felons can and will play a chief role in acquiring resources for their streets; and when they called on those same ex-felons to secure the attention of indifferent politicians. In sum, the Neighborhood Coalition considers the hidden virtues of the troublesome to be their secret weapon.[22]

Mrs. Dickerson cranks a loud engine that gets drowned out by even louder rap music. The song is called "I'm So Hood," and she raps along with it:

"I'm so hood
I got these gold [teeth] up in my mouth
If you get closer to my house
Then you'll know what I'm talking about
I'm from the hood."

My eyes meet Christina's, and we share a long laugh, the old ladies' wigs bobbing to the beat. "Give me the first address," Mrs. Pearl says, interrupting the song. Tamara reads from the city's acquisition list of thirty-three properties.

"It's interesting the logic they use to put houses on the acquisition list," Mrs. Pearl says. "I can't figure it out. Some of the houses are on the corner, next to vacant lots or commercial establishments. Others are already vacant, boarded up and for sale."

Christina explains that by listing vacant houses next to the ones they want to acquire, the city is trying to make the argument that the area itself is blighted. She instructs me to only take pictures of the "perfectly fine" houses, meaning those that aren't boarded up.

Soon we come to a home owned by a ninety-year-old woman named Mrs. Ida Conwell. Mrs. Conwell's parents came to Illinois as slaves, and she was proud to buy the house in which they lived in freedom. Her wish is to hand the house down to her children. The property is sandwiched between a church and a vacant lot. It is weather-beaten and humble, badly in need of painting, but appears structurally sound.

As the day progresses, we photograph several "perfectly fine" homes that the coalition plans to present as proof that the "unfit for living" label the city has attached to many residential units in its assessment is inaccurate. "See, young man," Mrs. Pearl says as we drive from house to house: "This is where you learn how to plan and how to fight. How to be a soldier. You ain't gonna learn this at the University of Chicago."

"Ain't nothing wrong with college, boy," Mrs. Dickerson says. "Don't let nobody—especially no old lady—tell you anything different. I went to Tilson College in Montgomery, Alabama, Valley High School in

Birmingham, Western Middle School, and Harper Hill Elementary. They changed the name, though. It used to be Harper Hill Elementary School for *Negroes*." Mrs. Pearl rolls her eyes, an indication she's heard this many times over.

"But Mrs. Pearl did get something right," Mrs. Dickerson continues. "You gotta be a fighter, like Harriet Tubman." Tubman, of course, is best known for helping slaves escape the South via the Underground Railroad, and less so for being the first female foot soldier to lead a military force into battle during the Civil War. "Old Harriet said, 'I might've been born a slave,'" — and here Mrs. Dickerson pauses, waiting for her friend to join her. Laughing, and in unison, the women finish what seems, for them, a favorite saying: "'But I ain't gonna *die* one.'"

On the day of the Eastwood Plan hearing, those dressed in red and those dressed in blue slowly file into the bustling City Hall courtroom. Tamara, Mrs. Pearl, Mrs. Dickerson, Mr. Otis, and Eric Childs are all there, on the right side of the courtroom. Pastor Tim is on the left side, in the front row, within earshot of the corporate lawyers, city council members, and local politicians who flank the judge. Everyone is eager to learn the fate of Eastwood's future. The hearings begin with testimony from the Delivery Development Corporation and the Eastwood Community Church; new housing in this blighted community is needed, both groups say. Some of the congregants, currently living in homes that Delivery has rehabilitated, speak about how the church's development arm has provided them with an affordable place to live. One church member states that being able to live in a new home on James Street was a crucial step in his recovery from drug addiction. Not having to walk past the hollow storefronts with illicit goods inside, he says, quite literally saved his life. Next, more than thirty residents from the Neighborhood Coalition present their case. They arrange poster-size pictures of structurally sound residential units that have been, in their opinion, wrongly labeled "dilapidated." Each of the thirty witnesses speaks about injustices they have experienced. They will defend their houses with their lives, they say—chain themselves to each others' porches, if need be.

The government officials' reactions are varied. Some nod in support of the blue-shirted men and the church's advocacy of redevelopment; others shake their heads as if the scene that the red-shirted residents paint—of sheriffs prying old women from their shacks—is too much to comprehend. One member of the city council chides the development corporation for not including the entire community in the process of neighborhood change. "This should be a good thing. Everyone wants a roof over their head and a safe place to live. How can I feel good about this legislation, knowing these people think they will soon be homeless because of it? I don't feel good about this," she says, then repeats. "For the sake of the public record, I must say that I do not feel good about this."

Regardless, all eight city council members vote in favor of the legislation. The Eastwood Plan is rubber-stamped into law. Over the next decade, the projected tax revenues from rising property values will fund a number of new projects for the church's development corporation. Many residents hope that the Eastwood Community Church will continue to transform lives through programs like the Rebirth Rehabilitation Center. But the question troubling the grandmothers is likely one that Tim Montgomery did not anticipate: Will my grandson have a place to call home once he's recovered?

During the testimony, some of the grandsons in blue polos manage to get the attention of their relatives and neighbors on the other side of the aisle. The men mouth, *I'm sorry*. And later, as everyone files out of the building, Eric Childs tells Mrs. Pearl that the men in blue polos want to make it known that they had not meant to betray their families and their neighbors. "They said they had no choice but to be there. The Rebirth Center mandated their attendance."

But Mrs. Pearl raises her hand, as if to say that no such apology is necessary. She then sets down one of the posters—a shabby-looking house with a strong foundation. She says, "I know what side of the room they were on. But more importantly, I know what's in their hearts."

Early Funerals

One day, I'm on Mr. Otis's stoop, scribbling in my notepad, trying to keep up as he tells me stories like his life depends on it. And I can't use my recorder. I have to write when he's talking, because Mr. Otis takes offense if you don't keep pace—he takes it as a sign that you don't think what he's saying is important. So, he's talking about gang history. And not the mythology you'd find in gang handbooks, but what the Knights actually did in the neighborhood—stories I've never heard before.

We're on his stoop until dark, Mr. Otis telling me about the old chiefs. Then he looks down and says today's leaders aren't like the leaders of old because they won't help you pull yourself up by your bootstraps. "Nope," he says. "They'll snatch the shoes off your feet."

The next day, as I'm headed downtown to the public library where Eric works part-time, I hear chanting as soon as I get off the El. It has to be over a thousand people, mostly teenagers. And it's loud. I mean, everyone is chanting. It takes a second to figure out what they're saying, but I finally make it out: "WE WANT FUTURES, NOT FUNERALS." I make my way through the crowd and move closer. Through an opening I see a stage and four rows of empty school desks. The desks have placards, each with a name. I recognize one name, and then another, and then another: the students in Chicago who've been shot and killed this year. Alongside the placards, pairs of gym shoes, once the property of the deceased students, are placed on the top of each desk.

—12/14/08, 1:22 AM

CHAPTER TWO

𝕹𝖔𝖘𝖙𝖆𝖑𝖌𝖎𝖆

———✳———

OR,

The Stories a Gang Tells about Itself

At the West Side Juvenile Detention Center, inmates hardly ever look you in the eyes. They almost never notice your face. Walk into a cell block at recreation time, for example, when young gang members are playing spades or sitting in the TV room watching a movie, and their attention quickly shifts to your shoes. They watch you walk to figure out why you came. I imagine what goes through their heads: *Navy blue leather boots, reinforced steel toe, at least a size twelve. Must be a guard.* That's an easy one. Then the glass door swings open again. *Expensive brown wingtips, creased khakis cover the tongue. A Northwestern law student come to talk about legal rights.* Yep.

Benjamin Gregory wears old shoes, the kind a young affiliate wouldn't be caught dead in. Still, the cheap patent leather shines, and, after sitting in the Detention Center's waiting room for nearly an hour and a half, the squeak of his wingtips is a relief. It's a muggy day, late in the spring of 2008. "I've been coming here for five years now," he says. Mr. Gregory is a Bible-study instructor. "It's a shame, but you can just tell which ones have their mothers and fathers, or someone who cares about them at home. Most of these kids don't. Their pants gotta sag below their waist, even in prison garbs. All they talk about is selling drugs and gym shoes."

Though I generally disagree with Mr. Gregory's assessment of today's young people—"hip hoppers," as he calls them, not knowing I'm young enough to be counted in that group—his observations are, if not quite accurate, at least astute. The relationship between jail clothes and gym shoes is direct, with gang renegades—young gang affiliates that seasoned members claim don't have the wherewithal to be in the gang—at the center. Until recently, Mr. Gregory couldn't tell you what a gang renegade was; I educated him on the topic when he overheard inmates tossing the term around for sport. According to gang leaders, I tell him, renegades are to blame for gang underperformance. They are the chief instigators of "senseless" violence, say the leaders, and thus deserve any form of harm that befalls them, be it death, debility, or incarceration.

Ironically, Mr. Gregory's generalized depiction of drug- and shoe-obsessed young inmates (shared by many prison guards, teachers, and even some scholars) can be compared to the way that gang members view renegades. Just as community leaders criticize the actions and affiliations of longtime Eastwoodians, older generations of gang members level critiques at young renegades. In what follows, I complicate the assumptions many have made about renegades by examining subjective versions of the Divine Knights' contested—and contestable—history. Investigating the gang's fraught past will help make clear the problems facing them at present. In the midst of unprecedented rates of incarceration, the anxieties that gang members harbor about the future of their organization are projected on to the youngest generation of gang members—and their gym shoes.

More precisely, in Eastwood gym shoes are emblems that embody historical consciousness. For gang members currently forty to sixty years old, the emergence of gym shoes signaled the end of an era in which affiliates pursued grassroots initiatives and involved themselves in local protest movements. Meanwhile, for the cohort of gang members who came of age in the "pre-renegade" era—those twenty-five to forty years old—gym shoes recall a time of rampant heroin trafficking, when battalions of young soldiers secured territories within a centralized leadership structure. As the younger of the two generations remembers it, this was the moment when loyalty began to translate into exorbitant profits. That these two elder generations of the Divine Knights hanker for a centralized and ordered system of governance places an enormous amount of pressure on the current generation, those gang members who are fifteen to twenty-five years old. We'll see that just like the game of shoe charades that inmates play in jail, a renegade's footwear can reveal his place in the world.[1]

In the Divine Knights' organization, wearing the latest pair of sneakers is considered the first status marker in the life and career of a gang member. For new members, having a fashionable pair of shoes signals one's position as a legitimate affiliate. Later, in your teens and twenties, success is measured by whether a person can afford a nice car or your own apartment.[2] Because most of the teenagers referred to as "renegades" have yet to progress to that stage, however, a fashionable pair of gym shoes is the pinnacle of possession.[3]

Even though gang leaders claim that nowadays fashion trends of young gang members are too beholden to mainstream dictates and don't represent Divine Knights culture, gym shoes remain the badge of prestige most coveted by renegades.[4] Exclusivity—whether or not the shoes can be easily purchased in ubiquitous commercial outlets like Foot Locker or only in signature boutiques—goes a long way in determining a shoe's worth, as does pattern complexity: the more colors and textures that are woven onto the canvas of the shoe, the more valued that shoe becomes.

Over a two-year period during which I listened to gang members in informal settings and in facilitated focus groups with Divine Knights affiliates, I was able to sketch an outline of attributes concerning the five most popular gym shoes worn by young gang members in Eastwood. In some cases, the most popular brands and fashion trends evoke a past that has ceased to exist. Behold, the renegades' "Top 5" (in ascending order of significance):

№ *5*

"Tims," or Timberland boots ($180),[5] are not technically a gym shoe. But in Chicago, the term is used as a catchall for various types of men's footwear. The construction boot of choice to tackle Chicago's harsh winters, Tims serve a functional purpose in addition to being appreciated aesthetically. The tan "butter-soft" suede atop a thick rubber sole with dark brown leather ankle supports are staples of any shoe collection (and are typically the first pair of boots a renegade purchases). If in addition to the tan suede variety a person has Tims in other colors, he or she is thought to be an adept hustler in any climate.

№ *4*

"Recs," or Creative Recreations ($150), are a relatively new brand of sneaker popular with young renegades because they are available in an array of bright colors. Multiple textures—metallics, suedes, rubbers, and plastics—are combined on the synthetic leather canvas of each shoe. Recs also have a distinctive Velcro strap that runs across the toe. Considered the trendy of-the-moment shoe, Recs are held in high esteem by young renegades because they can only be found in a select few of Chicago's signature boutiques.

№ *3*

As the Timberland boot is to winter, the Air Force One, commonly referred to as "Air Forces" or "Ones" ($90), is to the other three seasons. This shoe is a staple of the renegade's collection. If a young gang member has only one pair of gym shoes, they will likely be Ones. Although they come in a variety of color combinations, most affiliates begin with either white or black, with the expectation that their collection will grow in colorfulness. Moderately priced and available in a vast number of different styles, these might be the most popular gym shoes in the Divine Knights society.

№ *2*

Signature shoes ($165).[6] Young renegades are also likely to purchase the signature shoe of their favorite basketball player. For some, that's Le-

Bron James; for others, Kobe Bryant or, perhaps, Chicago-local Derrick Rose. As a gang member, one's affinity for a particular player can override the aesthetic judgment of his or her friends. Still, purchasing a signature shoe entails several calculations, including when the shoe was released, which company manufactures them, and the popularity of the player in question at the moment. Given the danger that one's signature shoe may prove undeserving of the time and effort invested in its purchase, no current player's footwear can surpass the model by which the success of his shoe will no doubt be measured: Michael Jordan's.

№ 1

"Jordans" ($230) are *the* signature shoe.[7] A pair of Jordans is valuable to the young renegade for a number of reasons, chief among them that Michael Jordan, considered the greatest basketball player of all time, made his name playing for the Chicago Bulls. Thus, a particular geographic pride is associated with his apparel. Second, the risks involved with purchasing this particular signature shoe are greatly reduced because Jordan's legacy is cemented in history. Third, since the first shoe one buys are not usually Jordans (because they are so expensive), there is a sense of achievement connected with finally being able to afford a pair.[8]

Pre-renegade era Divine Knights can recall down to the year—sometimes even the day—that they purchased the same model of shoes currently being worn by young renegades. That older gang members hypocritically hassle renegades for the same consumer fetishes they themselves once held dear bolsters the point that gym shoes have accrued additional symbolic value. At once, they point to the past and the future, similar to Eastwood's greystones. Recall that greystones reference the past, specifically an era of Great Migration during which blacks traveled from the South to the Midwest in search of manufacturing jobs. At the same time, greystones are the primary form of capital for governmental investment. Just as city planners project future tax revenues based on empty and abandoned domiciles, a young renegade speculates on his future by buying a pair of Jordans.

For the Divine Knights, this form of speculation has, historically, required a young affiliate to position himself as a noteworthy member, thereby attracting the attention of a gang leader. Ideally, that leader will take a young Knight under his wing, bestow that affiliate with responsibilities, and reward his hard work with a share of the organization's profits. In such a climate, adorning oneself with the most fashionable pair of shoes is a precondition for a person to prove himself worthy of the gang's investment. A symbol of speculative capital, gym shoes—like greystones—are endowed with a double quality: They express highly charged notions of social mobility for one generation; and for another, older generation, they evoke a sense of nostalgia.

To fully understand the way in which the renegade's gym shoes trigger an idealized notion of the past, it's productive to dwell for a moment on the idea of nostalgia itself. From the initial use of the term—in 1688, when Johannes Hofer, a Swiss doctor, coined the term in his medical dissertation—nostalgia has been used to connect forms of social injury to the physical reality of the body. Hofer combined two Greek roots to form the term for this newfound malady: *nostos* (return home) and *algia* (longing). It describes "a longing for a home that no longer exists or has never existed."⁹ Among the first to become debilitated by and diagnosed with this disease were Swiss soldiers who had been hired to fight in the French Revolution. Upon returning home, these soldiers were struck with "nausea, loss of appetite, pathological changes in the lungs, brain inflammation, cardiac arrests, high fever, and a propensity for suicide." One of nostalgia's most persistent symptoms was an ability to see ghosts.¹⁰

To cure nostalgia, doctors prescribed anything from a trip to the Swiss Alps to having leeches implanted and then pulled from the skin, to sizable doses of opium. Nothing seemed to work. The struggles of ensuing generations only confirmed the difficulty, if not impossibility, of a cure. By the end of the eighteenth century, the meaning of nostalgia had shifted from a curable, individual sickness to what, literature scholar Svetlana Boym once called an incurable "historical emotion."¹¹ The burdens of nostalgia—the pressing weight of its historical emotion—are still very much with us. Interrupting the present with incessant flashes of the past, nostalgia retroactively reformulates cause and effect, and thus our linear notions of history.

"I love this walking stick," Mr. Otis says to me. "And it's not just 'cause I'm an old man, either." He taps the stick on his stoop, adding, "I've had it since I was your age."

Of all the Divine Knights symbols, the cane is Mr. Otis's favorite. This is ironic, given that young gang members increasingly need canes as a consequence of the very violence Mr. Otis laments. Still, this seasoned gang veteran doesn't associate his cane with injury but with pride and a masterful breadth of knowledge about his organization. When he was young, Mr. Otis tells me, canes, a symbol of gang unity, were hand-drawn on the custom-made shirts the Knights wore. Nowadays, Mr. Otis's generation often contrasts the stability of the cane and its understated sophistication against the extravagance of sneakers. Why, I ask on a dusky October evening, is the cane his most cherished emblem? Mr. Otis clenches his hand into a fist, then releases one digit at a time, enumerating each of the gang's symbols.

"Well, the top hat represents our ability to make things happen, like magicians do," he says, wiggling his pinkie. Next comes the ring finger. "The dice represents our hustle. You know what they say: Every day as a Divine Knight is a gamble. The playboy rabbit," he continues, "represents that we're swift in thought, silent in movement, and *sm-o-o-th* in deliverance. Of course, the champagne glass represents celebration." Mr. Otis pauses briefly. "You can probably tell that all of these symbols have the young boys thinking that gang life is about trying to be pimps and players. But the cane"—signified by the pointer finger—"the cane represents consciousness. The knowledge that you must rely on the wisdom from your elders. The cane represents that we have to support one another—and support the community—to survive."[12]

We can't see much on nights like this, but that doesn't stop us from sitting on the stoop and watching the corner. The lights on Mr. Otis's street either don't work or are never on. In fact, were it not for the lamppost at the street's end that serves as a mount for a police camera, the streetlights wouldn't serve any purpose at all. Residents dismissively refer to the camera as the "blue light." The device, which rests in a white box topped with a neon blue half-sphere, lights up every few seconds. Stationed to surveil the neighborhood, the blue light fulfills another un-intended purpose: in the absence of working streetlights, the intermit-tent flash nearly illuminates the entire street. It is a vague luminescence, but just enough to make clear the molded boards of the vacant houses across the street. You can also distinguish the occasional trash bag blow-ing in the wind, like urban tumbleweed.

And you can spot the T-shirts—all of the young Eastwoodians in white tees—but that's about all the blue light at the end of the street can brighten for Mr. Otis and me. From where we sit, you can't identify the owners of those shirts; their faces aren't perceptible, not even their limbs—just clusters of white tees floating in the distance, ghost-like. Mr. Otis, a veteran both of Eastwood stoops and Eastwood's oldest gang, sees the ghosts as fleeting images of the "good ol' gang," as he calls it—a gang about to sink into oblivion.[13]

Mr. Otis watches the street intently, as if he's being paid for the task. And in a sense, he is: central to Mr. Otis's work at the House of Worship's homeless shelter is the supervision of his neighborhood. His street credentials, however, are far more valuable than anything he can see from his stoop. Mr. Otis was one of the first members to join the nascent gang in the 1950s. This was during the second Great Migration, when African Americans moved from the South to Chicago, settling in European immigrant neighborhoods. Back then, black youths traveled in packs for camaraderie, and to more safely navigate streets whose resi-dents resented their presence. Because they were known to fight their white peers over access to recreational spaces, the image of black gangs as groups of delinquents emerged.[14]

Mr. Otis became a leader of the Divine Knights in the 1960s, around the age of twenty-six. For the next forty years, he was—and remains—prominent both in the gang and in the community. Nowadays, he speaks about his youth with a mix of fondness and disdain. The two great narra-tives of his life, community decline and gang devolution, are also inter-woven. "Things were different when we were on the block," he says. "We did things for the community. We picked up trash, even had a motto:

'Where there is glass, there will be grass.' And white folks couldn't believe it. The media, they were shocked. Channel Five and Seven came around here, put us on the TV screen for picking up bottles."

In these lively recollections, Mr. Otis connects the Divine Knights' community-service initiatives to the political struggles of the civil rights movement. As a youngster, Mr. Otis was part of a gang whose stated goal was to end criminal activity. Around this time, in the mid-1960s, a radical new thesis articulated by criminologists and the prison-reform movement gained momentum. These researchers argued that people turned to crime because social institutions had largely failed them.[15] Major street gangs became recipients of private grants and public funds (most notably from President Johnson's War on Poverty) earmarked for community organization, the development of social welfare programs, and profit-making commercial enterprises.[16] The Divine Knights of the 1960s opened community centers, reform schools, and a number of small businesses and management programs. Such were the possibilities when Reverend Dr. Martin Luther King Jr. relocated his family to a home near Eastwood.

In local newspaper articles, King explained that his decision to live on the West Side was political as well as purposeful. "I don't want to be a missionary in Chicago, but an actual resident in a slum section so that we can deal firsthand with the problems," King said. "We want to be in a section that typifies all the problems that we're seeking to solve in Chicago."[17]

King's organization, the Southern Christian Leadership Conference (SCLC), geared up for a broad attack on racism in the North. Their first northern push focused on housing discrimination; and they referred to it as "the open-housing campaign" because the SCLC wanted to integrate Chicago's predominately white neighborhoods.[18] As the SCLC gathered community support for their cause in May 1966, they developed relationships with Chicago's street gangs. On Memorial Day, a riot broke out after a white man killed a black man with a baseball bat. Chaos ensued, resulting in the destruction of many local businesses. Gang members were rumored to be among the looters. Some civil rights leaders, in turn, feared that a spate of recent riots might jeopardize their campaign of nonviolence. When, during a rally at Soldier Field, a gang affiliate overheard a member of the SCLC state his reluctance to involve "gang fighters," Chicago gang members (including many Knights) took this as a sign of disrespect and threatened to abandon King. A Chicago gang member was quoted as saying:

> I brought it back to [a gang leader named] Pep and said if the dude feel this way and he's supposed to be King's number one man, then we don't know how King feels and I believe we're frontin' ourselves off. Pep say there wasn't no reason for us to stay there so we rapped with the other groups and when we gave our signal, all the [gang members] stood up and just split. When we left, the place was half empty and that left the King naked.[19]

Days after the Soldier Field incident, in an effort to mend fences, King set up a meeting in his apartment and reassured gang members that he "needed the troops." The Divine Knights were among the Chicago gangs to subsequently reaffirm their allegiance to King. After meeting with various gangs, top SCLC representatives were confident that gangs could not only be persuaded to refrain from rioting, but might also be convinced to help calm trouble that might arise on their respective turfs. Moreover, "the sheer numbers of youths loyal to these organizations made them useful to the Southern Christian Leadership Conference's objective of amassing an army of nonviolent protesters—even if including them came with the additional challenge of keeping them nonviolent."[20]

In June 1966, the Divine Knights were persuaded to participate in the two marches that Dr. King led into all-white neighborhoods during the Chicago Freedom Movement's open-housing campaign.[21] Inspired by the movement's demand that the Chicago City Council increase garbage collection, street cleaning, and building-inspection services in urban areas, the Knights organized their own platform for political action. They scheduled a press conference with local media outlets to unveil their agenda on April 4, 1968. But just before the reporters arrived, King was assassinated. Less than twenty-four hours later, Eastwood erupted in riots. The fires and looting following King's murder destroyed many of the establishments along Murphy Road, Eastwood's major commercial district at the time.

Many store owners left the neighborhood when insurance companies canceled their policies or prohibitively increased premiums, making it difficult to rebuild businesses in their previous location. This cycle of disinvestment, which peaked after King's murder but had been steadily increasing since 1950, affected all of Eastwood's retailers. By 1970, 75 percent of the businesses that had buoyed the community just two decades earlier were shuttered. There has not been a significant migration of jobs, or people, into Eastwood since World War II.[22]

In the decades after the massive fires and looting, Mr. Otis and other gang elders maintain that the Divine Knights saw their power decline because they could do little to stop the other factions of the Knights from rioting. Neighborhood residents not affiliated with the gang were likewise dismayed. Here was evidence, with King's murder, that the injustices allegedly being fought by the Divine Knights were, in fact, intractable. From Mr. Otis's perspective, the disillusionment that accompanied King's death, and the riots that followed—not to mention other assassinations, such as that of Black Panther leader Fred Hampton—all but ensured a downward spiral. The noble promise of the civil rights era was shattered, its decline as awful as its rise was glorious.

For Mr. Otis, the modern-day Divine Knights are as much about their forgotten history of activism as anything else. So on nights such as these—sitting on his stoop, watching the latest generation of gang members—he feels it his duty to share a finely honed civil rights legacy narrative with a novice researcher. "Take notes on *that*," he says. "Write *that* down. We, the Divine Knights, got government money to build a community center for the kids. We were just trying to show 'em all: gangs don't have to be bad, you know. Now these guys don't have no history. They're 'Anonymous,'" Mr. Otis says sarcastically, referring to the name of one of many factions in this new renegade landscape, the Anonymous Knights.

Out in front of Mr. Otis's stoop, ten or so gang members face each other like an offense about to break huddle. And then they do just that. The quarterback—Kemo Nostrand, the gang leader—approaches, retrieves a cell phone from his car, and then rejoins the loiterers. I ask Mr. Otis about Kemo and his crew: "Are they as disreputable as the younger gang members?"

"Look at 'em," Mr. Otis says. "They're all outside, ain't they? Drinking, smoking, wasting their lives away. They're all outside."

Nostalgia for the politically oriented gang is a desire for a different present as much as it is a yearning for the past. In Mr. Otis's lamentations about the contemporary state of the gang, structural changes in the American social order are reduced to poor decision making. Mr. Otis and gang members of his generation fail to acknowledge that the gang's latter-day embrace of the drug economy was not a simple matter of choice. The riots also marked the end of financial assistance for street organizations wanting to engage in community programming.[23] When drug dealing emerged as a viable economic alternative for urban youth in the late 1970s, politicians had more than enough ammunition to argue that the Knights would always be criminal, as opposed to a political organization. The fact that both the local and federal government feared gangs like the Divine Knights for their revolutionary potential is airbrushed out of the romantic histories that Mr. Otis tells, where he invokes civilized marches in criticism of the gang's present-day criminal involvement. In his version, for example, there is no mention of the gang members who, even during the civil rights heyday, were not at all civic-minded.[24]

Whether or not this glorious perception of a political gang persists (or if it ever existed in the way Mr. Otis imagines), it is deployed nevertheless. Like the shiny new surveillance technology responsible for transforming a person's visage into a ghostly specter at night, the rosy civil rights lens through which Mr. Otis views the gang helps fashion the image that haunts him. Nostalgia, this historical emotion, reorders his memory.

The interview unfolds in a West Side Chicago barbershop, long since closed. Red Walker, the short, stocky, tattoo-covered leader of the Roving Knights—a splinter group of the Divine Knights—reminisces about what it has been like growing up in a gang. Walker has been a member of the Roving Knights for twenty years (since he was nine). Now, as a captain of the gang set, Red feels that the organization's biggest problem is a lack of leadership.[25] Comparing the gang of old to the one he now commands, he says, wistfully, "When I was growing up, we had chiefs. We had honor. There were rules that Knights had to follow, a code that gang members were expected to respect."

A few of the Roving Knights' strictures, according to Red: If members of the gang were shooting dice and somebody's mom walked down the street, the Knights would move out of respect. When young kids were coming home from school, the Knights would temporarily suspend the sale of drugs. "We would take a break for a couple of hours," Red says. "Everybody understood that. And plus, when I was coming up in the gang, you had to go to school. You could face sanctions if you didn't. And nobody was exempt. Not even me."

Red's mother, he says, was a "hype"—the favored West Side term for drug addict. His father wasn't present, and he didn't have siblings. Red did, however, have a "soldier" assigned to him, whose responsibilities included taking him to school in the morning and greeting him when he got out. "Made sure I did my homework and everything," Red says. "These kids don't have that. There's no structure now. They govern themselves, so we call them renegades."

It's likely I will meet a lot of renegades on the streets of Eastwood, Red warns. Most are proudly independent, boisterous of their self-centered goals. Red says, "They'll even tell you, 'Yeah, I'm just out for self. I'm trying to get my paper. Fuck the gang, the gang is dead.' They'll tell you, straight up. But, you know what? They're the ones that's killing it, them renegades. I even had one in my crew." Plopping down in the barber's chair beside me, Red indicates that the story he's about to tell is somewhat confidential, but he's going to tell me anyway because he likes me—I'm a "studious motherfucker," he jokes.

"You know how niggers be in here selling everything, right?" Red says. (He is referring to the daily transactions involving bootleg cable, DVDs, CDs, and candy.) "Well, back in the day, a long, long, long time ago, niggers used to sell something the police didn't like us selling. We used to sell"—here Red searches for the right euphemism, settling on "muffins." "Yeah, we had a bakery in this motherfucker. And cops, they hate muffins. So they would come up in here, try to be friendly, they'd snoop around, get they free haircut, and try to catch someone eating muffins or selling muffins, or whatever. But they could never catch nobody with muffin-breath around here. Never."

One day, though, the police apprehended one of the "little shorties" working for Red, and the young man happened to have a muffin in his pocket. "Now, this wasn't even an entire muffin. It was like a piece of a muffin—a crumb," Red says. "Shorty wouldn't have got in a whole lot of trouble for a crumb, you know? But this nigger sung. The nigger was singing so much, the cops didn't have to turn on the radio. They let him out on the next block. He told about the whole bakery: the cooks, the clients. He told on everybody. And I had to do a little time behind that. That's why in my new shop," Red continues, glaring again at the recorder, "WE. DO. NOT. SELL. MUFFINS. *ANY.* MORE."

Red pauses, seemingly satisfied by his disavowal of any current illegal muffin activity, then adds, "But, real talk: That's how you know a renegade. No loyalty. They'll sell you down the river for a bag of weed and a pair of Jordans."

Red's rant, in my reading, is subtended by nostalgic yearnings for a different time, a different way of life, and a different gang. Such nostalgia produces a particular kind of injury. Red's romanticized notions of the past cover over the structural imbalances that, in the present, constrict people's life chances. Whether or not community outsiders buy into the idea that the gang provides both jobs and protection, Red uses this rationale to help justify the gang's existence.[26]

Sure, a gang leader like Red might entice a thirteen-year-old kid to deliver his "muffins" with a pistol and a pocket full of cash; but the social pressure that he's applying in his barbershop is subtler than convincing a teenager to stand on the corner—and even harder to anticipate. This social pressure surfaces through a lament leveled at the young person hired to sweep hair in the barbershop. This teenager is an inadequate affiliate, a self-governing renegade with no loyalty, in Red's opinion. More broadly, this teenager's presence ignites in Red a monologue on gang patriotism—or, perhaps, American patriotism more broadly.

"Obama?" Red says. "Really? I mean, I ain't got nothing against the brother. He's black. He's from the Chi. But I ain't gonna be walking around here with Obama shoes on like the campaign is paying me." Red is referring to the then-potential nominee's face as it had appeared, in hologram form, on the most popular sneakers some of the young renegades wear: Nike Air Force Ones. Speaking again about the teenage boy who has just left, Red says that when he was young, the gang was his nation. "We were a nation of Knights. I ain't wear no red, white, and blue Nikes with no politicians face on 'em. Nah. We kept it plain and simple. Our flag was orange and blue. Erving Russell Beamer was our president. He put food on our tables, clothes on our back."

Erving Russell Beamer is one of the most infamous Chicago gang members in the city's history. He is also a key architect of the Divine Knights' organizational system. In 1971 he was sentenced to fifteen years in prison for killing an Iowa City police officer. While incarcerated, he drafted internal gang documents such as "The Divine Knights Constitution" and "The Amalgamated Order of Knighthood," a text outlining the gang's expansive command structure in prison and on the streets. Beamer built the foundation for the "corporate" gang's reign.[27] He encouraged gang involvement by devising roles that catered to a young person's aspirations. Each Knight was assigned a rank, which were carefully demarcated so as to allow members to internalize distinctions in status. As a result, people who joined the gang not only saw the possibility that they might someday garner the social and economic prestige of a gang leader; they were also able to gauge progress based on their position in the Knight hierarchy.[28]

As he cuts hair, Red elaborates on the hazards that young renegades present to the gang. Taking advantage of Red's nostalgia for a leader, I continue to prod him about the differences between his and the latest generation of Divine Knights. "Mr. Otis, that's my neighbor," I say to Red. "I talk to him all the time. You call these young boys 'renegades'; you say they only care about gym shoes. But he told me that you guys were the same way. He said y'all were 'good-n-crazy' when you were younger."

Red switches off his clippers, and the man in his chair, hair half-cut, rolls his eyes. (Red's clients often joke that he can turn a twenty-minute haircut into a two-hour ordeal.) "Yeah, we were crazy," he admits. "But you know what the difference is? We were some close-knit crazy folk.

We used to wear colors. Remember that? What happened to colors?" All of Red's clothes, he claims, were orange and blue, head to foot. His era of Knights used to "represent." "We used to cock our hat to the side. When we rocked those expensive jewels, when we had on name-brand clothes and new shoes, it meant that we earned it. Hustling. We all looked fly 'cause we all got money. Together. We got it together." Red adds, "When I was a shorty, I could yell, *'Deeee-Vine!'*, and my crew would be around the corner yelling, 'Knights! Knights! Knights!'" He picks his clippers back up, waving them at me. "That's the difference. And you can tell old-ass Otis I said it."

That Red is bothered because one of his workers prefers Obama Nikes to orange-and-blue ones demonstrates the potency of the gym shoe as a historical symbol. For Red, the orange-and-blue outfits of his era recall a time when gang leaders commanded a centralized organization in Eastwood. Back then, every gang member knew his place. Just as Mr. Otis fails to acknowledge that political sentiment has shifted since his childhood (such that the modern gang couldn't solicit funds for community development, even if they were so inclined), Red fails to acknowledge that social transformations have contributed to the demise of the gang's centralized leadership structure.

The present-day demise of the 1980s gang structure can only be understood in terms of the context that gave rise to the corporate gang.[29] The gang's shift toward illicit entrepreneurialism was on par with systemic transformations in the American social order. The very composition of urban cities shifted, with increasing vehemence, starting in the 1960s, as businesses moved their investments from urban centers to the suburbs, and eventually overseas. Opportunities for illicit revenue blossomed just as opportunities in the legal labor market wilted.[30] With the dismantling of the Italian Mafia in the 1970s—due to the Racketeer Influenced and Corrupt Organizations (RICO) Act—and the lack of police presence in the inner city, black street gangs were well positioned to reap the financial rewards of drug trafficking.[31]

What's more, as members of the Divine Knights debated the gang's mission, other Chicago gang families—like the Snakes, who had secured drug markets in their respective neighborhoods—began to pull members of the Divine Knights to the South Side with the prospect of earning a lucrative income. Unwilling to be taken over by gangs that were growing in membership, the Divine Knights ran non-affiliated dealers out of their neighborhood, in the process claiming the West Side drug market as their own. When more and more urban youths (especially young black men) joined this thriving drug-distribution network, those individuals began to represent an increasing share of the Divine Knighthood. As the gang became more estranged from the legal labor market, the new membership continued to shift the gang's focus toward illicit entrepreneurship.[32]

By the late 1970s and early 1980s, the Divine Knights Gang was a full-fledged drug-dealing enterprise. But the emergence of the Knights as a criminal group is linked to the wider question of how to manage the gang problem. This question has itself to do with the politics of urban violence—not merely its empirical existence. In a business climate of deindustrialization that saw bustling factories turned into empty steel labyrinths, neighborhoods like Eastwood were conjured through the imagery of mass media. The predominant image was that of the evil drug dealer, which motivated an unprecedented amount of drug-related legislation.[33] In the late 1980s, the federal government deployed the RICO Act, once used to battle the Mafia, to dismantle urban street gangs. Additionally, as segments of the urban poor—particularly the mentally ill, alcoholics, drug addicts, and impoverished, low-wage workers—became increasingly visible on street corners, their presence precipitated legislative crackdowns in urban communities that were initiated by Ronald Reagan and continued by Presidents Bush and Clinton. A number of scholars have pointed out that during the 1980s and 1990s it was impossible to know the extent to which crime rates actually increased. One of the more maddening ironies of the period is that the growing politicization of crime itself contributed to higher reporting rates.[34]

In the last few decades, as government agencies have begun keeping reliable records, we've learned that violent crime has actually *declined* in the United States since 1993. This about-face has continued into the new millennium. Still, members of Red's generational cohort have been greatly impacted by drug legislation. From the time Red joined the gang, in 1988, to when he went to prison ten years later (for two years, due to a "muffin"-related offense), Illinois's prison population increased by 138 percent.[35] This number pales in comparison to the 400 percent rise in drug-offender incarcerations during the same stretch. In 1988, when Red was around the same age as the renegades he now rebukes, drug offenses made up less than 17 percent of all prison sentences in Illinois. By 1999, Red's final year in prison, drug offenses accounted for 40 percent.[36] The following year, when Red was promoted to gang leader, 29 percent of the inmates locked up in the state of Illinois hailed from Eastwood, whose population accounted for just three-tenths of 1 percent of the state's.[37]

These numbers are worth repeating: In 2000, thirteen thousand adults who would otherwise be living in Eastwood were serving hard time. The thirteen thousand Eastwood residents Red left behind when he was released weren't all gang members. Yet the drug legislation passed by pointing to the "drug problem" consequently transformed the community into a prison pipeline. Hence, whether he fully acknowledges it or not, Red's nostalgia for a golden era is not exclusively about his gang or a diminished ethic of collective hustling; rather, it's about an entire generation of adults exiled from a neighborhood via the scapegoat of urban violence.[38]

In Eastwood, no one quite recalls how exactly the term "renegade" came about. While people of Red's generation employ the label to describe their juniors, gang elders like Mr. Otis don't use it at all. Likewise, it is scarcely used in gang scholarship written in the 1980s and 1990s. This is not to say that researchers have not classified terms that refer to the self-interested affiliate. Street gangs have always had to deal with "defiantly individualistic" members, previously called "new jacks" or "independents."[39] Renegades, like new jacks and independents, are viewed as a shrewd class of youngsters who take advantage of the organization by amassing substantial revenues. Yet gang veterans do not worry that the renegade's end goal is to accrue enough power to engineer a gang take-over—after all, that would require a sense of the collective. The concern, rather, is that young affiliates' lack of self-control—not to mention indifference to gang custom—will lead to the Divine Knights' downfall.[40]

I consider it an ethnographic coup when, eight months into my time in Eastwood, I realize that several key leaders in local schools, churches, and gang-prevention agencies have become familiar with my research. Even if the leaders of these organizations do not know the full extent of my thesis, many are aware that my work involves gangs. Hannah Brady, a youth worker at Eastwood Community Church, one day asks me if I would be interested in talking to students at Brown High School as part of their Career Day. After I agree, Hannah informs me that I will be in a classroom with sophomores tagged by the administration as gang members.

The morning of Career Day is crisp and blue. After a continental breakfast of bagels, muffins, and hot coffee, I join nearly one hundred African American professionals in the school's library for a pep talk by Robert Edwards, Brown High's principal. It is February 22, 2008, the day after a presidential primary debate between Hillary Clinton and Barack Obama (and a couple of weeks after the latter's surprisingly competitive Super Tuesday: the midst of what would be twelve straight primary victories for the junior senator from Illinois).

The 2008 primary season, which brings with it the possibility that Barack Obama might secure the Democratic nomination, makes Principal Edwards optimistic. He is convinced this Career Day will be different from those that came before. Drawing from the previous day's political wrangle, he launches into a motivational speech: "I was watching the presidential debate yesterday, and I was smiling from ear to ear. My wife even said, 'Bobby, you look like our son on Christmas Day!' And you know what I said? 'No, sweetie, it's more like Christmas Eve"—because, Principal Edwards knew, today he would get to see many black professionals. "'That's my gift. That's a gift to our students.'

"But I have to admit," Principal Edwards continues, "I was smiling because of Obama, too. Barack offers hope. And that's all we really have here at Brown High School, a little bit of hope. And you know what? A little bit of hope goes a long way."

Last year was Edwards's first as principal of Brown. Ironically, the theme of Career Day was "Can a Black Person Be President?" The teachers present at the previous year's Career Day, Edwards says, left feeling defeated and discouraged because the kids said it wasn't possible, that it didn't matter who was president. The president didn't care about them or their lives and didn't have any personal effect on them. "But today," Principal Edwards says, "I stand here encouraged because I see that attitude starting to shift a little bit. That doubt is lifted a little bit with Barack. The theme of this year's career day is *Power*. I want you to talk about what it means to feel powerful—what it means in society and in your own lives."

The population at Brown is 99.9 percent black; most all of the professionals present are also black. Because of this, Principal Edwards says that it's imperative that we are positive examples for the kids. "Before you engage with the students," he says, "I want you to do one thing for me: raise your hand if you had a mentor when you were growing up." Every person in the library raises a hand. "The reality is that all of us needed one—or, in my case, *many*—to get to where we are now. These kids need one too." Edwards adds, "Today, when you're talking to these kids, some of them will be asleep, some of them will be talking or even fighting—but just remember that you have an opportunity to be a role model. The question is: Are you ready for the challenge?"

Rallying the troops with this rhetorical question, Principal Edwards dismisses us. I make my way up a concrete staircase to room 208, where two white male teachers greet me. One, Mr. Flynn, looks to be in his mid-twenties; the other, Mr. Drake, is a bit older. Both are wearing the kinds of ties that live in the back of a sock drawer, appearing in public only when the principal stresses that teachers should "look nice" for their guests. The older teacher is directing the class: fifteen black teenage boys sitting on plastic chairs. Gum wrappers and other paper scraps litter a floor that looks more like a locker room than a learning space. As we enter the room, thirty unimpressed eyes turn and stare at three "professional" black men—a graduate student, a corporate attorney, and a probation officer.

Mr. Randall, the probation officer, begins: "I work for Cook County Courts," he says. "Every day, I deal with kids that look like you. I'm talking about 'you' in the sense that they are around your age, they live in neighborhoods like this, they are black." One of the educational programs Mr. Randall oversees is called Jump Start. "Hopefully you won't have to go there," Mr. Randall says. "But if you do, you can still get an education. Another thing I do is monitor home incarceration."

"House arrest?" two kids from opposite ends of the class chime in simultaneously.

"Yeah, that's right. And I'm gonna let you in on a little secret"— Mr. Randall leans forward, cupping the right side of his mouth— "Probation officers who monitor people on house arrest are off every other weekend and on holidays. Do what you want with that information." The class erupts. Students begin bouncing on the edge of their plastic seats. One asks which weekend the officers are on. "It don't matter," says another student. "If they come one weekend, you know they're off the next, right?"

"That's right," Randall says. "Man, what's your name?"

"Danny," the boy replies.

"That's right, Danny."

Just then Mr. Flynn, the younger teacher, informs the class that, due to time constraints, we will be moving directly into the activity period. The first game we play is called the "Stand Up and Declare Activity." Four pieces of paper are taped around the classroom: On the north wall is "STRONGLY AGREE"; "AGREE" is on the south; "DISAGREE," the east; and "STRONGLY DISAGREE" on the west. The younger teacher opens a manila envelope, takes out a sheet of paper, and reads from it a printed statement. The game requires students to move to the wall on which their response is posted. The first statement: "I would feel more powerful if a black man were president." Most students angle toward the STRONGLY AGREE side of the room; one goes to the DISAGREE wall, and another to the STRONGLY DISAGREE side, where he is joined by the corporate lawyer. "I don't think race matters," the lawyer says. "As long as the president has the country's best interest in mind, we should all feel powerful. I have been voting in presidential elections since I was eighteen, and I'm forty-five now. I've voted in every election." He adds, "It's not the particular president that makes me feel powerful—it's the act of voting itself."

The kid alongside the attorney on the STRONGLY DISAGREE wall concurs, albeit for different reasons. "A black president ain't gonna make me feel more powerful 'cause the president ain't gonna do nothing for me," he says. "He ain't gonna stop people from being evicted, from getting shot. He ain't gonna put more money on their Link Cards." (This juxtaposition, between homelessness, death, and food-stamp cards, called Link Cards, triggers a ripple of giggles.) "Y'all laugh," he continues, "but the Link Card is important for me and my peoples. The president don't care about none of that, man. He just wanna be famous."

The next statement from the manila envelope: "Jay-Z is more powerful than Barack Obama." Once the room reaches equilibrium, the STRONGLY AGREE side has six people, as does the STRONGLY DISAGREE side, with the remainder of the population sprinkled proportionally in the middle range. The elder teacher, Mr. Drake, argues in favor of the rapper Jay-Z: "You guys know all his songs. You know everything about him. You don't know hardly anything about Barack or what he stands for. Last night was the nineteenth presidential debate. Who has seen a debate so far?"

All of the adults raise their hands; none of the students do.

"But I think Barack is more powerful," Danny Silver says. "He's trying to be president. Jay-Z's just trying to be rich. And plus, Barack, he got plans and stuff for how to improve our lives. He tells us about change, how to change the world, you know? All Jay-Z tells us about is how to hustle, how to sell drugs, how to live in the hood—which we already know." Danny gestures toward the window, which overlooks one of the poorest areas in Chicago.

Another student, Jemell Waters, chimes in: "Jay-Z got clothing lines. He got a record label, he produces movies, he got a restaurant, he got his own shoes." In making his case, Jemell gestures toward another student's feet adorned with pearl white "S. Carters"—Jay-Z's signature shoe. "People in the hood, we want that. We wanna dress like Jay-Z, eat what he eats, be on his label."

"But Jay-Z is a rapper," Danny roars. "A rapper can never be as powerful as the president. The president can raise taxes, lower taxes. A president can send us to war, make us go in the draft. A president can send *Jay-Z* to war if he wants to." Gaining steam, Danny adds, "I

know what you said earlier, but a president *can* put money on our Link
Cards, keep the heat on, keep us in our house. If we get evicted, what's
Jay-Z gonna do? When you're living in your car that don't have no gas,
and don't work—can't even turn on the radio. How you gonna listen to
Jay-Z? What then, huh?"

The room goes silent.

"Danny for President!" Mr. Randall yells out.

After a few more activities, a school assembly, and a keynote speech by
a local city councilman, Hannah and I leave Brown High through the
parking lot. One student, looking out the window from the school's
top floor, yells: "Good-bye, now. Have a nice day!" He talks in the
nasal voice that black comedians use in exaggerated imitations of white
people.

Another student, switching to his actual voice, howls, "Now get in
your car and drive home!"

"And don't come back," blasts another.

"Aye, man . . . aye . . . aye . . . aye! Is that your girl?" one continues to
heckle while we walk, stoic and unconvincingly deaf.

"You hear me talking to you, man! Why don't you get the fuck out
of here!"

"Bye-bye, now," another says, returning to his uptight white-person
voice.

Leaving Career Day, I feel a small blossom of nostalgia. I remember
why, as a teenager, I was drawn to education: those times when unexpected lessons from strangers became more meaningful than what I was
learning in history books. This created in me the sense that I could aug-
ment what I was being taught with a more experiential understanding
of how the world worked. Most of Career Day, it seemed that the kids
were barely listening to me—but I was still touched by a palpable sense
of accomplishment. The window hecklers, however, quickly deflate my
pride. And yet I am more surprised by the hecklers' resentment than I
should have been.

The students at Brown High, already targets of various community
interventions, are on this day expected to absorb the tutelage of a pro-

bation officer (a member of law enforcement and representative of the criminal justice system), a corporate attorney (one who accrues influence from straddling the domains of business and justice), and an anthropologist (an advocate and beneficiary of the American education system, who is trained to explain the very lives of these teenagers to the wider public).[41] We are supposed to serve as inspirational icons representing how far African Americans have come. Students in an almost entirely black, poor school are meant to learn from our experiences. They are encouraged to believe anything is possible. They are supposed to project our biographies on to a notion of their own limitless future — a future that the administrators hope the students will take ownership of. The irony is that, although we are supposed to bestow knowledge upon them, these youngsters have much to teach us about life's obstacles, especially regarding the sometimes-fatal pitfalls that accompany the pursuit of power. It is instructive, therefore, to linger awhile on the insights of these "at-risk" youth.

Although many people hope that Obama will serve as a emblem for boundless possibilities — political, personal, and social alike — gang affiliates like Jemell install him into the narrow frame reserved for successful athletes and rappers who "just want to be famous." Others, like Danny, recognize the distinction that Principal Edwards hopes for. Still, "professional" blacks and African American entertainers and politicians represent a paradoxical existence for Eastwood youth in that they are seemingly familiar in skin color and yet fundamentally unrecognizable in terms of future prospects. The students — specifically the small group who taunted me and Hannah as we left Brown High — articulate a struggle against the middle-class morality that conceives of Career Day as a viable response to permanent unemployment and escalating school dropout rates.[42]

Undoubtedly, part of the influence attributable to a gang leader, in terms of his influence over a young renegade, is that the gang leader's commitment extends far beyond a single day. His motives are no doubt self-serving, and yet the gang leader is a presence more constant than "successful" professional blacks in the daily lives of Eastwood teenagers. Nevertheless, gang leaders and Career Day speakers alike face resentment when attempting to socialize young urban residents. Our window hecklers offer one kind of resentment: a scornful disdain of our fly-by-night charity work. The second type of resentment—symbolized by re-fashioned gym shoes—helps young renegades establish their own brand of belonging during difficult times, times that prove to be confining.

When I tell Danny, a few weeks after Career Day, that I want to inter-view him for my research project, I never dream that the majority of our conversations will take place in the West Side Juvenile Detention Cen-ter. I have been waiting in the detention center for over an hour, largely unnoticed. I've tried making eye contact with a few of the inmates I recognize from Eastwood, but their heads are down, solemnly studying the floor while waiting for their loved ones.

The center has the stale smell of so many government buildings: cold, hard floors that reek of Pine-Sol, walls the hue of a mildewed sock, generic rectangular light panels that turn everything a dull yel-low. But sprinkled all around the miniature Big House—the "audition box for adult jail," as one police officer calls it—is evidence that learn-ing is taking place. Cutout letters that announce the "CIVIL RIGHTS MOVEMENT" blanket one wall, with quotes from Martin Luther King and Malcolm X taped underneath the title. "APARTHEID" labels the opposite wall, on which a portrait of Nelson Mandela hangs with an inspirational quote from the South African leader. Such colorful decor reminds people like me that children live here—even though some of them are considered adults by the law. Scanning the room, my eyes meet a guard's, and he views me suspiciously. His glare stands in striking con-trast to the perpetually diverted eyes of the inmates.

Upon entering the facility, every detainee is issued the same uniform: Dark gray khakis, a green T-shirt, and, in winter, a green sweatshirt. The clothes come in different sizes, some more worn than others, but all fix a person's status as that of inmate. As they travel with their peers in a single-file line, the confines of their Plexiglas encasements becoming home, these kids have only to look around to be reminded that they are incarcerated—that is, unless they look down. Because the county can't afford to equip each arrival with new shoes, those teenagers sent to the West Side Juvenile Detention Center are stripped of everything except the shoes they are wearing, which they keep until their trial date, when they are either transferred to a prison or released. As a result, icebreaker conversations center on what kind of shoes a person wears in his neighborhood, the number of pairs he has at home, and the type of footwear he plans to buy when he gets out.

Indeed, shoes are what breaks the ice with Danny. "At least you came in here with new Tims," I say. "They've gotta be giving you some kind of respect, right?"

"Could've been worse," Danny says playfully. "Scooter got arrested in flip-flops."

Danny informs me that the state is "trying to move [his] charges up to attempted murder." Mr. Randall, he says, is going to testify as a character witness. (Nelson Randall is the probation officer who was present at Career Day.) After the event, Mr. Randall developed a relationship with the youngster. He gave Danny a business card and mentioned a program he organizes for youth in Eastwood, the Eastwood Youth Action Committee (E-YAC), which is composed of Chicago-area high school students from different backgrounds. Some are honor students from elite charter schools. Others, like Danny, have already had multiple run-ins with the law and are gang-affiliated. Along with a fellow officer, Randall started the group as a mechanism through which youths can advocate, in court, on behalf of their peers. Members are also paid for attending two workshops a month that focus on the criminal justice system. Danny had attended five sessions and was active in E-YAC activities when he was arrested. Randall, a respected employee of the court, hoped to convince the judge that Danny was trying to turn his life around and break from his gang. But this proved difficult. Danny lives on the same block where the Divine Knights maintain their headquarters, a street where many lifetime gang members still maintain residence. His father is a member of the Knights, as is his older brother. Danny was, in his words, "born into the gang."

During the second semester of his sophomore year, Danny stopped selling drugs and began attending school on a regular basis. But because he was not dealing, he was expected to contribute to the gang in other ways—especially given his crew was currently bickering with a rival faction, the Bandits. Kemo, the leader of Danny's gang set, tasked Danny with carrying a weapon, in case a gunfight with the Bandits erupted. (Leaders like Kemo often roam the streets without drugs and guns, because the police recognize them and subject them to random searches. Plus, if a minor like Danny is caught with contraband, he will receive less time.) One day Danny was walking his girlfriend, Tasha Litch, home while holding Kemo's piece. He noticed that a squad car was tailing him, so he asked Tasha to pretend to drop her cell phone and then tell him if the gun was visible from behind. She confirmed that the handle was protruding from the small of his back. Danny kept walking, hoping the cops would fail to notice and drive away. But when the couple stopped at Tasha's doorstep, he heard the car door slam shut and realized the officers were approaching. He took off running.

Danny rounded a corner and threw Kemo's gun over the fence of an abandoned lot. The gun, which had a broken safety, discharged as it landed on a sea of empty liquor bottles. The prosecution claims that Danny was shooting at the police. Ironically enough, the sound of the gun blast led Danny to believe that the police were shooting at *him*, so he kicked into high gear and ducked through an alleyway. He evaded the officers and escaped to the apartment of his older brother, Devin (who is locked up, but Devin's girlfriend and son currently live in the apartment).

The next day Danny got word that Kemo was looking for him. Reluctantly, Danny went to Kemo's garage, where he was told that the incident had already brought unwanted attention to his drug operation and that, as a result, the Bandits were profiting and Kemo was losing money. He told Danny that he must face sanctions, then landed a swift right hook on the side of Danny's face, the force of which sent the youngster tumbling across a weight bench. Pleased with this exercise of brawn, the burly Kemo looked toward his team and began to snicker. With Kemo's back turned, Danny grabbed a pipe and told his fellow gang members to back up, swinging it in front of him to create a buffer. He walked backward until he reached a shelf where he was able to exchange the pipe for another of Kemo's guns. He pointed it at the owner.

"You motherfuckers are crazy," Kemo said. "Can't even take an ass whupping. "You run now, and it'll be ten times worse when we catch you." *Take it like a man*, was Kemo's advice.

"Fuck you!" Danny shouted, backpedaling through the garage. He reached the street and ran feverishly, as he had the day before. Only this time he dashed to the house of his best friend, Kwame "Cook" Robinson, who explained the day's events. "The police been at your mom's house and school with a warrant," Cook said. "Mr. Randall just called my cell saying you need to turn yourself in."

With the police and the gang after him, and after a brief deliberation, Danny returned Nelson Randall's call. "Can you come take me to the station?" he asked. "I'm ready." But before Randall arrived to escort him to jail, Danny borrowed Cook's brand-new boots. He knew what to expect inside the "audition box."

My time with Danny at the detention center exemplifies the social constraints under which young gang members struggle in the contemporary moment. On the one hand, renegades are considered disloyal to the gang; but, on the other, it is not as if their resistance improves their life conditions or permits them to reach middle-class standing. Instead, renegades are stuck. They run from law enforcement to their gang leader's garage, only to flee back into police custody, eventually returning to the juvenile detention center. There, mass incarceration lends a more pointed meaning to the mass production of their footwear.

It's easy to criticize young gang members and their obsession with shoes. Jail guards and Bible-study instructors and well-meaning university professors all seek to understand how these kids can spend so much time literally staring at their feet. The comparisons, of course, abound: *When I was your age*, many scholars and guards and preachers no doubt think, *I picked up trash and marched in picket lines*. These kids, by contrast, seem utterly confounding, self-obsessed, and directionless to boot. Their bearing, tough yet lackadaisical, suggests that their decision to sell drugs is simply a matter of personal choice. Indeed, renegades seem willfully ignorant of the larger social forces that have led gang members to hustling on the corner or into the confines of the detention center.

Spending time in Eastwood helped me to see how community leaders—and even a substantial portion of gang members themselves—fail to understand the youngest generation: They don't deem their jailhouse conversations as worthy of reflection, nor do they recognize the nostalgic forms of historical consciousness present in those conversations. More, they don't see how the attitudes, orientations, and behaviors of the gang's youngest members speak to anxieties about living in a society that contains no feasible fulfillment for their hopes and desires.[43] But, at the West Side Juvenile Detention Center, I hear on a daily basis conversations in which young renegades grapple with history through the objects they consume, fashioning their future out of what little material they have left.

"Those Air Force Ones?" Jimmie "Scooter" Matthews asks, as I'm about to leave for the day. He's inspecting my black Nikes, scrutinizing their green and yellow highlights. I hesitate because I know the make, but not the model, of my shoes. I could check the tongue, but don't want to seem insecure.

"Nah, man, those are some Dunks," Danny says, saving me. "Everybody on my block rocks them. Those are cool." He continues, eyes still glued to my feet. "But as soon as I get out, I'm gonna cop them new Jordans."

Scooter smiles and nods. "Yeah, me too."

Inside Jokes

I'm mad at myself. I just searched my notebook, looking for the time Tosh Tremont and I visited his nephew, Darryl "Blizzard" Tremont, in prison. Even though I took notes that day, somehow I didn't describe what happened. All I have are logistical details of the "Visitation Period." And now, of course, there's a discrepancy about what really went down.

The way Tosh remembers it, he was making fun of Blizzard and said something like: "At least now that you're locked up, Laurence can't write about how bad your music is." The joke, according to Tosh, made Blizzard laugh, even though he was obviously de-

pressed. I remember hearing the line, but from Blizzard, not Tosh. And Blizzard saying it in a self-deprecating way that wasn't funny. I don't recall Blizzard — or me or Tosh — laughing.

I remember Blizzard saying that he felt closer to the gang on the inside, because so many people from his neighborhood were locked up, too. Then he turned to me, proud of himself, and said that if I wanted to keep "following gang members around" (or engaging in those activities that I associated with ethnographic fieldwork), I would have to get arrested. That's when, I thought, we laughed. Then I recall saying, "I'm not sure about that because even when

I think I'm not doing research on the gang, it turns out I am." I'm pretty sure Blizzard agreed. "You're telling me," I thought he said. "I can't leave the gang either. No matter how hard I try."

—6/5/10, 4:22 PM

CHAPTER THREE

𝕬𝖚𝖙𝖍𝖊𝖓𝖙𝖎𝖈𝖎𝖙𝖞

———✳———

OR,

Why People Can't Leave the Gang

The recording studio of Gangsta City Entertainment is located in a cavernous basement in a historic Eastwood greystone, one of the time-worn but structurally sound buildings that the Neighborhood Coalition would have photographed. To access the studio, a person has to walk down a narrow flight of steps. Underneath this staircase are two torn couches for visitors to listen to the music being produced, but more so for all four members of Gangsta City—nineteen-year-old Blizzard and three other affiliates of the Divine Knights—who often occupy the studio at the same time. Just to the right of the stairs rests a mammoth desk with speakers, a computer, a drum machine, and two large monitors. And then the vocal booth proper, which would be a half-bathroom if the plumbing worked. Blizzard has sealed the toilet lid shut and ripped out the sink, replacing it with a microphone. For quality sound, he's insulated the walls with old eggshell mattresses. This dusty basement bathroom has been converted into a recording booth with the hope that disgruntled gang members, like Blizzard himself, might use the space to turn themselves into stars.

On a sweltering summer day in 2008, I'm sitting in front of a fan in his basement as he scribbles lyrics on a wrinkled Save-A-Lot receipt. In the tiny renovated bathroom, Blizzard raps "The Blizzard Is Here":

> You can call me a kingpin, you can call me a boss
> I move that Snow White, white snow, 'til she's gone
> And when she's gone I get more, man, I keep her for hard times
> My trunk is like a store, I procure what the hypes like
> I got what the hypes need, they shake when they see me
> They dream about seeing me, they steal to come be with me
> I'm a hotshot I got the whole block's attention,
> I got funds, guns, and drugs, for the low—did I *mention*?

In this song, the young rapper assumes the allegorical drug-dealer figure. He invites listeners to refer to him as a kingpin or boss, and suggests that he is well-known in his neighborhood for selling snow (powdered heroin or crack) out of his car trunk—this despite the fact that Blizzard doesn't have a driver's license, much less an automobile. He brags that when drug addicts—"hypes"—come around, they shake in his presence (not merely out of fear, he suggests, but also in Pavlovian anticipation of their next high). According to Blizzard, he is regarded as a hotshot because of his ability to "procure" and distribute drugs at low prices. Even the song's title, "The Blizzard Is Here," ratchets up his personal history of petty crime by calling attention to the rapper's inventories: not only does he have access to drugs, he has an overabundance—a blizzard of snow.[1]

How, I want to know, does being a rapper for Gangsta City Entertainment jibe with being a member of the Divine Knights? Although Blizzard claims that part of the reason he quit dealing drugs was because he no longer wanted to be a destructive force in Eastwood, his songs exalt the dealer figure and seem to delight in making people dependent on heroin. Does Blizzard wish he had been more successful as a drug dealer? Is he trying to close the gap between the kinds of criminal activity his gang is known for and his rap persona? If not, why is he fictionalizing his lyrics? Why isn't Blizzard, as they say, keeping it real?

The "keeping it real" discourse has proven to be lucrative for contemporary rap artists, and aspirants, like Blizzard and the rest of Gangsta City, have taken note. It's no mistake that Jay-Z, arguably the greatest current embodiment of the corporate rapper, was a focus of debate in Danny's classroom. Jay-Z's identity as a former drug dealer has become more relevant, and valuable, to him as his power in "legitimate" enterprise has increased. His career is proof positive that the credibility that drug dealing confers on rappers can be monetized.[2] (It also suggests that, for fans, "real" drug-dealing narratives carry great cultural value.) Rappers gain a different level of authenticity, or street cred, if they understand the ins and outs of drug dealing—and if, as formerly marginalized youths turned public figures, they are able to speak to this crucial part of urban life. That is, since descriptions of urban life often equate to glorious tales about drug dealing, a rapper's ability to assert economic control over his or her "product"—a term equally applied to drugs and songs—plays a pivotal role in discourses about drug dealing. Those rappers perceived as having the most control, through diverse realms of branding and marketing—such as Rick Ross, T.I., 50 Cent, and Jay-Z—are considered highly successful.

Perhaps ironically, hip hop's vast global influence is rooted in an incredibly specific locale: the narrowly conceived arena of black urban spaces, usually the inner city. Even as the hip hop industry has become increasingly profitable, hip hop artists have not released their urban anchors. They still ground their identity in the geography of their childhood neighborhoods.[3] In the hip hop world, a rapper's ability to trace and acknowledge his or her exact roots remains critical for staving off an inevitable accusation that he or she has compromised "an internal and interior real self."[4] More simply, if a rapper's origins are in the right area code, he or she is less likely to be accused of being inauthentic.

As much as "keeping it real" has transformed cultural capital into material wealth, the phrase has, by now, become cliché. This emphasis on realness has triggered even longtime fans to express disdain for the current state of hip hop. Nowadays, the outsize, larger-than-life boasts that sustain the genre inspire, it seems, equally exaggerated responses. "Keeping it real" invites criticism from across the spectrum—liberals and conservatives, scholars and pundits.

Social conservative Stanley Crouch argues that hip hop's reliance on urban poverty as currency fuels cycles of violence that are, ultimately, self-destructive. Addressing the late Tupac Shakur's claims to authenticity, Crouch says, "The thug mentality threatens the survival and moral health of poor black communities. . . . When you answer the chaos with more chaos, then that creates a double burden for everybody else."[5] Though you'd be hard-pressed to find middle ground for socially conservative black intellectuals and progressive urban scholars, today many in both camps would agree that the "keeping it real" discourse (with its vicious objectifications of women and its violent puns about gunplay) has become a liability for hip hop supporters and defenders of black urban youth.

While no self-respecting urban scholar would go so far as to say that rap music is a tumor eating away at the black community's ethical core, nearly all agree that "keeping it real" is a slippery slope leading nowhere good. In her latest book, *The Hip Hop Wars*, Tricia Rose underlines the controversy surrounding rappers' perpetual quest for authenticity. Rappers, Rose writes, claim that hip hop is "keeping it real" in response to the criticism that their lyrics are contributing to negative social conditions. The primary use of the "keeping it real" defense, then, is to prove hip hop's role as truth teller. Hip hop remains one of the most accessible platforms from which black urban youth might tell their life stories both in their own vernacular and on their own terms. But because many rappers perpetuate stereotypes about urban poverty in the process, Rose contends that rappers' arguments about authenticity are deeply flawed. Here, rappers feed a corporate structure that profits from "negative" representations of black people—as violent criminals, drug dealers, and sex fiends. Rose argues that by crowding out other notions of what it means to be black, these racist and sexist representations come to dominate the images of blackness that circulate globally. What's more, the failure of rappers to take responsibility for their music is dangerous for the black community as a whole. "What gets projected in hip hop has a particular impact on young people who already face heavy burdens, have little public support, and need as much help as they can possibly get," Rose writes.[6]

Urban scholars and critics often view the most commercially successful rap artists as "vulgar money-getters" whose personal quest for material wealth endangers the black community.[7] Impressionable black youth, in this interpretation, are diverted by empty, avaricious rhymes from the possibilities of post–civil rights fulfillment. By definition, rap music that relies on "negative" representations, say these critics, cannot be an authentic form of black cultural expression because real black art is not swayed by market dictates. Real black art seeks to uplift the marginalized black community. Real black art speaks truth to power.[8]

The problem here is how *truth* is defined. That is, by defining truth in relation to hip hop's—and by extension, a given rapper's—ability to elude market constraints, urban youth become primarily defined in terms of the forms of social control imposed on them by a capitalistic society, trafficking in gross cultural representations. The extent to which people are influenced by cultural representations can never be fully quantified, so there is no escaping this quagmire. Representations of blackness become quicksand that swallows urban futures in a sea of negativity. An alternative, less myopic, approach is to examine the ways in which urban youth search for room to maneuver even beneath the constraints that global forms of capital create—that is, to follow them as they travel down difficult roads in pursuit of their dreams. Such a perspective gives us a sense of an urban youth's resolve. It also gives us a sense of the potentially fatal pitfalls one encounters while embarking on this journey of self-discovery.[9]

We've already seen how the critique of "negative" rap is taken up and applied in Eastwood (through Mr. Gregory's discussion of the "hip hoppers" in the detention center). The assumption that urban residents (especially gang members and inmates) are disconnected and therefore "need as much help as they can get" from outside of their communities too often reproduces the frame of inner-city isolation. Throughout the book, we've seen how dangerous the presumption of a disconnected "underclass" can be. This is the logic that cleared the way for city planners and a prominent church to build a new community on behalf of their poorer counterparts without consulting those counterparts; this is also the logic that led older gang members to police younger gang affiliates in ways that fail to see the younger affiliates' struggles in the context of the contemporary moment. Hence, rather than merely articulating the ways in which hip hop contributes to the marginalized societal position of black urban youth, what follows is an ethnographic exegesis on the double bind that Cornel West has famously noted. His quote signals the paradox between the renegade who wears Obama Nikes and Obama himself: "The irony in our present moment," he writes, "is that just as young black people are murdered, maimed, and imprisoned in record numbers, their styles have become disproportionately influential in shaping popular culture."[10]

Too often the debate about authenticity in hip hop focuses on one-half of this double bind (the murdered, maimed, or imprisoned) or the other (the representations of influential rap artists), rather than examining how both halves shape the whole picture. As such, scholarship about hip hop becomes a way to talk about the urban poor without talking to them. Rather than taking a top-down approach, my analysis looks from the bottom up and tries to understand the travels that young Eastwoodians take in pursuit of their passions. Through aspiring artists' dreams to make it big, we'll see how the drug trade is localized and how the criminal justice system operates in urban communities. Examining authenticity from the bottom up helps us understand why the criminal-as-rapper becomes a vehicle to voice these connections: This figure's actions give us tremendous insights about the legitimacy of the law. Instead of dwelling on the danger that hip hop poses to urban communities, I will demonstrate how authenticity shapes urban youths' worldview, all the while revealing scars they've accumulated after numerous attempts to disentangle themselves from the gang—and the dense web of illicit commerce that has augmented to its influence. Authenticity proves critical to how we understand social life in Eastwood, where unsettled claims to the real reside at the nexus between the rap and drug trades.[11]

In 1895 the German pharmaceutical company Bayer began selling an over-the-counter pain reliever called Heroin. The name, a derivation of the German word *heroisch*, for "heroic," was meant to convey the drug's superhuman effects on its user. Developed as a morphine substitute, Bayer marketed heroin as a "non-addictive" cough suppressant. Researchers soon found, however, that despite the company's claim, users of the drug evidenced an extremely high rate of dependency. Heroin was essentially a faster-acting form of morphine, far more addictive than the dangerous substance it was intended to replace. Bayer was embarrassed by the findings. Ultimately, heroin—wonder drug turned fraud—proved to be a historic blunder for the company.[12]

More than one hundred years later, heroin is in wide circulation. It is famous for the transcendent relaxation and intense euphoria it offers, especially the initial "rush" it induces. In the first few seconds after injecting the drug, users report feeling heroic, capable of anything. In Eastwood, as in most African American communities, the primary method of heroin use is intravenous injection ("shooting up").[13] Addicts melt the drug from its clay-like form and then inject a liquid version of it into easily accessible veins in the arm. Over time these veins collapse (the acid found in heroin damages them), forcing users to continually locate new ones capable of sustaining injections. Other addicts, particularly those whose veins have given out, cook the drug and inhale its vapors. This is typically done by placing the substance on aluminum foil and heating it from underneath. When heated, the clay-like substance melts to a thick liquid, similar in consistency to molten wax, and in the process gives off a smoke that users inhale with a tube. These tubes are also made from foil; any heroin that collects on the inside of the tube can, in turn, be smoked afterward. This method is referred to as "chasing the dragon."

Just as the effects of heroin—its alternating states of rush and relaxation—elude a static, coherent form, so does our understanding of the roles that drugs play in poor communities. In Eastwood, authenticity often resembles Bayer's pharmaceutical blunder: the counterfeit becomes real, illuminating connections that have previously been obscured. The drug that was supposed to be a safe simulacrum becomes even more dangerous than its prototype. We've seen this throughout the book—inauthentic gang members (renegades) become a real danger to the Divine Knights' legacy; fake threats leveled by gang members at City Hall instill fear in a commissioner, prompting him to meet with more sensible-seeming members of the community. The blue lights that pulsate on dark streets, like the police incarnate, lead many East-woodians to deem their very innocence illusory. To hear these residents tell it, government resources are being devoted to keeping thousands of Eastwoodians incarcerated each year instead of regulating the international drug markets that help transform this neighborhood from a half a world away. A symbol of everyday debates about the "real" heroin's history provides clues for how we might understand authenticity in poor urban communities.

Like an addict who must tap uncollapsed veins for new highs, global distributors of the drug must continually tap new markets in search of new profits. The billions of dollars in heroin profits amassed each year have grave implications for inner-city Chicago. More prevalent on the West Side of Chicago than on the North and South Sides, heroin has grown increasingly lucrative in recent years. It was enticing temptation for a young gang member, which suggested to me that Blizzard's decision to give up the drug trade to pursue his music career was no small sacrifice.[14] Arrests for possession of more than fifteen grams of heroin were up nearly 50 percent in 2010 (the year Blizzard stopped selling drugs, compared to 2009, when he began). By the end of 2010, the Narcotics Division of the Chicago Police Department had seized nearly a quarter of a billion dollars' worth of heroin, an increase from the year before of more than seventy million dollars. The Divine Knights currently control a large part of this market; their network extends beyond Chicago's West Side east to New York; south through Indiana, Missouri, and Tennessee; and west to Iowa. Over the past decade, competition in Latin America and the Middle East has increased the supply of the narcotic, generating two injurious results: the cost of heroin has come down, and the drug has become purer.

The United States' fight against the Taliban, no matter what one thinks of the benefits, has produced unexpected side effects; chief among them, for our purposes, is that the increasingly pure heroin now available in Eastwood is the direct result of military occupation abroad, particularly in Afghanistan.[15] The cultivation of opium in Afghanistan reached its peak in 1999, when farmers sowed 225,000 acres of poppy. The following year, the Taliban banned poppy cultivation, a move that cut production by 94 percent. One year later, American and British troops removed the Taliban and installed an interim government. And Afghanistan became the world's largest opium-producing nation.[16]

Global heroin-distribution chains are labyrinthine and extraordinarily fluid. As a hub of heroin distribution, inner-city Chicago is entangled with U.S. military strategies that have unintentionally stimulated narcotics production. Compared to the clandestine systems required to transport these narcotics, hip hop is loud, in our face, and easily identifiable. No surprise, then, that hip hop is an easy scapegoat for the inner city's many ills. Consider, though, the lack of research devoted to linking the global war and urban crime, and, conversely, the sizable amount of scholarly attention devoted to the connection between hip hop and black criminality.[17] If hip hop music is the soundtrack for this study of rappers and heroin dealers in Eastwood, the war in Afghanistan certainly provides a backbeat. As the United States has committed itself to this war, it has unwittingly aided in the cultivation of a more robust heroin trade at home.

Susan Hutchison's mother, Cynthia, was a war veteran, one of the first army members deployed to Afghanistan in 2002. On a breezy autumn day eight years later, Susan tells me, with pride, that her mother's story prompted her boyfriend, Blizzard, to stop selling drugs. After years of prodding, Susan was finally able to convince Blizzard to scrap that part of his business. He did so just weeks ago and, to offset the lost income, he is now pushing various forms of pirated media.

It is a surprisingly chilly afternoon in October. On the stoop outside Blizzard's basement studio, Susan is telling me about her mother, Cynthia, who, in addition to being a soldier, was also a heroin addict. Until she was eleven, Susan was kept in the dark about her mother's addiction. She lived with her aunt Nicky Conroy, who told her that Cynthia was stationed at an army post overseas. "She would say that my mother was a war hero," Susan explains. "She would say that she was off saving lives. Sometimes I even got postcards from my mom. And pictures too. But I should've known something was wrong 'cause the pictures looked kind of old."

Her mother looked beautiful in those pictures, Susan tells me, but she herself has always resembled her aunt Nicky more than Cynthia, so much so that her friends often assumed she was Nicky's daughter. "They would say, 'Here your momma comes,' and after a while I stopped correcting them because my aunt was raising me. She was like my mother."

One day while riding the train home with her cousin and her cousin's friends, Susan spotted Cynthia under a bridge close to the West Side. "My cousin Tasha and her friends were making fun of each other. Joking around. Then," Susan continues, "someone said, 'Look at that dope fiend.'" Susan looked out of the train window and, shocked, recognized her mother. "I jumped off the train and ran to the bridge that she was under. I wiped the drool from her mouth."

Susan, her cousin, and her cousin's friends carried Cynthia to her aunt Nicky's house. Two months later Cynthia died from a drug overdose. Those two months were filled with pain and shame, as Cynthia panhandled in order to fund her habit. "She hustled and got high until she died," Susan says. Her mother's death happened three years ago, but in Susan's voice you can still hear the profound disappointment when she speaks of Cynthia's struggles.

Cynthia's story, and Susan's relationship with her, rested on a set of interconnected white lies. To hide the truth, Susan's aunt Nicky copied her sister's handwriting, creating a series of fraudulent postcards. Ironically, the old photos of Cynthia that Nicky sometimes attached provided Susan just enough of an image of her mother to be recognizable from a moving train. Susan told me that were it not for the army jacket that the "dope fiend" under the bridge had on, she might not have taken a second look. Despite, however, the stripes of a ranking officer stitched on her sleeves, Susan never again thought of her mother as a war hero. In the disjunctive space between the fabricated memory of her mother as veteran and the reality of her mother as heroin addict, Susan found a con artist.

The ersatz memories constructed to hide Cynthia's downfall from soldier to addict created very real, and very difficult, emotions that Susan was forced to confront—betrayal, shame, abandonment. Beyond the heartbreak, however, this deceit did serve a useful purpose: Susan strengthened her relationship with her aunt. And, in a roundabout way, Cynthia's tragic end helped convince Blizzard to stop selling drugs. Such consolations can seem small, though, especially when juxtaposed against the tale of a war veteran who fought to suppress the Taliban, only to open the floodgates of heroin production that contributed to her death.[18]

In the fall of 2010, Blizzard is not yet ready to concede that the story of Susan's mother has anything to do with why he's stopped selling heroin. Nevertheless, he has been focusing instead on media pirated from the Internet. Sometimes I follow him along his routes of distribution, and a few days after Susan told me the story of her mother, Blizzard and I are walking through an abandoned lot on the edge of Eastwood that is controlled by the Anonymous Knights. At the far end of the lot, six gang members are slouched in folding chairs. This patch of undeveloped land, a bare stretch of dirt graveled with broken glass, is a common meeting spot for the Knights when secrecy is required. The lot is well away from the blue lights and abandoned buildings. "If someone is around, they know," Blizzard says. "No surprises."

As a member of the Anonymous Knights, Blizzard has every right to pull up a chair; but because he is with me—a non-affiliate—we stop about twenty feet away, on the other side of the fence. Once the meeting is over, Blizzard is hoping to sell the gang members some of his goods. We lean against the chain-link fence waiting for the Knights' commanding officer, Kemo, to conclude his call to arms. Kemo is twenty-eight years old and has a massive presence in terms of physicality and charisma. He stands about six four and weighs at least 250 pounds. His voice booms; you often hear him before you see him. He speaks in short, authoritative bursts. When he yells—and he often yells—Kemo's words pierce the air like bullets. And yet he has been known to help an old lady cross the street, to buy a homeless man a meal, to hand a needy kid money for school clothes. Alongside the violent incidents and venomous outbursts on which Kemo has built his reputation, these acts of chivalry and kindness give him an air of sincerity.[19]

Blizzard could not be more different than Kemo: he's roughly ten years younger, almost a foot shorter, and at least one hundred pounds lighter than the gang leader. When Blizzard yells, his voice squeaks. It's hard to take his threats seriously (his words don't carry the same weight as Kemo's; they sound more like bird chirps than bullets). In public,

Blizzard wouldn't be caught dead helping an old lady or spending his hard-earned money on the homeless. But away from the street—where reputations are made and broken—he tutors his younger cousins when they are having trouble with their homework, and he cooks dinner when his mother works late. For four years now, Blizzard has been the primary caretaker for his disabled uncle, Tosh. People depend on Blizzard.

Not that a person would have much sense of this if, say, she happened to listen to him rattle off curse words on the corner. One might assume that Blizzard is lazy, immature, unmotivated, or simply posturing. Standing by the fence, I get the impression that part of the reason he picks this particular location to sell DVDs is because he admires Kemo. Blizzard, it seems, would gladly have a group of foot soldiers looking up to him, hanging on his every word as if their lives depend on it.

Meanwhile, on the other side of the chain link, Kemo is enraged. In recent weeks, three gang members have gotten locked up or shot, and by the sound of it, Kemo has concluded that the Knights must be doing something wrong. "When the Bandits come back around," he says, "someone is gonna have to step up. I'm looking for soldiers who are gonna represent this set."

Aside from the Bandits, Kemo's chief concern is the police. Pacing, he instructs his charges to "rotate the corner" when cops patrol. "You all can't stay in the same spot. If you stand here together, then you're gonna get locked up together or shot together. Who wants that? *Anybody?*"

Blizzard is less than a year removed from being a full-time foot soldier. Yet because his world now revolves around rap music, he speaks as if it—the other side of the fence—was a lifetime ago. His former and current industries do, however, contain fascinating parallels—specifically, new blood. Just as record-company executives must identify, sign, and develop new talent in order to make a commission, the Divine Knights' hierarchical network of drug distribution requires each affiliate to recruit new members into the organization—this in addition to selling product. Gang leaders do the bulk of the recruiting.[20]

New recruits are assigned a few blocks on which to deal, and, as street-level dealers, each must buy his or her product from the gang leader. Each gang leader is entitled to a percentage of every product sold in his respective section of Eastwood, just as a record-label owner like

Jay-Z is entitled to a percentage of every album sold from the artists he signs. On Eighteenth and James Streets, Kemo is both a higher-level distributor and dealer, dealing and selling to the dozen or so street-level teenagers in his set. When Blizzard used to sell heroin, he would purchase a "pack" (about two grams) from Kemo for seventy dollars. Blizzard would then divide the pack into smaller "bags" or "books" that were about one-tenth of a gram in weight; these he would sell for five dollars. Kemo made a profit from each pack he sold, which he received at wholesale price from the Divine Knights' team of central distributors.

Kemo also collects an additional source of revenue: a percentage of the sales from any gang members he allows to operate on James Street. This "street tax" is levied on sales of heroin, pills, and marijuana, as well as on pirated movies and music.[21] Blizzard resented having to share his profits with Kemo. So as a way to reassert control over his labor, he would include rhymes he had written in the DVD sleeves with a link to his website, where his music could be purchased. Kemo might've staked claim to a share of his profits, Blizzard reasoned, but he could not stake claim to his dreams.

Following the meeting, Blizzard and I leave the lot after the Knights do. Blizzard's sales are steady, impressive even. When I slip Blizzard ten dollars for a bootleg copy of the film *American Gangster*, he tells me he's sold out. He hands me back the bill, but I tell him to hold on to it. He'll drop it off later, Blizzard says, but he never does deliver the movie—at least not that day.

As we walk, I see that the money in Blizzard's pocket has given him a boost. Now emboldened, Blizzard mocks Kemo in the sternest voice he can muster: "Rotate the corner," he says again and again, turning Kemo's exhortation into a racket of envious scorn. "He used to tell us the same thing. We used to be rhyming, battling each other. Kemo would pull up in a car and get mad 'cause we wasn't hustling. But even when I used to sell drugs, I still liked music better."[22]

That Blizzard contrasts becoming a rapper and record-label executive with his stint as a heroin dealer is somewhat disingenuous, as are his lyrics, not to mention the grand persona he is trying to create. He relishes being categorized as a criminal. Blizzard's gravitation toward the criminal figure was inspired by a number of factors—prominent among them, his not-so-secret admiration for Kemo, his belief that rapping about street life endows him with authenticity, and also the subject broached in the first chapter: the threat of redevelopment.

By the winter of 2008, new government money is flowing into Eastwood and, with it, safety concerns. A new police precinct opens on James Street, blocks away from Eastwood Community Church. While city planners view Eastwood's poorest residents as unfortunate anchors, weighing down both property values and the neighborhood's future, drug-dealing gangbangers pose the biggest threat and are regarded as the worst group—a distinct subset of negatively valued black urbanites. Gang leaders like Kemo (who are primarily focused on the Knights' drug operation) are forced to adjust to the threat of redevelopment.

Kemo, in anticipation of major changes in Eastwood's demographics, overhauls his drug-dealing business. For years part of the appeal of dealing drugs was that one could earn an income while exhibiting explicit markers of gang affiliation—tattoos, gang colors, a brash street vernacular.[23] Starting in 2008, though, Kemo begins to prize members who can navigate not only Eastwood but the newly gentrified areas springing up east and north of town. Shortly after his altercation with Danny, Kemo made it clear that he was fed up with "renegades." Well-mannered, well-educated gang members now hold greater value for him; they are less conspicuous and more successful dealing to the growing number of whites who are buying drugs. This shift breeds resentment and rivalry among members of the Knights, as more traditionally "authentic" gang members see their chances to climb the gang's ladder to power diminishing.

Blizzard, Jonny "Champ" Wilson, Kenneth "Expo" Shipley, and Boris "Precise" Katz—the founding members of Gangsta City Entertainment—are among the Knights who find themselves on the outside looking in following Kemo's new mandate. None of the four have beyond a high school education, and each has been arrested at least once. On many occasions the rappers, especially Champ and Expo, openly lament their lack of money, the fact of which often tempted them to start selling again. While Champ and Expo still consider being drug dealers, Blizzard and Precise declare they are no longer interested. Because Kemo has more affiliates who want to sell than street corners to put them on, Blizzard and Precise are not pressured. Still, during the nine months I listened to all four of the founding members brainstorming and recording songs, dealing was always a central theme. Like so many fledgling hip hop artists, the archetypal drug-dealer figure had become an essential symbol for the Gangsta City rappers. Through the inhabitation of this figure, Blizzard, Precise, Champ, and Expo have given themselves freedom to voice their anxieties, and aspirations, regarding future prospects.

For Blizzard, this has as much to do with creating rap songs as it does producing them. Since 2005, when he bought his first computer, he has been slowly adding to his recording studio, and although it is located in the basement of Blizzard's mother's house, the studio is clearly his domain. Blizzard is the leader of Gangsta City Entertainment, meaning he is tasked with recruiting rappers and with inspiring them. To do this, he often compares aspirants to established rappers, all the while catering to "the real."

In the world of the studio, Blizzard is the coach who knows how to motivate each player. He knows Expo is self-conscious about his raspy voice (which, folks say, doesn't match his diminutive frame), so he assures him that his voice commands respect and tells him: "I made a beat last night that would be perfect for your voice." He knows Precise is extremely competitive, so he compares Precise's skills to those of local artists. "Did you hear his song?" Blizzard says, referring to a rising local talent. "You're a much better rapper than him." He knows that Champ, like himself, has a tendency to get preoccupied with authenticity, so Blizzard argues that Champ is uniquely qualified to talk about street life. "We've been struggling our whole lives," Blizzard says. "Can't nobody talk about these streets like us."

Since many Divine Knights regard Blizzard as Kemo's polar opposite, it's ironic, in this regard, that the talent-management skills Blizzard has honed at Gangsta City are also critical for leading a gang set. What's more, since Blizzard would be considered Clark Kent to Kemo's Superman, it's also ironic—though not so surprising—that in Blizzard's songs he invokes the figure of the criminal as a heroic ideal.

In African American communities, criminals for a long time have been at the heart of debates about authenticity. When trickster and out-law personas surface through cultural practices like "toasting," "signify-ing," and "playing the dozens," they serve as models of heroic action.[24] Worried that these models of heroism might translate into criminal activities, scholars have long warned black communities against emu-lating the criminal figure in the real world.[25] As mentioned, the more recent incarnations of this kind of warning resides in Stanley Crouch insistence that glorifying the criminal "threatens the moral health of the black community," or Tricia Rose's suggestion that exalting the black criminal feeds corporate America's racist impulses.[26] While both Crouch and Rose seek to examine how the figure of the criminal affects black urban youth, the flip side of this perspective examines the ways in which black urban youth mobilize such figures in the first place, and why these figures have become culturally significant.

Along these lines, Walter Benjamin hypothesizes that "great crimi-nals," like mafia bosses or drug kingpins, are secretly admired for not only the violence they enact, but also for the injustice to which this vio-lence bears witness.[27] Blizzard is attracted to hip hop, in part, because it allows him to bear witness to violence through song rather than en-acting violence in the drug trade. On a number of occasions, Blizzard has suggested that the criminal persona he's created is not based wholly on his experiences as a street hustler. He often incorporates his friends' stories, specifically those whom he believes have been unjustly incar-cerated. In addition, Blizzard draws from the short-lived infamy of his older brother, Andre, who was able to carve out a substantial sphere of authority as a street-level heroin dealer in Eastwood. Once part of the Divine Knights' central leadership tribunal, Andre is currently in prison. Blizzard claims his decision to rap about selling drugs as op-posed to actually selling drugs—a calculated, conscious one, to hear him tell it—was deeply influenced by his desire to avoid Andre's fate.

Many in Eastwood, however, suggest that Blizzard has always wanted to be a well-respected drug dealer, but he just didn't have what it takes. According to Tosh, Blizzard's uncle, when Blizzard was in middle school, high-schoolers ridiculed him for "pretending to sell drugs." As the story goes, Blizzard would roll loose tobacco in translucent paper and then sell these cigarettes to old men on their way to construction sites. One day the cops stopped Blizzard as he was walking away from a customer. They had to let him go, though, after finding only a bundle of loosies, not the heroin they were expecting. Nobody faulted Blizzard for trying to make a few dollars selling his cigarettes; the mockery that ensued was a result of his outsize reaction to being stopped by the police. "The crazy thing is that Blizzard was excited that he was mistaken for a drug dealer," Tosh says.

In the winter of 2008, during a pickup basketball game at Eastwood Community Church, two boys—one a Bandit; the other, Dario Hopfield, a member of the Anonymous Knights—started fighting following a particularly hard foul. When dirty looks progressed to physical confrontation, the crowd of onlookers rushed the court, assembling behind the feuding gang members based on affiliation. Clearly the fight was about far more than a foul. Such a feud was no rare occurrence. These brawls happened so frequently, in fact, that Eastwood Community Church and other churches had established a protocol for defusing tensions. Typically, one side was forced to go home—*actually* home, not lying in wait around the corner for the other side. Departures were closely monitored. After a half an hour or so, once the coast was deemed clear, Pastor Tim would dismiss the side that wasn't allowed to leave.

On this particular Thursday, though, the group of gang members made to exit first—the Bandits—were so worked up that they turned over the shelves in the church where everyone places their personal belongings. Book bags, cell phones, and bundles of clothes that belonged to the players still in the gym came crashing to the floor. Members of the Anonymous Knights, insulted by the blatant disregard for their personal belongings, swept toward the overturned shelves in a tornado-like swirl. By the time they reached the mess, the instigators had skipped out of the gym.

The church staff promptly locked the doors to prevent a brawl, but the Bandits did not leave the premises. Instead, they taunted the Anonymous Knights from outside. As the church staff waved from inside of the gym for the Bandits to leave the area, Blizzard jumped from the bleachers onto the gym floor, pulled a shotgun from his trench coat, and charged the doors. Luckily, the assistant pastor, Curtis Gaines, and one of the men from the church's rehab center were able to wrestle the gun away from Blizzard before he could aim and shoot. Not that it would have mattered if he had: the gun wasn't loaded.

When Eastwoodians (especially members of the Anonymous Knights) found out that Blizzard went to an open gym with an unloaded gun, rumors about him spread through the neighborhood like wildfire. They hinged on one crucial question: Would Blizzard really shoot someone, or was he just play-acting for attention? Blizzard's criminal pronouncements, long avoided or outright ignored by most in Eastwood, suddenly gained real dimension. For many, the open gym incident turned indifference into resentment; Blizzard was no longer a mere blowhard, but something far worse: a charlatan.

"Everybody knows the story, so they think he's just trying to be like Kemo," Tosh tells me. In wielding an empty shotgun, Blizzard became a poor man's version of Kemo, who once brandished a loaded shotgun in an incident that gained him infamy in Eastwood. When he was fourteen, rumor has it that Kemo kicked in the very same gym doors with a shotgun on his shoulder. At that time, the Roving Knights, not the Bandits, were the Anonymous Knights' main rival. After a brawl had broken out, Kemo left the premises, returning minutes later with the firearm. When the Roving Knights scattered at the sight of an adolescent with a deadly weapon, a legend was born. Since then, Kemo has grown from a skinny teenager whose "gun was bigger than him," says Tosh, to a linebacker-size adult. Many gang members claim it was the brashness displayed in Kemo's formative years that propelled him to the position of gang leader.

The uncanny similarity between the two shotgun-wielding events leads many gang members to view Blizzard's actions as a deliberate attempt to bolster his street credibility. For many, Blizzard's actions (and, by extension, his raps) are disingenuous. To be clear, these gang members did not want Blizzard to actually shoot one of the offending Bandits. Rather, they resent the fact that Blizzard attempted to pass as someone who *would* shoot a rival, and then try to profit from his dangerous reputation through his music. In Eastwood, reputations are a measure of value, especially when that reputation is tied to one's rank and achievement in a gang. Those who would impersonate a recognized member of the collective, who would attempt to enhance their own value by fraudulent means, are not only impostors—they're thieves.

I noted earlier that Tosh is Blizzard's uncle (though, since he's only five years older, they consider themselves peers). Like Blizzard, Tosh wants to steer clear of engaging in criminal activity. He prefers to write about it, as a novelist, and, by and large, other active gang members—some of them bona fide hustlers—support his dream. Tosh's allegiance to the Knights, unlike Blizzard's, has never been questioned. During a shoot-out in 2000, Tosh was hit and, as previously mentioned, is now paralyzed from the waist down—a virtuous disability, as many gang members see it. Tosh has demonstrated a willingness to sacrifice his body on behalf of his gang. Absent the nagging pressure of having to prove his loyalty to the Anonymous Knights (namely, by selling drugs), Tosh has time to craft a new reality through his writing.

When I first described my work to Tosh—the ways in which writing a dissertation is similar to writing a book—he grew excited and told me he was crafting a memoir based on his exploits as a gang member. His writing is inspired by the literary stylizations of Donald Goines, who is renowned for his vivid depictions of ghetto and prison life. Goines died in 1974, shot to death by neighborhood criminals in his hometown of Detroit. His killers allegedly objected to characters and story lines in his novels, which they feared could be used as clues in exposing their crimes. Today Goines's books remain popular, in part because of the vast number of rappers referencing them in songs.[28]

During the course of my research, my relationship with Tosh intensifies. We brainstorm ideas about our respective projects at a local restaurant called Big Al's over a Chicago-style pizza—stuffed deep dish. As I proofread his manuscript, Tosh shares his perspective on my field notes. A purist when it comes to the hip hop subgenre of gangsta rap, Tosh cannot understand why I spend so much time in the makeshift studio with Blizzard. Tosh believes rappers ought to speak on behalf of a marginalized public, spinning gripping tales linked to an authentic street experience. And because Blizzard doesn't have a celebrated career as a gang member, in Tosh's opinion there's no way he can be a good rapper.

"If you wanna study gangs and rap," Tosh says, "I know what you should do. I'll take you around the guys that robbed Bullet"—a well-known Chicago rapper, Reed "Bullet" Taylor. "They still got his chain. It's a platinum medallion of a twelve-gauge bullet with diamonds everywhere."

And what should I ask them—how does it feel to rob a Grammy-award winner?

"Real funny," he sneers. "You could start with the simple questions—like why they did it." According to Tosh, one night after a concert in the city, Bullet entered a Chicago nightclub. A few Anonymous Knights, including Kemo, were also in the club. Kemo introduced himself to Bullet, and they became friends. A couple of months later, the gang leader convinced Bullet to film a music video in the part of town controlled by his gang set. When members of the Bandits saw the video, they were incredulous. Bullet was supposed to be an Anonymous Knight?

"So that's why the next time Bullet came to the West Side, he got robbed," Tosh explains. Stealing the rapper's diamond-encrusted bullet was more about sending a message than it was snatching a valuable trophy. The member of the Bandits credited with the robbery, Shawn Harris (previously known as Shawna)—one of the few prominent females in the gang—doesn't wear the medallion. And she hasn't sold it. Rather, the theft made a powerful statement, says Tosh: "First off, the Knights aren't shit. And second, come hang with the Bandits when you want some credibility."

Tosh promises me an audience with Shawn so that I might hear her story firsthand. She apparently loves to talk about the day the Bandits looked Bullet in the eye and said, "If you want your chain back, tell Kemo a little girl stole it." The use of "little girl" is key, Tosh reminds me: Kemo often uses the term to dismiss Shawn's authority and thus denigrate the Bandits.

The Bandits control Oliver Street, a thoroughfare directly adjacent to James Street, which is adamantly guarded by Kemo and his Anonymous Knight foot soldiers. (Shawn's crew was the source of Kemo's frustration the day I watched him scold his set in the abandoned lot.)

I ask why the Anonymous Knights didn't reclaim the medallion.

"Word is, Kemo wanted to charge him a shitload of money to do the deed. So, Bullet took the loss. Now he basically stays in the suburbs where he belongs."

In Eastwood, what passes for an authentic gang experience is always disputed and contested. Even commercially successful rap artists can become entangled in the webs of feuding gang sets. Indeed, the pull of authenticity is so strong that Bullet still feels compelled to cultivate an image of himself as being from the street.

As someone familiar with the other kind of "shooting up" prevalent in Eastwood, Tosh is the first to admit that his notion of the real is rooted in his disability. Being a paraplegic prevents him from selling drugs in an open-air market; and yet his condition is an embodiment of the danger that the open-air market represents. His wheelchair, in other words, is a symbol of authenticity—a reminder to everyone that he's been shot. What's more, Tosh claims that his wounds make his writing more authoritative than Blizzard's raps.

Months before the winter of 2008, when the gym incident became another case in point for discounting Blizzard's authenticity claims, a gang war was ignited in front of his mother's house. We are in Blizzard's studio on a muggy night in June when the session is interrupted by gunshots. Blizzard stops recording. I look through the window and see people running up James Street. A car in front of the greystone screeches away. Blizzard's sister, Kathy Tremont, runs into the house just as the rappers from the studio run out to the porch. "I'm too young to die," she says melodramatically.

Blizzard steps into the doorway, peers down the dark street in the direction of the burnt-tire fumes. Champ, Expo, and Precise mumble about where they think the shots came from. Nobody seems to know anything. The porch is uncomfortably silent. Just then, a shirtless boy approaches. "Two people got hit: Eddie and Pete," he says breathlessly. The assumption is that the Bandits were behind the attack. Blizzard calls Kemo, using the untraceable walkie-talkie function of his phone. His debrief: "Two guys. Eddie and Pete. Bandits, we think."

After the shooting, I ask gang members what started the feud between the Bandits and the Anonymous Knights. A territory dispute was my best guess — Kemo encroaching on Shawn's territory, or vice versa. Not so, however. The tale of the turmoil begins, always, when the leaders of the two warring factions were in high school. Tosh: "Believe it or not, they" — Kemo and Shawn — "used to be close. *Real* close, if you know what I mean. And let me tell you something, back in the day — "

I cut Tosh off, finishing the sentence for him. *Back in the day, Shawn was the finest thing in Eastwood. She was beau-ti-ful.* I'd heard this many times before. Gang members, years ago, viewed Shawn as the paragon of femininity, and most seem eager to recall those days. I suspect it is because many of them want to believe that deep down she is still the innocent girl they insist on remembering and not the openly gay woman she's become. Both members of the Anonymous Knights and the Bandits tend to associate what they deem a newfound masculine disposition with the events that led to her father's incarceration.

Shawn's father, Ronnie Harris, was a high-ranking gang official in the 1980s, before the Bandits, as such, even existed. Like many high-ranking officials from that era, he was, allegedly, motivated by money; consequently, Ronnie was instrumental in overhauling the Divine Knights Gang, transforming them from a community-based political action group to a corporate enterprise. In the mid-1980s, politicians passed beefed-up federal legislation targeting drug traffickers; soon after, Ronnie was sentenced to sixty years for drug possession with the intent to distribute. Upon his incarceration, Ronnie's wife, Shawn's mother, took over his role in the gang. But she was arrested under the RICO Act for transporting drugs across state lines and was also sent to prison. Now Shawn runs what has become the family business. Still, although she commands a gang set whose primary job is to sell drugs and also performs the duties of a gang leader, Shawn does not have an official role or rank in the gang. In Kemo's eyes, for instance, she is merely running her father's drug operation in his absence. This despite the fact that, as mentioned, the Bandits as we know them today didn't exist when Ronnie went to prison. He will be eighty-seven years old before he is eligible for parole.

That Shawn is a lesbian bolsters the argument that she is only pretending to be part of a gang in which the presence of women is largely erased and taken for granted. Females in the Bandits are seldom compensated for their time in prison the way men are. When a high-ranking gang member goes to prison, gang leaders often pay the member's family's rent and, if children are involved, make sure they're fed and clothed. Female affiliates are less likely to have these privileges extended to them, despite playing substantial roles in processing drugs and transporting heroin ("runners"), meaning they are just as likely as the men to go to jail. Just like the video vixen who is silenced on stage sets, yet whose presence is an unavoidable prerequisite for hip hop music videos, female gang members are necessary to the operation yet seldom share in the spoils.

"If you ask Kemo," Tosh says, continuing his explanation of the rivalry, "Shawn's just got a chip on her shoulder 'cause she's a woman playing a man's game. If you ask me, Kemo's just mad 'cause Shawn gets more money *and* women than him." Tosh laughs to himself, then assures me that Shawn, because she is a woman, can never reach the heights her father did (who was once second in command, with only the Supreme Chief of the Divine Knights outranking him.) More accurately, though, Shawn can never assume her father's power because his position in the gang no longer exists. No longer is there a single leader; accordingly, there is no second-in-command.[29]

Two days after Eddie Jamieson and Pete Hughes are shot, Kemo convenes the fragmented central leadership of the Divine Knights and decides to declare war on the Bandits. In practical terms, this means that Blizzard's studio, located just next to the alley behind James Street (an ideal spot to retreat to in the event that the street is overtaken by a rival gang or the police), will become part of the "rotation"—that is, one of the many houses where the gang will store its guns. The "rotation"—the continuous relocation of the gang's illicit resources—is a practice that was born in prison, where the Divine Knights are likewise highly organized. To avoid the random searches that guards carry out on each prisoner's cell, one gang member at a time is tasked with housing everyone's weapons. The chances that your bunk will get searched on the particular day you happen to be on call are slim. Of course, this is only an estimation: if a person is unlucky enough to get searched on the day he has "shank duty," a substantial amount of prison time could be added to his term. (On the outside, the term is still shank duty—this despite loca-tion and the fact that the weapons in question have evolved significantly from hand-whittled knifes.)

Shank duty has been a staple of the Divine Knights operational pro-cedure since at least the 1980s, when members of the gang began serving long prison sentences. As a gang leader, it is Kemo's job to decide which houses and businesses become part of the rotating arsenal. Word on the street is that Kemo has decided to make Blizzard's studio a "stash house." For compensation, Blizzard will receive five hundred dollars in cash each time Kemo uses his basement to store weapons.

Much as he wants to, Tosh can't tell anyone—friends, neighbors, relatives—when he and Blizzard are on shank duty.

"If it was up to me," he says, "I would post a sign on the door that says 'Shank Duty: Enter at Your Own Risk.' But I can't do that because we can't trust people around here." Tosh fears someone getting arrested on an unrelated matter, and then disclosing the stash house in order to get a reduced sentence. So, instead of making it known to the public, Tosh decides to come up with a signal for people like me that he wants to keep out of harm's way. "When you call, I'll just say my stomach hurts and you know not to come to the studio 'cause it's shank day," he says. But that's no good—what if he really does want to hang out? Tosh goes on and on like this, suggesting a code phrase and then retracting it himself. Forty-five minutes later, he finds his solution: wheelchair basketball.

"I'll say: 'Don't come to the studio. Just meet me at the gym 'cause I feel like playing wheelchair basketball.' Then you'll know what the deal is."

For months I keep my distance from Blizzard's studio. Tosh never calls with the code phrase. I invite the Gangsta City rappers over to my apartment to rehearse each time they catch wind of a possible tal-ent show, and sometimes Tosh comes with them. Otherwise, we meet at Big Al's, where we continue to exchange notes on writing. One day at Big Al's, Tosh is a no-show. When I ask one of the employees if she has heard from him, she informs me that Blizzard's house had been raided the night before. I rush out of the restaurant and head straight to the studio. Tosh is on the front porch, seated in his wheelchair. He

says, "Neighbors called the police and said that there was a drug operation in the basement. They didn't find any drugs, but they still arrested
Blizzard."

"For what?" I ask. "Guns?"

"Nope. The warrant was for guns, but they arrested him for selling
bootleg DVDs."

During Blizzard's trial, it comes to light that the police had been watching his basement for months. They had received tips that gang members were congregating at the greystone during "peak drug-trafficking
hours." On the basis of information received from a gang member in
which Blizzard's basement was fingered as a storage facility for drugs
and guns, the police were able to procure a search warrant. Little did
this informant know that Kemo, concerned that Blizzard would not
be able to keep the location of the stash house discreet, had ultimately
decided against a rotating arsenal. Blizzard, however, in an attempt to
bolster his street cred, bragged to friends that his basement was in fact
a stash house in the rotation.

When the cops broke down Blizzard's door, they found an archive of
over one thousand downloaded movie files, blank DVDs, and computer
printouts of miniature film advertisements he planned to insert in the
DVD jewel cases. No guns or drugs were found; Blizzard was charged
with copyright infringement. The police seized all of his studio equipment. Unable to afford bond, he was sent to jail. While Blizzard waited
for his trial date, Gangsta City Entertainment—without its leader or
recording equipment—disbanded.

The Blizzard I visited in jail was noticeably, and understandably,
frustrated. Though he was no longer selling drugs, he had still man-
aged to wind up behind bars. To make matters worse, no one seemed to
notice his sacrifice. On the street, gang members were still ridiculing
him, Blizzard said, because his arrest fit perfectly the profile of a "studio
gangsta." Being incarcerated for selling movies, and not for the drugs
and guns he rapped about, added to the idea that Blizzard's gangsterism
was largely self-invention.

Blizzard's subsequent conviction (he was sentenced to eight months
in prison) had much more to do with a history of criminal behavior than

his current offense. His drug-dealing past did, in the end, figure into his sentencing; still, Blizzard was taunted so much after his release that instead of moving back into the apartment on James Street, he packed his things and headed across town to live with his girlfriend, Susan.

The last time I see Susan is a year after Blizzard's release. "I kicked Blizzard out because I found a bag of heroin in his coat pocket," she says. "I don't know if he was using or selling, but I gave him a choice: Either you can leave, or I can call your parole officer and tell her what I found. He left." Susan shakes her head.

Since Blizzard left Susan's, Tosh has only seen him a few times. He will not speculate as to whether his nephew is using heroin, though Tosh admits to hearing rumors. Quickly, Tosh turns the conversation toward how much his nephew means to him, and how his own life has been altered by Blizzard's absence. Tosh reminds me that after his injury, Blizzard volunteered to be his caretaker. "He helped me get out of bed in the morning. He helped me take baths. He listened to my screams when I couldn't hold a goddamned fork."

Tosh claims the real reason he made fun of Blizzard for trying to be a gangster was because he didn't want his nephew to go down that path. Blizzard had a lot more to offer the world than peddling heroin in Eastwood, Tosh thinks. I mention Blizzard's name again, and Tosh, almost teary-eyed, waves his hand in front of his face as if to clear the air. Then he changes the subject: the first draft of his memoir, *Trapped*, is complete. "It's about me—my life," Tosh says. "But more than that, it's about 'the trap.' The trap, that's the area of town where you get drugs. They say that down South. So this is our Midwest trap. Eastwood is a trap."

I wonder, though, if the title relates to Tosh being paralyzed, to him getting shot.

"What do you think?" he says, extinguishing a potentially sentimental moment with sarcasm. "Of course it's about getting shot. But I don't really talk about my rehab in the book. It doesn't end with rehab. It ends with a dream."

In that dream, Tosh is still in the trauma center, after finding out that he's been paralyzed. He's in the hospital bed, and he's waiting until the doctor leaves the room. He waits until the middle of the night when no one is paying attention and the entire hospital is quiet. Then he gets up. He gets up and walks down the long trauma center hallway. It's like he's in a tunnel that's getting brighter and brighter until he reaches the door. He opens the door to leave the trauma center and then wakes up. "I'm back in the hospital bed," he says. "I'm still paralyzed. It was all a dream."[30]

As Tosh tells me about his book's ending, I think about the human potential embedded in his idea of being "trapped." This was a potential of possibility that I had neglected before. Through his work, Tosh positioned himself at a crossroads between the real and imaginary, and these faces of existence interchanged with one another like a coin flipping through the air. The fact that Tosh wasn't paralyzed by his thoughts, sharing a lucid moment in which his disability was undone, suggests that the fork in the road where Tosh was temporarily stationed just might lead to an alternative pathway.

About six months after Tosh tells me about feeling "trapped," I receive an envelope in the mail from an Illinois correctional facility. I open it, expecting to see a letter. Instead there's a bootleg copy of *American Gangster*. Someone has slipped an untitled poem inside of the DVD case. If I had my way, I would call it "A Wish":

> There's a wish that sits on a candle, inside of its flame
> The flame dances a seductive dance
> And by the flickering light—
> Men see shoe boxes full of hundred-dollar bills
> All the men in Eastwood
> With stuffed shoe boxes in their rooms
> But this cell is not a bedroom
> And there are no shoe boxes here
> I was you, before I knew, what being you really was
> There's no "Why" to your reasoning, you hustle just "Because"
> The O.G.'s in this prison shake their heads when you're around
> 'Cause they understand what you fail to catch on to:
> The only thing that matters is a wish
> And if you have a breath left to make it come true

After reading this cautionary poem about the allure of hustling and the pitfalls of the street, the first thing I think about is how different it is from the boastful raps that poured out of Blizzard in Gangsta City's basement studio. Reflecting on his words, I smile with the realization that I no longer needed to worry about the cocky young rapper who taught me about Eastwood's heroin trade, and so much more. He might've been locked up, but he hadn't lost his desire to dream—or, in his words, to make his wishes "come true."

But perhaps, more than the poem itself, what comforts me most is what is written underneath. It is signed *Darryl Tremont*—Blizzard's real name.

Two

———✳———

The Resilience of Dreams

Getting In

Today, for the second day in a row, I ran into Mr. Randall. Yesterday he passed by the window at Big Al's; I waved and he waved back. This afternoon at the House of Worship, where I was meeting with Kemo, Mr. Randall tells me he's impressed to see me breaking bread with a gang leader. (At the same time, a little worried.) He used to be Kemo's probation officer, Mr. Randall says.

He wants to know how I "got in." Mr. Randall asks this as I'm sitting across the table from Kemo — and it isn't just the two of us, Kemo and me. Also present: Justin, Tiko, Pete, and Steve (not "Psycho" Steve —

either, it's "Skinny" Steve, who's harmless; Fatima's older brother). Not that Mr. Randall seems to care — he doesn't acknowledge anybody else at that table.

Instead, he hones in on my "relationship" with Kemo, which is ironic: To this day, Kemo's never spoken a word to me. He's made fun of me but only in passing, his taunts always loud enough for me to hear. Kemo has yet to address me directly, though, even when I've asked him questions. So the idea that I've gotten "in" is particularly amusing to me. I tell Mr. Randall that he has nothing to worry about, that I'm not being recruited into the gang. As a

matter of fact, Kemo and I were meeting about organizing a forum to *stop* the
violence, all without saying a word to
one another.

—1/17/09, 11:07 PM

CHAPTER FOUR

𝔇𝔦𝔰𝔞𝔟𝔦𝔩𝔦𝔱𝔶

———✳———

OR,

Why a Gang Leader Helps Stop the Violence

Justin and I are waiting in Kemo's garage for the gang leader himself, who's about a quarter of an hour late. Near where I'm sitting there are piles of DVD players, cell phones, car stereos, laptops, and Internet routers. Justin explains: In wintertime, when severe weather makes it hard to convince foot soldiers to stand on the corner and deal, Kemo "goes all bootleg," selling a wide variety of contraband. Hot merchandise means it's cold outside, says Justin, who is gripping the armrests of his wheelchair and raising his body up and down in a slow, fluid motion. His triceps bulge as he finishes his third set of inverted push-ups.

When Kemo finally arrives, he closes a side door someone had left ajar, relieving Justin and me of the sting of winter. "What's Urkel doing here?" Kemo says, staring me down. He refuses to reciprocate the customary head nod.

"I told you: He's helping out with the forum," Justin says. "He's here to take notes." Suspicious, Kemo keeps his eyes trained on me. Then he casually snaps open a chair and straddles it, ready to spell out, in meticulous detail, what can and cannot be discussed at the upcoming forum.

"I don't want you guys mentioning any gang leaders or any sets by name," Kemo says, looking back and forth between Justin and me. "No blocks, no streets, nothing like that. I don't know who's gonna be around, you know."

"Nah, I don't do that," Justin replies. "That's not the point of what I do." Kemo seems pleased by this. "But," Justin continues, "I am going to talk about the consequences of gang banging. I am going to talk about what happened to me, and how it's affected my life."

"I ain't got no problem with that," Kemo says with a smirk. "But good luck getting them to listen. I'll do my part. I'll get them there. Then they're all yours."

Upon leaving Kemo's garage, a number of questions floated in my mind: Why would Justin, a paralyzed former gang member turned activist, team up with a gang leader like Kemo to organize a community forum on violence? And why would Kemo agree to play along? What can this forum and the collaboration that allows it to take place teach us about the concept of disability?

In 2009 the rate of violent crime in Chicago was almost double those of New York City and Los Angeles.[1] Among the nation's ten largest cities, each with a population of at least one million, only Philadelphia had higher rates of murder and violent crime than the Windy City. In the 2008–9 academic year, a record number of public school students (thirty-eight) were murdered.[2] The grim severity of these numbers naturally focuses our attention on death, but unacknowledged in statistics like these is a more complex reality: Most victims of gun violence do not die. In fact, a wounded victim of gun violence is four times more likely to end up disabled than dead. Gunshot injuries constitute the second most common cause of disability in urban areas (only car accidents rank higher).[3] For our purposes, we must note that gun violence is the *primary* cause of disability among Latinos and blacks—the two most heavily represented populations in Chicago gangs.[4]

In Eastwood, it isn't uncommon to see a young person pushing himself here to there in a wheelchair or walking unsteadily with the aid of a cane. This chapter is an attempt to understand why disabilities are disproportionately visited on communities like Eastwood. More generally, I consider the multifaceted ideas about what injury means among disabled populations. My argument is that, while admirable, the Disability Rights movement has focused too emphatically on assuaging social difference within disabled communities; in so doing, the movement has obscured key distinctions along the axes of race and socioeconomic status. We will examine two models of disability: the social, in which there are multiple ways to view ability, and where physical capacities are not devalued (the larger community of disabled activists in Chicago tends to observe this model); and the medical, which highlights physical differences rather than seeking to diminish them (disabled ex-gang members rely on this model).

That disabled African American ex-gang members are willing to insist on the defectiveness of their own bodies points to the crushing burden that violence creates in communities like Eastwood. This burden, as well as the dilemmas of the disabled, will be examined with the following (seemingly obscure) lenses attached: notions of debt and obligation. Critical aspects of gang sociality revolve around what one owes, and what one is owed. To the reader, the sequence of gang violence may seem predictable: One gang member shoots an affiliate of a rival gang, and, in response, members of the rival gang retaliate. In this way, death and injury are forms of debt exchange. Because social bonds between gang members are so often solidified through violence, the testimony of a disabled gang member can be strategically deployed—as we will later see—to disrupt a cycle of vengeance. Within this violent world, wounds become the precondition for enabling social transformation.

Days after meeting with Kemo in his garage, I find him holding court in an abandoned lot. A group of eight teenage boys that the gang leader has handpicked to sell drugs in his domain sit on the glass-strewn ground at his feet. Kemo is waving his arms, punctuating his admonishment (the boys are failing to properly police their neighborhood turf) with menacing stares. He looks like an urban griot.

"Y'all lack discipline," Kemo says. "That's why you got the Bandits coming in here shooting up the place." Recently, members of the Bandits, the Knights' rivals, injured two of Kemo's set. Pete, an affiliate shot in the leg during the incursion, sits next to Kemo, the cane he will use for the rest of his life between them. Kemo praises Pete for his bravery. Pete is one of the few among them who has "what it takes" to be a gang leader one day, Kemo says. He then reaches for the curved handle of Pete's cane and drags the rubber tip through the dirt, sketching the boundaries of the Knights' block. X's mark the places he predicts rival gangs will attempt to invade; around these, Kemo draws a series of arrows—routes the gang members should travel to safeguard their territory. Kemo's depiction of his commercial strategy literally relies on a marker of disability: the cane. It is at once a convenient prop used to diagram a strategy for maintaining economic control, and a reminder of the potential consequences of such a mission.

The "land of promise" that's celebrated in the Constitution of the United States has an unsavory flip side: the construction of the "defective" black subject.[5] The discourse of American exceptionalism has long masked its most vulgar side. In the 1890s, anthropologists measured the skulls of African descendants to show how behaviors (like criminality) and abilities (like intelligence) corresponded differently to blacks and whites. More recently, scholars and government agencies have suggested that the socioeconomic plight of urban blacks could be linked to degenerate cultural values.[6] These notions of the defective body born in the nineteenth century continue to shape the leading perspectives of social and cultural difference in the twenty-first.[7] And yet, as Philippe Bourgois and Jeff Schonberg have recently suggested, there remains a dearth of urban scholarship examining the relationship between injuries both physical and social.[8]

We can understand how the concept of injury operates in Eastwood, how this concept gains vitality, by examining the productive tension between injury and enabling.[9] Gang cultures often coalesce around the strategies required for protecting turf (territory, property, access). Successful strategies, of course, can lead to the accretion of good standing and wealth. Indeed, many gang members in Eastwood consider their turf as the primary ground on which they can "get ahead" in a society where young Eastwoodians are frequently excluded from participation in the American polity.[10] Similar to the war veteran in contemporary American society, the violent event in which a person experiences injury allows the disabled gang member to rise in social stature and moral standing (recall Kemo's praise of Pete, the injured affiliate). And like the war veteran, the rhetorical effect of this patriotism stands in sharp relief to reality. Disabled gang members in Eastwood are released from service with gratitude—the military equivalent of an honorable discharge.

Of course, disabled gang members who would rather continue their drug-dealing activities are likely to be forgotten about, marginalized, and neglected within the active gang member strata. In contrast to members killed and martyrized in gang wars, the disabled gang member, unable to contribute monetarily in the manner most valued (that is, as a street-corner drug dealer), becomes like Susan's mother, Cynthia, the supposedly "honored" war veteran begging for change by day, and by night bedding down beneath an inner-city bridge.

Erving Beamer, the most infamous Divine Knight of all time, embodies this point. In 2001 Beamer was released from prison for weapons violations only to discover that the exponential increase of competing gang sets had greatly diminished his authority in Eastwood. As Beamer attempted to wrestle power from a number of local gang leaders now in control of smaller gang units, intra-gang feuding increased. By 2003 the infighting had reached a boiling point; that year Beamer was paralyzed after being hit by four bullets. Nearly a year after the attempt on Beamer's life, a local news channel discussed the implications of the shooting. In an "ABC exclusive" on November 17, 2004, television anchor Charles Thomas summarized Beamer's situation: The former Supreme Chief of the Divine Knights, who had spent over half his life in state and federal prisons (Beamer was fifty-five at the time), was now imprisoned by his own body. Some of the assassins who effectively turned Beamer into a paraplegic were henchmen formerly under his command, Beamer believes.

"They felt that I was threatening their way of life," Beamer says in the exclusive. Thomas, narrating, states that "Beamer knows who his shooters are, but will not give an order to retaliate."

"I don't want to take control again," Beamer says. "It ain't for Erving Beamer no more. There's no benefit to joining the gang. I see myself as Dr. Frankenstein: the monster I created turned on me."

The last Supreme Chief of the Divine Knights is currently hidden away in exile far from his hometown, presumably. (In Eastwood, there's a bounty on Beamer's head.) At the conclusion of the exclusive, Beamer's wife pushes him in his wheelchair down an unidentified hospital hallway.

While the majority of gang violence pits subsets of the same gang against one another, the Divine Knights members' conceptions of their involvement with the gang is based on an opposition to the Snakes, their rivals operating in South Side Chicago. The Knights, in marking their territory, use sets of symbols that include the Snake insignia, which are either crossed out or drawn upside down. When confronted by a fellow gang member on the street, one proves affiliation to the Knights by stating the name of his or her gang set followed by the word "love," or by saying the name of a gang set associated with the Snakes followed by the word "killer." (The Snakes, for their part, harbor similar hatred for the Divine Knights; and their gang has also been split into sets since the 1990s.)

Divine Knights only claim allegiance to the larger organization when facing off against the Snakes. On an everyday basis, Knights think and act as members of much smaller, localized gang sets. It might seem that gang unification would inspire violence between the Knights and the Snakes, but gang members in Eastwood seldom leave their neighborhood. The local sets are capable of combining to form a united force when other gangs threaten their organization as a whole; but when internal social relations are disturbed, those same sets are prone to considerable fracture. Each new local territorial dispute threatens gang accord; often at the middle of these disputes are the physically injured members, their wheelchairs turned into paradigmatic symbols of injury. In many ways, the gang set devalues injured affiliates, as they are unable to physically respond to threats. But, at the same time, the injuries that gang members like Tosh, Pete, or Justin have suffered help constitute the turf that their respective gang set will control and profit from. Injury is a fundamental precondition that provides a certain amount of structure for the Divine Knights' geography of commerce. Disability, in other words, gives shape to the Divine Knights' organizational configuration.[11]

In 2009, in response to the extraordinary number of public school students killed by guns, community forums on violence became commonplace in Eastwood. These forums were typically sponsored by nonprofit organizations, schools, or churches, and coordinated by adults who—though well-intentioned—had only tangential relationships to the young black men they were targeting.[12]

Justin, having attended many such forums over the past year, worries about their efficacy, as he sees very few young men in the audience. "The guys who really need to be there, them boys who really need to hear those stories, they're out on the street," he tells me. We're putting away basketballs at the after-school program where Justin works, and I volunteer. The gang, he says, is still a major influence on the young men of Eastwood despite best efforts of the forums' organizers. Too many of those forums, in Justin's opinion, are "out of touch." According to Justin, the way to remedy this, to get through to the young men the forums aren't currently reaching, is to offer sessions led by men like him: streetwise males in their early to mid-twenties (young enough to relate to teenagers) who have real relationships with members of the Divine Knights and who, most importantly, are in wheelchairs. These ex-gang members, it turns out, have much to teach scholars about the importance of examining how and why certain populations in certain areas are disabled in certain ways.[13]

Disability scholars have long rejected the medical model of disability. Instead, they champion a rights-based model, which "emphasizes people's personal adjustment to impairment and their adaptation to a medical-rehabilitative regimen of treatment."[14] These scholars view disability as an institutionalized source of oppression, comparable to inequalities based on race, gender, and sexual orientation. They argue that it is not an individual's actual "impairments" that render that individual subordinate in terms of social status, but socially imposed barriers—anything from inaccessible buildings, to limited modes of transportation and communication, to prejudicial attitudes.[15]

This "social model" is a radical departure from the medical model of illness, which has dominated Western thinking since the early twentieth century.[16] (The medical model, in summary: Disabilities are physical conditions that reduce a person's quality of life and thus pose clear disadvantages to that person.) In *The Wounded Storyteller*, for example, Arthur Frank discusses how medical culture is often an unsettling, almost foreign experience for the ill and injured—largely because doctors are trained to reinterpret personal feelings of suffering into symptoms. Medical treatment facilities use technical language that is "unfamiliar and overwhelming," thereby leading the disabled patient to "surrender" his narrative to medical authority.

For Frank, the wounded storyteller's disavowal of medical expertise is the basis by which he voices his own experience of suffering.[17] The notion that as opposed to abiding by medical classifications of impairment, people should embrace their own wounded bodies as an act of empowerment has been greatly influenced by the Americans with Disabilities Act of 1990. The act makes discrimination based on disability illegal. Just as important, it has advanced awareness of the systemic societal barriers that people with disabilities must contend with— obstructions impacting their worldview and drastically altering their social navigational systems.[18]

The Americans with Disabilities Act has greatly increased the flow of resources to disabled people. But in striving to mitigate the biases against those with physical and mental impairments, scholars of physical impairment have glossed over the ways that race operates within disabled communities. My time in Eastwood reveals the perils of such an omission. Justin's wheelchair-bound life and the way he makes sense of his disability would be nearly unrecognizable—not to mention incomprehensible—to, for example, a well-off, white, middle-aged person who is paralyzed in a car crash.[19]

Paralyzed ex–gang members in Chicago—the ones Justin admires, at least—do not subscribe to Arthur Frank's thesis that medical treatment facilities mute the injured patient's voice. In fact, since meeting at Eastwood Hospital around 2003, Justin's friends have participated in a rehabilitation program designed to teach those suffering from spinal cord injuries how to adapt. At the conclusion of the rehab course, a few of the men petitioned the hospital to sponsor a program they developed. Referred to as the "Crippled Footprint Collective," the program sends former gang affiliates—themselves the victims of violence—to schools to discuss what it feels like to have your life permanently altered by a disability. This is the group previously mentioned that motivated Justin to dream of a career in violence prevention.

One Monday I travel with Justin to Jackson High, located blocks away from the House of Worship, where school administrators have blocked off the bulk of the school day to violence prevention programming. The sessions are separated by gender: the girls will hear from a group of women on leave from an Illinois Correctional facility; the boys, from Justin's group of disabled ex-gang members. Darius Gilbert, the leader of this group, welcomes some 250 students to the Crippled Footprint Collective, which is, as he explains, "a little different from other programs. Like, we're not here to scare you or anything like that. We're basically here to educate you about the consequences of drug activities and gang life." The students fidget in their creaky wooden seats, the backs of which are scarred with hastily carved Divine Knight canes.

Darius continues, "As you can see, all of us here have wheelchairs. And the reason we have wheelchairs is because we were out in the streets gang banging, selling drugs. We got shot, and ultimately we got paralyzed." Today, Darius says, the students will learn what happens to the body when the spinal cord is injured. By educating the students about the grim realities of being wheelchair bound, the Crippled Footprint Collective speakers hope to get current gang members thinking about their lives outside the gang—specifically, if they become paralyzed and have to care for themselves. Eventually, the gang deserts gunshot victims, the speakers argue. If this message resonates with the students, Darius and company are well on their way to achieving their primary goal: Reversing the foundational belief that the perpetuation of violence unifies the gang—the belief that to be a member of the Divine Knights means to unite with allied gang sets against a threat that's unrelenting.

"There's two types of spinal cord injuries," Darius says. "There's a paraplegic and a quadriplegic. *Par* means two: It means two of your limbs are affected. I'm a paraplegic. I'm paralyzed from the waist down.

A quadriplegic is paralyzed from the neck down." A practiced speaker, Darius establishes authority by demonstrating medical expertise. He educates the high-schoolers about the spine, how it doesn't naturally heal itself (similar to the brain in that respect). "Ain't no medicine or no doctor in the world that can fix that."

The audience is still fidgeting, hesitant to look directly at the wounded bodies onstage. The unease only increases when Darius begins revealing specific indelicate ways his life has changed since becoming paralyzed. Aside from mobility, one of the primary bodily functions affected is the bladder. "Y'all know when you gotta use the washroom—you get that feeling, right? Well, when you're in a situation like ours, you no longer get that sensation." Darius adds, "So, what happens is that you gotta be on the clock. You know every four to six hours, you have to manually extract the urine. And that's done with one of these. This right here is a catheter."

The cloudy plastic bag is met with a collective groan from the crowd. Next, Darius places his thumb and index finger a couple of inches apart—the length the needle must be inserted into the urethra "before it starts draining." An eruption of gags and grimaces. Knowing he has their attention, Darius continues: "And this gotta be done every four to six hours for the rest of your life. 'Cause what can happen is, either you're gonna pee all over yourself . . . and you can imagine you're on the corner chilling and all of a sudden: You're wet."

More groans. Then, laughter—nervous, embarrassed laughter. Darius waits out the chuckles, smiling with the kids, willing to indulge their nervousness and for a moment to play the role of the hapless, disabled person.[20] Next, having illustrated the sad fate of one's biological representation of manhood after being paralyzed, Darius gives way to Aaron Sparks, another activist from the Crippled Footprint Collective. Like Darius, Aaron goes heavy on coarse personal details, focusing first on pressure sores—also known as bedsores or ubiquitous ulcers. Simply put, pressure sores are the result of sitting in a fixed position for a prolonged period of time; eventually, the bone begins to dig through skin.

"It starts off as a little pimple. But this is one pimple you don't wanna pop, 'cause you could make it worse," Aaron says.

"See, in a situation like ours," Aaron continues, "we can't feel our butts. So what we have to do is, we have to be constantly lifting off our chairs, doing 'pressure reliefs.' So you'll see me every once and a while do this"—he grabs the armrests of his chair and lifts his body above it, an inverted push-up. Pressure sores can develop in a matter of hours but can take two months to a year to fully recover from. "So you can imagine if summer just kicked off. And I got a pressure sore—now I gotta stay in bed to heal it."

Oscar Dyson, another of the activists, takes the reins and invokes the tragic legacy of Christopher Reeves. "You know the actor that played Superman?" Oscar asks the audience. "He actually passed away from a pressure sore. His got infected—the infection reached his bloodstream and made its way to his heart. He had a heart attack," Oscar says. "What I try to tell people is that this is Christopher Reeves—this is Superman. He had Superman money. And he couldn't prevent one of these sores? What's gonna happen to one of us from the hood? We don't have that kind of money. We don't have that kind of around-the-clock care."

Oscar's message is twofold: A wide gulf separates the level of access to medical resources available to a world-renowned actor and a poor person of color; and, more subtly, the notion that no one is actually fast enough to dodge a speeding bullet. Even Superman can die from a pimple.

Arthur and Joan Kleinman, in their study "The Appeal of Experience, the Dismay of Images," argue that illness stories transcend the bodies of the ill. It is not merely that culture "infolds" into the body through differing ways to define disease, or varying access to, and attitudes toward, health care. Our physical processes also "outfold" into social space, giving shape and meaning to the society of which we are part. Likewise, the stories told by disabled ex–gang members are not just about the interpersonal impact of disability. Their stories outfold as well, inviting teenage black males to recognize themselves in them.[21] In offering testimonial about the disabled life, former gang members signal the ways in which the practices of injury and enabling rely upon and help shape each other, and how the mutual constitution between injury and enabling is a means to respond to the gang's far-reaching influence in Eastwood.

In contrast to Frank's notion of "narrative surrender" to medical authority, the Crippled Footprint Collective speakers at Jackson High exhibit no anger or resentment toward the medical establishment for labeling them as disabled or even "impaired." Rather, disabled ex–gang members construct their narratives around the medical model of disability in order to emphasize the biological reality of their now "broken" bodies. This approach amplifies the magnitude of urban violence. For members of racial groups who are prone to debilitation through gun violence, drawing attention to the broken body is a political act. Here, the comparison with refugees is appropriate: Though the political ends are different, the method by which a person highlights his or her wounds is similar.[22] Comparable to how refugees (or asylum seekers) have deployed the language of trauma to gain political asylum, members of the Crippled Footprint Collective borrow narrative techniques from one another; they rehearse constantly. They learn through repetition and by absorbing one another's reactions.[23]

At Jackson High, for example, Dwight Davis, one of the disabled ex–gang members, did not speak. He listened and watched, still honing his own illness narrative in preparation for the next school assembly—when, perhaps, he might feel ready to testify. In this way, the Crippled Footprint Collective speakers draw on presuppositions of illness that enable collectively salient descriptions of disability. Disabled ex–gang members hope that by presenting an altered version of the gang narrative—a version in which injury isn't noble but preventable—these inner-city students will come to see the effects of violence more clearly.[24]

A couple of days after the assembly, Marcus Cooper, a senior at Jackson High, invites me into his house. His mother is cooking dinner and asks if I want to stay. At the dining-room table, Marcus tells me how the assembly has altered his perspective on gang life. "It was real deep to hear them speak," he says. "My mom kept telling me that my associations will lead me to one day, God forbid, be in the same predicament. And my heart was beating like a hundred miles an hour, 'cause I could just see myself in the position they're in."

Most of the people Marcus hangs out with are, in his words, "gangbangers." He claims he's always wanted to do right but couldn't, or didn't. He fought regularly, sometimes leading the charge. Now, however, his school is so violent that his focus is less on fighting and more on survival.

For many like Marcus in Eastwood, gangs are commonly imagined as stand-in family units. Even a teenager who opts not to join the Divine Knights will be cognizant of who belongs with which set, as well as the jurisdictional boundaries of each. Young people are well aware that although most of the gang sets in their neighborhood fall under the Divine Knights umbrella, at any given moment two of the sets can become hostile.[25]

"We have all the rival gangs," Marcus says. "I actually got pulled out of my last high school 'cause me and my friends got into it with some Bandits. My mother feared for my life. And I noticed when she took me out of school that most of the fights I was getting into wasn't because of me or something I did. It was because of my friends." In the past three weeks, two of Marcus's friends have died and one of his cousin's friends. "I know you heard about the fifteen-year-old boy that was found in the Dumpster. That was him."

Marcus's assertion that he doesn't always start the fights in which he becomes engaged could be read as a convenient excuse (especially with his mother within earshot). Even so, the peer pressure he describes is all too real, the stakes—teenagers being murdered and maimed on a regular basis—much too high. Trade in injury is so common that even a hospital bed doesn't necessarily occasion a person to orient his life away from the gang; it may simply lead him to seek revenge. In Marcus's case, a trip to the trauma center after getting jumped did nothing to dampen his enthusiasm for fighting. He says, "When my mother came in there, I was talking to the doctor like, 'So, umm, what's up? What's your son's name? Can I play video games?' I was having fun—not knowing that something could've seriously been wrong with me. When my friends came, I was jumping on the bed like, 'Yeah, man, they ain't do nothing to me! They ain't do nothing to me!'"[26]

Feeling invincible, Marcus's first reaction was to seek revenge. "I even put the hospital band—the one that was on my arm—I put it around my neck, and I wore it as a chain, like a trophy," he says. "My mother said that scared her. She told me that I could be dead, 'cause I blacked out for a second while I was fighting."

Once out of the hospital, Marcus received a visit from his friends, who wanted to plot an assault on members of the rival gang who had jumped Marcus. "Inside my head I'm like, 'Do I really want to go with them?'" Marcus says. "'Or do I wanna listen to my mother?'" His main concern was appearing weak if he chose not to retaliate. It wasn't simply Marcus's reputation that was on the line, his friends argued—the whole set's was. And yet Marcus insists that he remained adamant that he and his friends not strike back.[27]

In the days after Marcus's beating, as he chose to listen to his mother, a curious thing happened: After school, he came home. He didn't dawdle on the corner. Instead, he stayed inside. And his friends stopped talking to him; soon, he was getting dirty looks. At one point, the leader of his local set visited Marcus at home to relay the message that Marcus had turned his back on his friends and his community. In the eyes of the gang, Marcus was abandoning them. By refusing to retaliate and by removing himself from social activities, Marcus forwent the opportunity to cultivate bonds with his brethren. He voluntarily withdrew from a system in which injury serves as motivation for debt settlement and was therefore viewed as a deserter.

Intimately felt obligations deeply impact the ways in which a teenager like Marcus navigates the social world. Still, this sense of indebtedness does not always have to lead to injury. By rechanneling gang notions of reciprocity—and in the process allowing his wounds to engender peace, rather than violence—Justin, through his work with the Crippled Footprint Collective, frames the community forum as a harmonious way to settle debts between gang members.

In the winter of 2008, Justin designs a Crippled Footprint Collective program aimed at the most unlikely audience to attend a seminar on violence: gang members. The gathering will specifically cater to different factions of the Divine Knights. Even though he is not one of the Crippled Footprint Collective speakers, he appreciates their approach. But when Justin brings his proposal to the administrators at Eastwood

Hospital, they decline. The institution is "low on funds," they tell him. In fact, the hospital administrators say that the Crippled Footprint Collective program now has to institute a $250 fee for public appearances. Dismayed by the constraints, Justin decides to organize an independent forum. From Darius and Aaron, Justin receives tips about how best to craft his message. He studies video recordings from the Crippled Footprint Collective speakers, all the while seeking other sources of sponsorship. An improbable benefactor emerges: Kemo. On behalf of the Divine Knights, Kemo pledges to donate funds for the purchase of food and promises to make the event a mandatory meeting for his constituency.

Justin and Kemo have a long history together; it dates back seventeen years, when the two were budding gangbangers. Why, though, would a gang leader contribute to a forum on the hazards of gang life? "Kemo doesn't want the killings either," Justin explains. "You gotta remember—some of those boys are his cousins and the little brothers of people we grew up with. Besides Kemo *owes me*, and now I'm cashing in."

On a brisk Saturday morning in May 2009, three days after the thirty-sixth murder that year of a Chicago public school student, Kemo delivers. He deposits an Escalade's worth of young gang members at the House of Worship, the same church that sponsors the recovery center where Mr. Otis works. Kemo, along with a few of the leaders of gang sets in the neighborhood, linger outside of the church as members of their respective constituencies file in. The gang leaders are prepared to quell any confrontations, Justin tells me.

In addition to soliciting help from gang leaders, Justin has also asked a number of probation officers and high school counselors to attend. The event begins with a performance in the church auditorium. Franco "Dr. Deep," Carr a local Chicago emcee, raps in front of a brick backdrop onto which pictures of slain students are projected. The name and age of each victim is written across the photos, accompanied, in some cases, by a description of the cause of death ("beaten with a bat"; "bullet to the head") and the age of the assailant ("killed by a 15-year-old youth"). After Dr. Deep's performance, Pastor Ray, the master of ceremonies, instructs the group of almost one hundred youths to reach under their seats for a half-sheet of paper—the "Violence Truce."

This truce is adapted from a "Proclamation," written by the California Crips' cofounder Stanley "Tookie" Williams. In 2005, after clemency and a stay of execution were both rejected, Williams died from lethal injection. It was hotly debated even at his death whether or not Williams's anti-gang advocacy represented genuine atonement. In awe of his enormous influence and life story of redemption, a number of activists and celebrities watched as the former gang leader—and Nobel Peace Prize nominee—was executed.

By adapting Tookie's "Proclamation," Justin hopes that the violence forum will yield similar successes as the negotiations between the Bloods and the Crips of California. At the same time, he wants the "Violence Truce" to be specific to the Divine Knights' extensive legacy—a legacy that, from Justin's perspective, has not always been synonymous with pain and suffering.

"What we're gonna do," Pastor Ray says, "is read this truce together. Then, if you all agree with it, I want everyone to sign their names on the bottom and leave some contact information so we can hold each other accountable. Right now, though, I want everybody to look at the paper and read with me."

The crowd reads in unison, their adolescent voices sounding measured, less certain than they do on the street corner.

WE WILL *stop all shootings, ambushes, murder, drug deals, robbery, vandalism, kidnapping, extortion, and any other acts of crime, which afflict our communities.*
WE WILL *help restore order and to rebuild the community.*
WE WILL *use every nonviolent measure to resolve all past, present, and future conflicts.*

The list continues. I wonder if Kemo and the other gang leaders milling about in the parking lot realize that their sets are just then reciting twelve statements that, in theory, at least, bind them with the force of a brotherly oath to create a more peaceful future.

It is symbolic that the meeting during which the "Violence Truce" is read aloud occurs in Eastwood—the "Sacred City," birthplace of the Divine Knights. Anytime the gang has official business, its fractured leadership convenes at their headquarters located only minutes away

from the House of Worship. What's more, the text that the young affiliates read from—just like the literature they receive upon initiation into
the Divine Knights—is approved by Kemo. (Justin's imprimatur carries
weight as well, as he is a well-respected former affiliate. Days prior to
the event, Kemo told his young affiliates how Justin sacrificed his body
so that Kemo could flee in a gun battle.) Thus, given its official autho-
rization and the context in which it circulates, the "Violence Truce"
imbues Justin's event with a more specific meaning than, say, the high
school assembly previously mentioned.

Dr. Deep had opened the forum with pictures of students killed that
year projected on a backdrop behind the stage. Photos from the 1960s,
by contrast, accompanied the reading of the Truce. They pictured the
Divine Knights of that era cleaning their neighborhood with shovels
and brooms; they showed the community center and reform school that
the Knights once built. Here, the juxtaposition between the crimes that
the gang has become known for and the "restore and rebuild" legacy
on which it was reputedly founded is stark. These images, immediately
recognizable to me (and most likely would have been to the majority
of gang members in the audience), are taken from a book about the
gang's community-service initiatives during the civil rights era. This
book, which circulates widely in the community, is read by young gang
members as a rite of passage.[28] By projecting nostalgic visions for how
the gang ought to be, these images substantiate the communal bonds
that the Divine Knights have built through the years; also, the positive imagery suggests that the gang is not inherently a violent criminal
organization.

After leaving the main session, the teenagers attend breakout sessions where facilitators address specific topics related to gang violence.
Kemo's boys, like those of other sets, travel in a pack. The gang leader
has demanded that his entire set sees Justin, so some fifteen teenage
boys shuffle to the church library, where they sprawl in cushioned arm-
chairs and steel folding chairs to accommodate the overflow crowd.
Some of the boys appear nervous, others too tough to sit for Justin's
speech. By the time he begins, forty gang members are stuffed into the
library. With so many of Eastwood's affiliates in attendance, the setting
reminds me of the spirited summer nights when respected elders gather

on a stoop or corner and recount gang lore. Only, instead of a notorious Divine Knight standing and holding court, Justin is seated in his wheelchair.

"I was raised right here in Eastwood," Justin begins. "And, just like today, there was a lot of violence when I was growing up. It was real bad over here." Despite being a small community, Justin explains, Eastwood was rife with warring gang sets back when he was an active Knight. Compounding the tension was the fact that there was only one high school in the area. "I remember in the ninth grade—before I was even in the gang—I would get frustrated because I had to cross rival territories to get to school. I was getting chased, beat up, and robbed constantly. Sometimes the people from my block would stick up for me. Because of that, members of the rival gangs would assume I was in the same gang as the guys from my block. So now they started treating me like opposition. It got to the point where I was already marked as a gang member, so I just decided to join the gang."

Justin goes on to describe the devotion he found within his new fraternity. Being that the Knights were a generational influence on Justin's family (his cousins, uncles, and even his grandfather were all involved), he took to it quickly. Soon he was skipping school often, the violence around him escalating. He witnessed the deaths of close family members and good friends. "I thought, if my boys, my friends, my cousins, they all died for the gang, then why not me?" Justin says. "What makes me better than them? I started telling myself, 'Man, I'm willing to die for this.'"

At the time, Justin says, he needed that mentality because he'd started dealing drugs. His two closest friends were becoming gang leaders and big-time drug dealers; they were supplying product to everyone in his neighborhood. Then, following a meeting with high-ranking gang officials, the gang captain who was supplying both of Justin's friends said that the two would have to consolidate their gang sets. They could play Rock, Paper, Scissors for all the supplier cared, but someone had to step up and someone had to fall back. It had to be done, the supplier said.

"So my two boys decided to set up a meeting," Justin continues. "It was January 3, 2000. That day the friend who I worked for picked me up and told me what they decided. They were gonna do it like the old-timers: meet and fight, one-on-one. Whoever won the fight would get the neighborhood drug market. The other person would be the right-hand man and make his crew fall in line. They would even shake hands afterwards."

It was agreed that the fight would happen in an abandoned lot. Justin and his friend arrived first and got out of their car to wait. A few minutes later, Justin spotted a car coming down the street but couldn't make out the driver. The car continued past them. When it reached the dead end, it circled back around. "It was creeping up slowly," Justin says, "so my boy said, 'Let's get out of here.' But by the time we got back inside, the car was right beside us. I look up and the person in the passenger seat had pulled out a pistol.

"*Tink . . . Tink . . . t-t-tink. Tink. Tink.* That's all I heard. I saw flashes. My boy said, 'Pull off. Pull off,' so I started driving. But I was already hit, so I lost control of the vehicle. We were swerving and weaving. Eventually, I crashed. That's when I noticed that I was bleeding from my shoulder and my thigh. I started screaming: 'I got shot. I got shot.' Next thing you know, I hear the car door slam shut. Just then I realized: One of my friends had left me, and my other friend wanted me dead."

Justin's voice is shaky. His elbow is on the armrest of his wheelchair, and he's covering his mouth with his hand, concealing an expression I can only assume conveys disappointment. The room is riveted. Even the kids who pretended that they could care less about what Justin had to say are pitched forward in their seats, eagerly anticipating the rest of the story. While Justin regains his composure, I recall how weeks ago he told me that Kemo "owes" him because they were together when Justin was shot. It hadn't registered before now: the person in the car with Justin was Kemo.

And he was desperate to retaliate against the shooter, another affiliate later told me, but Justin forbade it. In the hospital, on what he thought was his deathbed, Justin made a commitment to God to turn his life around. The most he allowed Kemo to do was to confront the perpetrator, tell him to leave the neighborhood and never come back. Because Kemo hoped that one day Justin would change his mind and authorize revenge, the gang never identified the shooter to the police. The assailant escaped. In this light, Kemo's commitment to the forum makes all the more sense—as does Justin's willingness to accept his help.

"I just got out of the car and started running," Justin continues. "I cut through an alleyway and stopped at the first house I saw. I knocked on the door. Then I knocked harder. And harder." Next, the porch lights up and Justin gets excited, thinking someone inside the house was about to help. But what he really saw were headlights beaming on the door, the car from before approaching fast. "Someone got out and started running toward me with a gun, so I hopped over the porch railing. I almost reached the back of the house when I heard a shot go off—*BANG.*"

Justin fell to the ground. He wasn't in pain, he says; he was in shock. He realized his legs weren't working. "I was trying and trying," he says, "but I couldn't move my legs. I couldn't get up. I just couldn't." His head on the grass and the attackers fleeing, Justin began screaming for help—and for all the people he "was willing to die for." "I was screaming my boys' names," Justin says. "One by one, I screamed my cousins' names."

While waiting for help, Justin grabbed a nearby storm drain and tried to hoist himself up: "I remember looking at my legs and they were dangling. They were dead. When I saw that, I fell back down." Before long, the home owner emerged; she called an ambulance and tried her best to comfort Justin. "'Everything's gonna be all right,' she said. 'Don't worry, everything's gonna be all right.'

"As she's telling me this, I see her eyes watering. Tears are coming down her face. And I just remember thinking, like, 'Man, I don't wanna die.' I remember thinking that in my head. All my life I told myself that I'm willing to die for this. I was willing to get shot. I didn't care. But when I was lying there, I was scared to die. I didn't want to die. I don't know why, but I didn't want to die."

Justin ends his story with his doctor's words, "You'll never walk again"—a somber description of the day a surgeon informed him that he would be paralyzed for the rest of his life. As he recounts his early days in a wheelchair, what strikes me is how abandoned Justin felt. The pain of Kemo running from his car, and his recitation of the names of his gang brethren while lying in the woman's yard, rivals the pain of the bullets lodged in his body, Justin once confessed to me. The injury of abandonment is inextricably linked to physical injury.

Justin's testimony—which combines physical injury and social abandonment—forces a dialogue about the pressures of gang membership. In this way, the trope of injury complicates the standard emphasis among gang affiliates, about the potential for money and notoriety, about all that membership enables by emphasizing the social relationships that hold the gang together. Justin and Kemo's bond, for instance, mirrors the sense of debt and obligation intrinsic to their own lifelong friendship. With this in mind, it is critical to acknowledge that the transformation of a young affiliate takes place over and through a disabled gang member's body. Injured gang members' stories of catheters and enemas, pressure sores and bed rest, illuminate an often-overlooked aspect of gang sociality: Disability is a distinct possibility, yet frequently invisible, reality.

At the conclusion of Justin's breakout session, I observe that many of the young gang members are unable to look Justin in the face; instead Kemo's boys stare, stoically, at the spokes of his wheelchair. Maybe it is out of fear that they might become emotional, as many in the room already have. Justin's powerful story has elicited rare shades of empathy and sorrow from otherwise unshakable young gang members. Not only did Justin sacrifice himself, but after doing so, he forgave the debt owed to him and transformed it into a communal project to stop the killings. This sacrifice, Justin hopes, will help youngsters like Marcus break free from the crippling currency of obligation upon which gang life is built. Justin's life story, in other words, is the conduit through which an alternative pathway for a more peaceful gang just might be opened up and imagined, against all odds.

Resilience

Today, I visited Amy at her group home, and Mark Buckley showed up while I was there. He scans back and forth between Amy and me, as if to confirm with her that this is a conversation appropriate for me to overhear. Amy says that I can stay. Then Mark begins what seems like a routine exchange:

"How are you feeling?" he says. "Have you been filling your prescriptions?"

"I'm good," Amy says. "I've been taking my pills."

"Any side effects?"

"I'm not nauseous anymore. Maybe a little sluggish."

"Have you told Dr. Tyson?"

"No," Amy says. "This is new. The sluggishness is new. She knows about the nausea."

"You haven't told her yet because you haven't had a chance? Or because you've been missing appointments?"

"I just haven't had a chance," Amy says.

"Well, make sure you make your appointments," Mark says. "This is not a doctor's appointment, you know? It's just a friendly visit."

"I know," Amy says.

Mark adds, "And you're helping me as much as I'm helping you. Because I

can't tell you to do things that I'm not
doing. If I did, then what would that
make me?"

"A hypocrite," Amy says.

"That's right: a hypocrite." Mark
smiles. "And if there's one thing I'm
not—"

"—it's a hypocrite," they say together. Mark gives Amy a hug before
turning to leave. After he descends the
tattered steps of the group home, he
turns around to face the porch.

"Stay strong, Amy," he says.

—6/3/10, 1:18 PM

CHAPTER FIVE

Disease

---✳︎---

OR,

How a Will to Survive Helps the Healing

In cellblock 3B, Amy O'Neal is one of a half-dozen girls gathered around a table awaiting the start of Bible study. I sit across from her. This is December 2007, at the female wing of the West Side Juvenile Detention Center. Monica Namba, a twenty-two-year-old volunteer for Eastwood Community Church's outreach ministry, has brought freshmen from a nearby Bible college to the detention center for the first time. She is introducing them to Amy, one of her favorite inmates. "Amy has HIV," Monica says to the college group. "But she has the strongest spirit."

The Bible study begins abruptly when Monica instructs everyone to turn to John, chapter eight, verse four. Amy reads:

"'Teacher,' they said to Jesus, 'this woman was caught in the very act of committing adultery. In our Law Moses commanded that such a woman must be stoned to death. Now what do you say?' They said this to trap Jesus, so that they could accuse him. But he bent over and wrote on the ground with his finger. As they stood there asking him questions, he straightened up and said to them, 'Whichever one of you has committed no sin may throw the first stone at her.' Then he bent over again and wrote on the ground."

At the end of the sentence the next young woman around the table begins reading in seamless transition:

"When they heard this, they all left, one by one, the older ones first. Jesus was left alone, with the woman still standing there. He straightened up and said to her, 'Where are they? Is there no one left to condemn you?' 'No one, sir,' she answered. 'Well, then,' Jesus said, 'I do not condemn you either. Go, but do not sin again.'"

Every few months, Monica makes sure that every incarcerated young woman who's willing recites this verse; doing so offers different sets of teenagers who find themselves in the same cell a steadfast message of redemption.

After Bible study, the guards suggest that the teenagers spend the rest of the recreational period, about fifteen minutes, working on their creative projects. Some write poems or songs, others pen letters to loved ones. Monica encourages me to talk to Amy—the least shy of the bunch. I approach Amy, her head resting on the table, a tattoo of a woman's face visible on her forearm. Above the likeness of the woman, the words "R.I.P Sue-Anne Green" are written in an Old English font. As I'm studying the tattoo, Amy suddenly shoots up: an elderly nurse has called her name from a clipboard. Immediately, Amy begins a seven-pill regimen, the nurse checking under her tongue after each one she swallows. "That a girl," the nurse says.

Meanwhile, Monica rounds up the Bible college students. I leave the detention center with them, unaware that over a year would pass before I would have my first conversation with Amy.

Leaders of the Eastwood Community Church's outreach program have a seemingly straightforward goal: Convert nonbelievers into followers of Jesus Christ. For them, the fact that a teenager like Amy attends

Bible study every week suggests that one day she'll dedicate herself to personal transformation. And yet embedded in the church's outreach initiatives are a number of ideas about sin and healing (and injury and redemption) that can easily become conflated. By examining this outreach within the context of the church's community mission, we can begin to understand the ways in which disparate institutional notions of healing bleed into one another.

Members of the church's outreach ministry equate HIV with sexual deviance and sexual deviance with sin. And sin, in their view, is the impetus for moral transformation as well as social reform. It shouldn't surprise us that in Eastwood—as in many urban communities—rates of diseases and addictions are disproportionately high; for this reason, finding ways to contain their influence becomes the basis for both governmental intervention and economic investment. For the church, though, addressing disease and addiction now means grappling with new interpretations of how the body heals from injury. No longer, from a medical standpoint, is healing defined as either a full recovery or a terminal diagnosis (or, from a religious perspective, bodily transcendence). Rather, healing is an ongoing process. Increasingly, the concept of healing is associated with those who must manage chronic illness.[1]

One of the ways that the church helps patients heal is by fostering an environment that prizes willingness—a willingness to remain faithful or sober or loyal to an antiretroviral drug treatment regimen. The challenge that this church encounters is that some Eastwoodians do not merely wish to transcend addiction and disease through religion and leave their past behind. Residents like Amy dwell within a space of injury and harness the resolve it affords. I would come to learn that Amy, for instance, doesn't merely wish to develop a religious-based will, but an extra-religious "renegade will," akin to the brazen attempts to escape life's constraints already discussed.

The "renegade will" plays a vital role in helping leaders of both religious and medical institutions understand the ways that injury is linked to urban poverty; and in a community like Eastwood, where many are susceptible to the same kinds of diseases and addictions, narrating one's experiences of injury become a vital resource. In what follows, we'll see that when healing translates to the management of myriad injuries, the sixteen-year-old HIV-positive drug addict with the tattoo on her forearm is well positioned to teach us about resiliency.

Mark is a health worker. He is employed by Healing Hearts, a non-profit organization that provides support to HIV-positive teenagers. Three weeks after Amy's release from the detention center, Mark was assigned to her case. In the year that they have known each other, Mark has built a strong relationship with her. Case in point: I first met Mark, a gay black man in his forties, at Eastwood Community Church when he came to visit Amy. "You know I love Amy, right?" he said. "'Cause I haven't stepped into a church in years."

Although he considers himself a Christian, Mark hasn't felt comfortable in a church for some time, given that most of those he has attended associate homosexuality with sin. Months ago, however, Mark broke his promise to not step foot in a religious institution until he is free to marry in one—this was after Amy convinced him to listen to her speech at a local church. That she wants him to hear her story is a feat in itself, Mark explains, because they didn't always get along. The breakthrough came when Mark proved himself to be more than just Amy's health worker—specifically, the day he confided in her. Like Amy, Mark is living with HIV and has been for five years. His personal stake in Amy's health, he confesses, stems from seeing many young people die.[2]

HIV-positive teenagers like Amy, many of whom have difficulty adhering to a treatment regimen, are extremely vulnerable for premature death. Mark explains: "They get sick. They don't tell anyone. Now, that's problematic." He angles forward in his seat. "But that's not even the main set of issues we're worried about. Most of the time, they don't have any symptoms at all. Then they stop taking their medication altogether. By the time they get *really* sick, it's too late to prolong their lives."

Mark pauses for a moment, shaking his head contemplatively before continuing: "And don't let me get started on the drugs. Now that's adding insult to injury.[3] It's hard enough to get a drug addict to tell you what day of the week it is, much less the hour of the day. And that's what you gotta know: It's extremely important to take your pills at the right time—and to make appointments."[4]

Mark fears that combined with the threat of relapse with heroin addicts like Amy, a high-risk lifestyle associated with drug abuse will justify the withdrawal of antiretroviral drugs. Over the next several months, Mark will spend time helping Amy develop the skill for identifying which drugs relate to which physical experiences. He will encourage her to speak with her physician about the effects that the antiretroviral cocktail therapy will have on her bodily chemistry, to schedule doctor's appointments so that her physician will be able to adjust the regimen relative to the progression of the disease, and to monitor her exercise and eating habits. For Amy, maintaining a healthy diet, taking her medication regularly, going to sleep at the right time, learning to be alert to her physical symptoms, and scheduling regular medical appointments are all vital to maintaining the kind of lifestyle that could not have been imaginable a few decades ago with patients diagnosed with HIV.[5]

Over the past several years, antiretroviral drugs (drugs that work to maintain function of the immune system by preventing infections and thus extend an HIV patient's life span) have headlined the burgeoning research on HIV and AIDS. In both Western and non-Western contexts, antiretroviral drugs have dramatically changed the social landscape in disease-infected regions: present-day generations are able to take part in society in a way that was previously unthinkable. As social scientists have pointed out, however, having the drugs is merely the first step; even armed with this medicine, the barriers for treating populations vulnerable for acquiring HIV are substantial, as are the risks associated with improper use. The assumption that a supply of antiretroviral drugs is a panacea for infected populations, in other words, has proven to be overly optimistic.[6]

This new era of healing through the management of chronic illness has made the issue of adherence ever more salient. Non-adherence poses health risks not only for the individual, but for the entire community. If a patient misses doses of an antiretroviral drug regimen, drug resistance can develop. This term refers to strains of the virus initially resistant to the drug treatment that eventually become dominant in an infected person's bloodstream. The prevalence of drug-resistant strains makes it more difficult to treat the infected individual, as well as anyone else that

148 † CHAPTER FIVE

person may infect. Doctors stress that those who initiate antiretroviral therapy must be prepared to commit to lifelong treatment.[7]

"Folks have got it all wrong," Mark says. "They think people find out they're HIV positive, wake up the next morning, and then — *boom* — like magic, start living a disciplined life. Nope. Truth is — being *willing* — being willing to adhere," he repeats, "is just as important as adherence itself."[8]

Healing, as defined by Mark, resides at the intersection between clinical and moral understandings of illness. Although Mark is trained to understand the progression of HIV, like many community experts his effectiveness is limited by the fact that the willingness he seeks to inspire must take hold in an African American Eastwood, a neighborhood whose sizable population of young black inhabitants are thought to lack moral resolve. The fact that they must deal with a community that is characterized by its "reckless will" is what pairs the priorities of Mark's institution, Healing Hearts, with that of Pastor Tim's.[9]

Many times I have witnessed the dismay on Pastor Tim's face when he opens the *Eastwood Gazette* to dire HIV statistics in his area.[10] He explains the numbers as a result of the infected persons buying into "street" culture. But unlike many Eastwoodians who locate danger in an abstract notion of inner-city dysfunction, Pastor Tim does not just complain. He feels it his duty to take a hands-on approach and help develop strength of character in Eastwood's youth, fortifying their will with religious resolve.

Each week Pastor Tim traverses James Street and tries to convince the gang members who rotate through each corner to attend Youth Night at "The Temple," a social program sponsored by Eastwood Community Church. In addition to owning and operating a community redevelopment company and a drug rehabilitation center, the church has numerous other social programs. Every day of the week is dedicated to a different cause. In the church's Saturday night hip hop worship service, young Eastwood residents perform gospel-rap hybrids; they sing and dance for the Lord; and they stage skits about certain circumstances that may test a teenager's faith. At the end of each service, Pastor Tim gives a sermon.

On Mondays, in preparation for the Saturday service, all of the teen-agers and young adults associated with the event meet for "Temple Practice." After a thirty-minute Bible study, those in attendance break off into small groups: Pastor Tim meets with the planning commit-tee in the church library, the gospel rappers meet in the conference room, and the interpretive dancers along with young men who engage in a Chicago-style dance called "footworkin'" share the day-care center. While the "Temple Leaders" who help run these meetings are typically in their twenties and thirties and may have been involved with gangs at some point in their lives, the majority of the teenage students who at-tend Temple Practice would be considered upstanding youths—except for the young men who "footwork."

Footworkin' is a seemingly chaotic style of dance characterized by fast movements of the feet. It is specific to Chicago. In the 1980s, street gangs created it during the explosion of violence that coincided with the drug boom; quickly, it became one of the many expressions of gang rivalry. The frenzied, fleet-footed quickstep is performed by frenetically stomping or kicking one's feet in a stutter-stepped pattern. It fuses African dance moves with tap dance and is comparable to "krumping" in Compton, or "chickenhead" in St. Louis—distinctive regional out-growths of break-dancing. Whereas break-dancing movements high-light flow, layering, and ruptures in line (movements in which the joints are snapped abruptly into angular positions to create a "semi-liquid effect"), footworkin' prizes rupture over fluidity. Footworkers vigorously dribble their sneakered feet in ways that capture the repetitive, hyper-accelerated samples of a local musical genre known as "juke."[11]

In recent years there have been efforts to capitalize on the appeal of footworkin'. Dancers have posted their latest moves on the Inter-net, and one group of street dancers, the FootworkKINGz have made two documentaries on the genre, which they circulate via the web. De-spite these efforts, footworkin' remains a marginalized social practice—particularly because of its association with gang life.

The footworkers who attend Temple Practice are not all gang mem-bers. In many instances, though, the best footworkers are. Because the high school dropout rate is so high in Eastwood (71 percent), foot-workin' gang members often have a surplus of free time. At any hour, day or night, a person might see them outside practicing their craft. Additionally, footworkin' is closely associated with underground "juke" parties, which are often the refuge of high school dropouts in Eastwood. (The upstanding student, who also happens to footwork, is far less likely to attend.) Footworkers from particular streets and belonging to certain gangs are thought to be consistently better than those from other areas; understandably, this sense of rivalry has been known to spark feuds.

It is not surprising, then, that less than a month after Pastor Tim invites street dancers to participate in the hip hop worship service, gang-affiliated footworkers begin attending Temple Practice. Not only does this dress rehearsal provide a venue for footwork battles between various male-dominated crews; the footworkers also get to use the church's state-of-the-art sound system. And during Chicago's harsh winters, the dancers are afforded shelter and heat. There is a catch, though: they have to sit through Bible study.

He never formally theorized the ritual of Bible study, but in examining the spheres of social life that produce the kind of order in which certain rituals are based, Emile Durkheim defined religion as such: A unified system of beliefs and rituals that unite a "moral community."[12] Indeed, part of the power of religious-based rituals is that everyone participates; even if someone is a nonbeliever, his or her presence does not detract from the spiritual potency of the service. In Pastor Tim's Bible study, however, the principle that Durkheim describes works in reverse.

The footworkers frequently disrupt biblical teachings with groans, sighs, and jokes. They spend the majority of their time signaling to one another in coded language, not so subtly communicating that they would rather be elsewhere. Even the upstanding footworker is pressured to, say, giggle mischievously alongside his more demonstrative peers.

Two months into my volunteer work at Eastwood Community Church, I am in the day-care center with Fatima Kearns, a teenager who does interpretive dance. She is showing me several interpretations of a dance sequence she plans to perform. Church groups from Portland, Oregon, to San Antonio, Texas, have staged versions of it, and as I watch alongside Fatima on the same desktop that the footworkers use to master the latest dance moves, I begin to notice how each interpretation centers on which temptations a given congregation should avoid. Just as Fatima begins outlining her plans for the performance, a rumble of laughter interrupts our YouTube session. On the other side of the door, the footworkers are making a spoof out of Fatima's cherished song. Tiko stands on his toes and waves his arms dramatically, pretending to be a ballerina. The rest of the footworkers cackle. One by one, they form a queue behind Tiko, flailing their limbs and eventually collapsing.

The following week, another, more serious incident occurs. It begins when the forty or so footworkers who have come for Temple Practice are asked by Pastor Tim to state their name and what school they attend. The footworkers start to snicker after Tiko says that he doesn't even go to school, and Pastor Tim, visibly annoyed, instructs Tiko to separate from the boys he came with.

"I wasn't doing anything," Tiko says. "So I shouldn't have to move."

"Either move or leave," Pastor Tim says.

Next, Tiko walks out, and a stream of teenage boys follows his lead. Soon only three footworkers remain. Shortly thereafter, we hear a familiar ruckus: a crowd of footworkers engaged in a dance battle outside of the church. Pastor Tim approaches the glass door and waves them off. "Go home," he yells.

Tiko, in the heat of battle against a young man named John Sage, jitters forward toward the door, pauses, allowing everyone watching to become transfixed by the rhythmic flashes of his gym shoes, and then kicks the door violently, shattering the glass. The footworkers flee. It takes a couple of weeks (and a fainthearted apology) before street dancers are permitted to return to Temple Practice. In the interim, church patrons debate the pros and cons of continuing to grant gang members use of their facilities. It is clear that for some churchgoers, footworkin' is a malevolent social practice that fuels gang rivalries and violence; for others, it's a way to avoid gang activity by channeling aggression into an expressive outlet.

The more time I spent at the Temple, the more I began to understand: it is because footworkers are habitual—yet far from ideal—churchgoers that their sporadic dances discomfort the institutional processes of moral transformation. Even if a footworker identifies as Christian, he or she is likely to be skeptical of the church's self-conscious, reflexive narrative of transformation. Many gang members I talk with read the advice of church congregants as criticisms of their actions, their affiliations, and the geography of commerce in which they circulate. (Oftentimes, this is true.) On the other side of the argument, many churchgoers feel that the gang's drug-dealing network—and the intravenous injection needles that come along with it—are the two major reasons diseases like HIV are prevalent in Eastwood. In the context of the church, footworkin' symbolizes their wider disdain with gang activity.

And to make matters worse: Every Monday the footworkers disrupt Bible study with uncannily consistent outbursts. (The Temple Leaders say: "If they hate being here so much, if they are *so unhappy*, they should just *go home*.") On many occasions, in fact, the footworkers are so unruly that they're dismissed before they can take advantage of a booming sound system and a warm place to dance—their two key incentives for being at Eastwood Community Church. And yet every week they come anyway, even though the vast majority of them do not attend the church service on Saturday that they are supposedly practicing for.

The crucial point: When urban residents who harbor disdain for the gang are the same people who inhabit positions of authority in neighborhood institutions or programs (such as the Temple), gang members often feel censored. The gang members' protests, from Tiko's well-aimed kick to many more subtle outbursts, correspond to an index of injuries they feel and the ways they feel that the church broadly paints them and their actions as reckless.

The door still isn't fixed by Saturday evening. Jagged shards of shattered glass are frozen in the frame, a disfigured snowflake. Just before the Youth Night festivities start, Pastor Tim replaces the fractured glass with a large piece of wood. In addition to the fifteen or so footworkers who attend Youth Night, the church has a large and loyal constituency of young people in their congregation (around sixty); tonight, in total, nearly one hundred teenagers are in attendance. Kids from nearby churches who occasionally attend the Temple, one of the only churches in the area to have a Saturday-night service, bolster the crowd.

"Tonight we're gonna talk about the temptations that test our commitment to God," Pastor Tim begins. "I want to start with a dance performance. Everyone, please welcome our performers with a round of applause."

As the pastor exits, the interpretive dancers I have watched rehearse for weeks take the stage. Fatima is, perhaps, the most dedicated of them all. She organized this week's interpretive dance rehearsals, and Pastor Tim is especially happy to have her engage in activities at the church. A little over a month ago, Fatima's older brother, Steve Kearns, a twenty-two-year-old member of the Divine Knights, hung himself in his prison cell after being denied parole. Because of the recent tragedy she's endured, Pastor Tim hopes that surrounding her with a supportive community will provide the emotional foundation Fatima needs to tackle an arduous grieving process.

Tonight's performance is about developing the resolve it takes to heal from injury. It begins with Fatima lying on her back onstage. Two other Temple Leaders are behind her: Peter Olson, wearing a brown vest and army fatigues; and Olivia Arnold, dressed in black pants and a black hooded sweatshirt. Only Blake Pietz, who's playing the role of the Christ figure, has yet to make an appearance; when he does, robed in white, he stands behind Fatima, placing his hand above her head. She rises. He then aims both hands to the ground, keeping them parallel while raising them vertically: a tree trunk. He picks an imaginary piece of fruit from this tree and then gives Fatima a bite. Blake takes her hand and they dance, their movements choreographed to a contemporary gospel song called "Everything," by the band Lifehouse: "Find me here, / And speak to me / I want to feel you, / I need to hear you / You are the light / That's leading me / To the place / Where I find peace again."

I half expect Tiko to be ridiculing the performance just as he did Fatima's rehearsal, but, to my surprise, the footworkin' gang member watches with what appears to be reverence.[13] Onstage Peter, the young man in the brown vest and army fatigues, cuts in on Fatima and Blake's dance. Littering the stage with dollar bills, Peter leads her away from the Christ figure. Fatima drops to recover the bills. A young woman behind me blurts out, "No, girl. Don't let him con-trol you." Fatima collects the money and pretends to be satisfied, smiling just as brightly as when the Christ figure gave her fruit.

But Peter soon snatches the money, and Fatima, clearly dismayed, turns from him only to be greeted by Olivia, the young woman in the black hooded sweatshirt. Olivia is carrying a knife. She demonstrates how to take the blade to her wrist; Fatima follows Olivia's lead, slicing both before dropping the knife. She tries to push Olivia away, but Olivia pulls a gun from her waistband and points it at our protagonist. She doesn't shoot, though. Instead, Olivia hands Fatima the gun, who turns the barrel toward her own head and is about to pull the trigger. Just as the song reaches its crescendo, however, Fatima slams the gun down and jumps in the direction of the Christ figure. The Lifehouse song booms:

'Cause you're all I want
You're all I need
You're everything, everything
You're all I want
You're all I need
You're everything, everything

Music blaring, the antagonists who visited Fatima onstage wrestle for control over her horizontally outstretched body. She is surfing on the extended arms of her enemies, all of whom are pushing her backward. As Fatima struggles with the villains, I have to admit that I am moved by her performance, despite its heavy-handed symbolism. Fatima's struggle with the Grim Reaper and her rejection of suicide are reminders of how hard it must be for her to deal with her brother's death. Judging from the lack of stray chatter, I can only assume that some of the teenagers—many of whom know Fatima personally and are aware of her loss—feel the same way.

Crying out to Jesus onstage, Fatima's efforts to reconnect with him are palpable. Her face is covered with sweat, her biceps bulging. As the villains repeatedly push her backward, they rip her shirt to shreds. Just as the tempters descend on her exhausted body, the Christ figure re-enters, shielding her from the villains. He fends them off while Fatima throws both arms in the air, relieved. The audience applauds, and Blake helps her to a standing position. Fatima's friends do not even wait until she's offstage to congratulate her: they whistle and yell, unambiguously indicating that they found the performance riveting.

Pastor Tim meets her in the aisle and gives her a hug. "Now, that would've made Steve proud," he says. Overhearing him, I am reminded that Youth Night performances are designed to aid in the cultivation of a communal sense of healing. Indeed, the Lifehouse song "Everything" calls out to God repeatedly, imploring him to speak to the congregation, to lead them to peace. And there is no knowable timeline for when a person will attain that peace. She must submit to God's will in order to find it—this is the message.[14] Notice that unlike Tiko and the footworkers, Fatima is not vigorously contesting the church's narrative of transformation. Even so, the absence of a knee-jerk dismissal does not mean Fatima accepts the narrative wholeheartedly. By taking it upon herself to choreograph a dance for others to witness, she is making sense of what it means to transform—to heal—in the context of her own life.

Once the applause dies down, Pastor Tim taps the microphone, ready to make an announcement that, as I interpret it, means the following: As a part of the institutional nexus interconnecting an array of influential local organizations, each of which is interested in social reform, Eastwood Community Church is obliged to make a Christian understanding of healing and injury compatible with another nonprofit that deals specifically with health concerns. "Right now I have something extremely important to say," Pastor Tim says. "We have the good people from Healing Hearts with us. And we want to let all of you know that behind the stage, inside of the church library, you can be tested for HIV. You can be tested right here."

Chicago has one of the highest rates of HIV in the nation, Pastor Tim explains. Worse, Eastwood has one of the highest rates of HIV in Chicago. "Believe it or not, all of you are especially susceptible to this disease. You're young. You're black. And you grew up right here." He adds, "You all—well, all of us—we're in the middle of a fight right now, a fight to save our communities, our families, our lives. Knowing your status is a key weapon in this fight. Know your status. I beg you."

Days before Youth Night, I heard Pastor Tim inform the Temple

Leaders to get tested for HIV along with the teenage participants. He wanted to send the message to the teenagers that there's no stigma attached to getting tested. After his public service announcement tonight, Pastor Tim encourages us to follow him to the church's gymnasium, which Healing Hearts volunteers have set up as an HIV-testing site. Everyone in the crowd leaves the sanctuary. Today, in solidarity with those who are brave enough to enter the testing center, I wait with about eighty young congregants. A single bedsheet serves as a door. It offers little barrier between an adolescent and the line of her peers waiting patiently for a health worker to wave them in, swab the inside of their mouth, and, twenty minutes later, inform them of their status.

On this night, two girls and two boys are told that they are HIV positive. They attended Youth Night presumably to have a good time and left knowing they are infected with a chronic virus. Unfortunately, these urban youths are proof positive that injury is pervasive in urban communities like Eastwood—and that it can emerge without warning.

"These are what I call blue blessings," Pastor Tim says. He feels anguish, he tells me, but is also grateful that tonight nearly eighty teenagers got tested. Meanwhile, Mark focuses on caring for the newly diagnosed. He is worried about the initial bout of depression they will likely endure. He stresses his commitment to stay in touch with these youth, and the hard work it will take to make sure they do not get swept up in denial or disconnect from their loved ones. Or worse, attempt to escape the reality of their diagnosis with alcohol and narcotics.

"I want to help them come to terms with the fact that they have HIV—you know, the way I did with Amy," Mark says. "'Cause accepting their positive status as a part of who they are is the first major challenge of their new lives." The new life of the patient to which Mark refers dovetails with the Christian concept of being born again. The difference is that rebirth will be grounded in injury. It entails the rigorous management of a chronic disease.

In Eastwood, healing—both in the religious and medicalized sense of the word—is processed and interpreted in different ways. In some cases, injuries are detected through biomedical technologies that analyze DNA from the inside of a person's cheek; in others, the collective experience of injury is based more on empathy (as in Fatima's performance, which could be viewed through the prism of her brother's suicide).[15] Here, modes of examining injury, as opposed to being at odds with one another, reveal that help is mutually constitutive. Community leaders like Mark and Pastor Tim depend on the injured to convey the missions of their respective institutions. (In addition, the injured also help keep these institutions attuned to social issues that are relevant to the neighborhood.) I learn this lesson—and others—about a month after Youth Night, when I accept Pastor Tim's invitation to attend the Rebirth Center Breakfast.

An important annual community event, the Rebirth Center Breakfast celebrates the men who have successfully matriculated in and transitioned out of the church's drug-rehabilitation program. At the breakfast I run into Noel Reyes, a former official in the Divine Knights Gang. When I first began my research, I interviewed Noel about his previous position in the gang. Noel was born and raised on James Street, and he was a childhood friend of Kemo, Red, and Shawn. Although he didn't have Kemo's prowess, Red's charisma, or Shawn's pedigree, he was an astute thinker. His job was preparing and assigning "G-packs"—large quantities of prepackaged heroin or cocaine that street-level dealers sell on the blocks that the Divine Knights control—to gang leaders. Because new members are continuously recruited into the fold to sell narcotics, the person responsible for providing them drugs to distribute and determining who gets what kind of product (marijuana or heroin, prescription drugs or cocaine) has substantial power. Ten years ago Noel lost a prestigious job, and nearly his life, when he began using the heroin that he was supposed to be divvying up for his fellow affiliates.

Six months after I arrived in Eastwood, Noel confided in me, while describing his fall from a high-ranking Divine Knight to a drug addict. "That job meant everything to me," he said. "I was on top of the world, making real money for the first time in my life. It meant everything." Noel shook his head, as if trying to erase the memories of the days when he privileged the gang over what he now holds dear: God and his family.

Now he sits among the proud alums of the Rebirth Center, preparing to deliver his speech, his notes beside a freshly polished plate of chicken and waffles. One of the highlights of the annual banquet is that spouses of these men don smocks and hairnets, serving up all the food their husbands can eat. Pastor Tim begins the event with a brief introduction, after which Monica performs a medley of gospel music. Adorned in an all-white choir robe, her voice fills the air, aligning the injury of addiction with a notion of spiritual redemption: "Redeemed, how I love to proclaim it / Redeemed by the blood of the Lamb / Redeemed through His infinite mercy / His child, and forever I am."

When Monica finishes her performance, Noel approaches the podium. A recent graduate from the Rebirth Rehabilitation Center where he was a resident for twelve months, Noel addresses current participants about what they can do with their lives after they graduate. "The most important thing," he says, "is to have a plan. You gotta know what you want to do. But you can't just want any old job. You gotta be familiar with the qualifications it takes to get a particular kind of job. You may need college. But, then again, you may not. The first step is to find out exactly what kind of training you need."

At first, Noel paces in an upright posture. Soon, though, he grabs a stool from the corner of the stage, sits down, and relaxes—a signal, perhaps, that he is preparing the audience for a dialogue (a conversation among a group of peers, many of whom don't know what it is like to reenter society after leaving a rehab clinic). It's a dialogue that's much less formal than a Pastor Tim sermon.

"Most of you know that I want to be a chef," Noel continues. "I'll be finishing my associate's degree in culinary arts in a couple of months." This is met with resounding applause. "My favorite dish to prepare is Cajun-baked catfish. It's the dish my wife likes most. But I had to master this dish, you understand? I had to cook it over and over. At first I put in too much paprika. Then too little garlic. See the balance has to be just right to stimulate the taste buds. And that only happens by preparing a dish over and over again."

Noel is building toward an analogy: The same discipline required to learn to cook well is also required to wake up every day and surrender to God's will. As Noel makes this connection, Pastor Tim smiles. He seems pleased that Noel is emphasizing God's role in preparing him, psychologically, for rehabilitation. "I was lost when I first came to the

Rebirth Center," Noel says. "I thought I knew it all. And let me tell you, it's hard for someone like me who was a gang leader back in the day to humble himself and let someone tell me when to eat, when to go to bed, and how to spend my money."

Continuing, Noel says, "You see, in the Rebirth Center, after you get rid of that monkey on your back, you're eligible to get a job in the community. I started working at Big Al's, the soul food restaurant down the street. I remember when I first got paid, Pastor Tim took my check. It was the first legitimate money I had made in a long, long time. And he said I couldn't spend it. He said that he would give me what I needed for the week and he would save the rest."

A self-described headstrong "grown-ass *man*," Noel didn't easily submit to such treatment. ("How you gonna tell me how I can spend *my* own hard-*earned* money.") Pastor Tim allotting Noel his money was, somewhat ironically, a reversal of the power that Noel once had over young gang members. Prior to Rebirth, the last time someone rationed Noel's money stream he was likely a fresh-faced Divine Knight hoping to make a name for himself.

"I was really upset," Noel says. "But then I remembered the lessons we learned in the Rebirth Center about letting go—the lessons about letting God take over. And it was a blessing, because a couple months after I had that argument, I got hit with child support. The only reason—and I mean the *only* reason—that I was okay was because I had all of that money saved up."

Noel, acknowledging that he should've been paying child support all along, scans the room, trying to gauge everyone's facial expressions. "But you gotta understand," he says, "I had a resentful character before. I was extremely childish. The way I acted with Pastor Tim was the same way I acted with everybody. There were times when my child's mother asked for money—times when she tried to get places to garnish my wages. and I wouldn't let her do it. I've quit jobs before because she was taking money out of my check but wouldn't let me see my son."

Because he quit so many jobs, Noel was often broke. To maintain even a modicum of hygiene, he stole things like soap and bubble gum. Once he was caught for the petty theft. "I was in County and they were asking me, 'Hey, B, what you in for this time?' I said, 'Man, I had about five packs.'" I laugh with the crowd at the pun between bundles of heroin (G-Packs) and bubble gum.

Wrapping up, Noel gets serious once again. "All jokes aside, I owe everything to the Rebirth Center and to my family for sticking by my side. To my wife, Grace, I thank you for helping to change me into the man I am today. We men don't know what these women go through, putting up with our mess. Grace probably didn't know what she was getting into."

"No way," Grace Reyes yells from behind the serving table. "But I'd do it all over again."

Noel's testimony illustrates the importance of a "renegade will" as a resource for resilience. Such performances of redemption—performances in which urban residents display a willingness to heal—are the basis for institutional collaboration. What's more, his speech shows that institutional efforts to help people heal from disease and addiction culminate at the very moment an urban resident internalizes a story of redemption, makes it his or her own, and a polished, vigorously rehearsed illness narrative becomes an asset for others. At Eastwood Community Church, part of making a resource out of personal pain and suffering means teaching others to develop the necessary willpower to recover from injurious events. Noel now considers his tenure as a gang member misguided, his previous exploits destructive. These were the years when his rank in the Divine Knights determined his self-worth, when he was too "childish" to see the value in providing for his family.

Once again Eastwood Community Church proves to be a site where medical notions of healing (in terms of managing addiction) and religious notions of healing (in terms of maintaining faith in God) are fostered, and the reiteration of a willingness to heal becomes a critical component in this process. Only this time, instead of a crowd full of teenage boys and girls, the audience is male drug addicts—many of whom are former gang members—and their families, who can't hear too many times that the people who once disappointed them are willing to change. Here, the discipline and patience it takes to replicate a meal

again and again is consonant with the disciplin.
necessary to harness injury in order to heal.   tience deemed

Three weeks after the Rebirth Center Breakfast, P.
to take this message of redemption and communal he   m decides
church walls. On Monday night he unveils his idea t   eyond the
planning committee: a worship service in the style of a bl   Temple's
stage on Murphy Road, right in front of the church. There   rty on a
and large speakers to entice residents to leave their homes, an   e food
she can bridge the gap between believers and nonbelievers, A   cause
headline the pastor's event.   will

By the time Amy is due to speak on an unseasonably warm Satu ay
in March, around two hundred residents are seated in foldout chairs n
front of the makeshift stage. For the past hour, Eastwood Community
Church's choir has been performing. Another fifty or so Eastwoodians stand in the general vicinity of the church, making idle convers-
tion. Amy has spoken at the church before (she has even told her story
at a local middle school and a recreation center), but this is by far her
largest audience. Standing behind Pastor Tim, she appears nervous. She
is positioned to tell the crowd about the resolve it takes to manage injury on a daily basis. "Hello, everyone," Amy says, taking the mic with
far less confidence than the seasoned preacher. "I'm eighteen years old
and I'm here to talk about how I contracted HIV, the virus that causes
AIDS." As she emerges from the shadows, I realize that I haven't seen
her since she was released from the juvenile detention center.

Growing up, Amy was a tomboy, she says. She loved playing basketball, which she learned from her mom. "She was my best friend. The
turning point in my life came when I was fourteen and my mother
died." Here, Amy's throat cracks, but she continues: "My mother, Sue-
Ann Green, was six months pregnant when she was killed in a drive-
by shooting. The baby also died. Her boyfriend was a member of the
Knights. He was also a drug dealer. And one day someone decided to
take his life. My mother happened to be with him, and he used her as a
human shield. He lived. She didn't."

Recounting the circumstances of her mother's death in a staccato of

...s, Amy's eyes remain fixed on her spiral notebook.
measured ...e that when she goes off script she becomes teary-eyed
Later An ...bly impassioned, unable to make it through her speech.
and unc ...other's death, Amy lived with her aunt. But as soon as she
Afte ...her aunt started using drugs. Heroin was her drug of choice.
moved ...
In her ...se, Amy says of her aunt, "She used to say that she was so
distr ...over my mom's death that she turned to drugs to deal with
her ...and pain. I don't make those kinds of excuses. But somewhere
do ...he line, I started using too. I would steal drugs and needles from
m ...nt; and I was only sixteen when I used heroin for the first time."

...ne day Amy woke up, walked into the bathroom, and found her
...nt on the ground, dead of a drug overdose. After she died, Amy began
...oing to a drug-rehabilitation center. Before starting treatment, she was
tested for sexually transmitted diseases, the results of which revealed
that she was HIV positive. "I still don't know how I contracted the
virus," she says. "It could've been from having sex. It could've been from
sharing needles with my aunt. I think it was from my aunt because she
was skinny; and toward the end of her life she started getting sores and
abrasions on her skin—"

As Amy is speaking, I hear a familiar voice punctuating her words.
Behind me, Mark, her health worker and friend, has once again come
to lend Amy moral support, delivering words of encouragement like,
"Yes, that's right," and, "Please, child, tell 'em." As he deploys the call-
and-response interactions that accompany Sunday sermons to affirm the
diagnostic techniques that he's taught Amy, medical and religious discourses intersect once again.

"Nobody knows whether or not my aunt had AIDS," Amy adds. "But
the point is: I don't want to die young like her. Or like my mother."
Rolling up her left sleeve to expose her forearm, she says, "You probably can't see this. But it's a tattoo. This is a tattoo of my mother, and it
covers up the places where I used to inject. As an addict, I can't think
about death. Thinking about death is easy. Death doesn't even scare me.
It's living that's hard. For me, every single day is a struggle."

Amy's story personalizes an already-valuable healing narrative. As
someone who is well equipped to discuss an onerous and ongoing pro-

cess of healing, she is an expert at eliciting empathy. On the one hand, Amy's illness narrative is similar, formally, to Fatima's dance performance: both are built on a framework that would be familiar to an audience of churchgoers. But, like Noel's speech, the point of it all is not merely personal transformation, but to focus the audience's attention on the daily rigors of managing injury. Like "renegade dreams," the "renegade wills" that Fatima, Noel, and Amy have developed are grounded in injury and seek to refigure the pain experienced through addiction and disease into newfound aspirations or a radical reorientation to the world (in this case related to sobriety and drug adherence).

By making a story of redemption her own, Amy reminds us all that, as an HIV patient, survival means a lifelong commitment to adhere. The resiliency that Amy has developed makes multiple institutional understandings of healing commensurate. As such, both believers and non-believers can make sense of the willpower cultivated in this communal space. In this way, Amy's narrative speaks to how people in Eastwood make sense of volition in light of the kind of injuries you have to think about every day for the rest of your life (or at least until your will to adhere becomes stronger than the disease that threatens it). In this context, developing the will it takes to cope with the injury of addiction and disease ceases to be solely a single-minded cognitive relationship with a higher power. It is a far more radical endeavor. Allowing other Eastwoodians to see you managing various forms of injury is both action and strategy that can be adopted in adverse times—a collective asset others might draw on. This is the very resource on which many of their lives may depend.

The day after Amy's speech, I visit her at a group home for girls where she now lives. While I am there, discussing the impact of Amy's illness narrative, Mark arrives. Sitting on the shabby steps of a group home with Mark and Amy, I witness the narration of experience, as Mark helps Amy develop the language she needs to attune herself to any side effects of her antiretroviral treatment. He encourages her to talk with her physician about the side effects of her cocktail therapy (nausea, sluggishness). He reminds her to schedule doctor's appointments, since doing so will allow her doctor to change the drug regimen in relation to the progression of the disease. His efforts are crucial. The will that

Mark encourages Amy to harness and maintain is both a general power to overcome obstacles in life, and also specifically related to adhering to a drug-treatment regimen.

Moments later we watch Mark drive away. Then Amy reminds me of our first encounter in cellblock 3B, just over a year ago, though it seems like an eternity, she says, because of what she's learned in the meantime. As we watch the overcast sky turn bright, she confesses that a sense of willingness is rebooted in her every day at noon—when there's no nurse in flowery scrubs to check under her tongue, and she shuts off her cell phone reminder, opens her purse, and swallows seven pills that, she hopes, will sustain her.

Framing

This morning Mr. Otis tells me that the police are going to check the blue-light footage from his street, to try and figure out why the eighteen-year-old Eastwood boy was shot last week. Mr. Otis paces in front of me, gripping the community newspaper, the *Eastwood Gazette*, which features a photograph of the slain teenager. Glancing at the paper, then shaking his head, Mr. Otis tells me the part of the story that is not in the newspaper: "Police say the boy ran from them"—he says, still pacing—"ducked and dodged through an alleyway when he saw them, right? When the officers cornered him, they say he pointed a gun at them, so they shot to kill. And believe me, they succeeded. But, get this, man: The kid was shot in the back. The boy's mama says he was scared stiff of the police. A couple days ago, before he was shot and all, she said some cops told the boy, 'We're gonna get you.' So, now she's trying to sue the city. She says the police planted the gun. She says the police wanna turn her son into a criminal, you know, justify the shooting—make it seem okay."

After I left Mr. Otis's stoop, I take the paper from him and read it. Mr. Otis is right. Both the city of Chicago and the family of the slain boy are waiting for footage from the blue-light video, waiting for the footage to prove that the boy was either a criminal or unjustifiably killed. But who's to say what the footage actually reveals? Does a blurry image of a teenage boy running from the police prove that he's guilty? Or does the frame capture a boy who knows he is always *presumed* to be guilty? And maybe that's why he's running.

  —3/3/09, 10:11 PM

—————— ✳ ——————

OR,

How to Get Out of an Isolated Space

On September 24, 2009, a transfixed bystander uses her cell phone from the passenger side of a car to record a series of violent altercations. Before we see any fighting in the grainy video, we hear car horns. Drivers try to maneuver their vehicles around a large, scattered mass of teenagers who occupy the street and surrounding sidewalks.

"Get out of the car," a woman in the passenger seat says to the driver. Meanwhile, in the background, we hear young girls screaming. Kids in black school uniforms are hurdling cars, presumably to assist their friends who are fighting just past the camera's edge. The camera pans up the block. Several fights are happening all at once. The woman behind the camera phone has positioned herself as the director. She is no longer handling the device herself, but telling her male companion what should be captured on the video.

"Zoom in. Zoom in. *Zoom in,*" she says.

On the sidewalk, we see a boy holding a long piece of a railroad tie—part of the foundation from a nearby railroad track. He handles it like a baseball bat and strikes another boy (who, we later discover, is Derrion Albert) on the head. Derrion's back was turned when he received the blow. Unable to brace himself, he falls to the ground. Derrion attempts to regain his composure, gets to his knees, and then another boy hits him with a balled fist. The camera pans out. We can see two teenage boys in a fighter's stance, facing each other. Each is waiting for the other to flinch. They, too, are holding wooden railroad ties. "Oh my God. Get closer," the woman directing the scene shouts.

Heeding her order, the cameraman focuses once again on Derrion, who is curled up in a fetal position on the street. Boys are running past his immobilized body, kicking him on the ground while he lies there, still.

"Get a close-up on him," the woman is imploring. "They're *killing* him," she says, now screaming, *"Look."*

"Get up, sir," an older woman says.

This woman, who has come out of the nearby recreation center, is bent over and trying to speak to an unresponsive Derrion. Soon more Good Samaritans (young women in school uniforms) come to Derrion's aid, taking the place of his assailants who by now have fled.

"Pick him up. Pick him up," the woman behind the camera phone says—for the first time speaking directly to the people involved in the melee. The group of students who now surrounds Derrion manage to flop his limp arms around their necks and drag him into the doorway of the community center.

"Get up, Derrion. Get *up*," a young girl says. "Derrion. Get up. *Please.*"

Out of the frame, we can hear an adult talking. "Officer," he says, "we got a kid beat to death in here—

"—We got a guy *dying* in here."

Should the reader view this scene as simply another "senseless" murder, if the reader views the wood-wielding assailants described above as faceless aggressors—and Derrion, just another unfortunate victim—then my efforts here have failed. Derrion could've been any one of the young people whom I've described in Eastwood. He could've been Danny or Justin, Blizzard or Amy, Susan or Tiko. Worse still, Danny, Justin, Blizzard, Amy, Susan, or Tiko could've been among those teenagers hurdling cars, among the adolescents swinging wooden railroad ties. We know by now that there is not some innate difference that separates Derrion and his aggressors—some inherent distinction between injured and assailant. But *Renegade Dreams* has attempted to convey something we know little of: the sensibility—the alternate frame—that Eastwoodians cultivate out of being seen both as highly susceptible to experience injury and extremely likely to enact it. In this regard, it's only fitting that I end where I began—the frame of the "socially isolated" community—because this enduring trope helps explain why Derrion's violent murder became a media event that went viral on the Internet, that was re-broadcast on national news networks like CNN and ABC, and that resonated with millions of Americans.

My argument is straightforward. We should not allow the specter of urban violence—made more palpable with each news special and each viral video—to reify the notion of the "isolated" ghetto. That notion grows increasingly outmoded with each passing day. Instead, we should embrace the opportunities to reframe seemingly familiar narratives that, because of their familiarity, impede our understanding of how injury is experienced. This means that when presented with the images like those captured in the footage of Derrion's murder, the object of analysis cannot merely be the fight itself, but the camera phone that captured it, since the framing of the event is what we need to examine when seeking to illuminate the inner city's connections to broader social worlds. Attention to how multiple frameworks on the inner city collapse upon one another and become conflated will lead us to ask new questions: What are the ways in which the cell phone, in this instance, proves critical in disseminating images of (and frameworks about) gang violence?

The footage of the gang fight became so popular that days after the incident, United States Attorney General Eric Holder was moved to comment. He said that he hoped Derrion's death would serve as a "stark wake-up call to a reality that can be easy for too many to ignore as they go about their daily lives." The ongoing onslaught of youth-on-youth attacks, the attorney general argued, must be understood within a universal context: "Youth violence is not a Chicago problem any more than it is a black problem, a white problem, or a Hispanic problem. . . . It is an American problem."

Yet news outlets seemed oblivious to Eric Holder's plea. They did not adhere to his careful choice to describe the incident as a form of "youth" violence rather than "gang" violence. It did not seem to bother local news anchors that the latter descriptor brings to mind a threatening public, comfortably distant from the lifestyle and values of the American "mainstream." On the afternoon that Derrion died, Chicago news reporters asserted that the conflict stemmed from a feud between "two rival street gangs," later adding that Derrion was "pummeled to death by a local mob," before referring to the event as a "savage" beating. Initially presumed to have died amidst the quotidian "savagery" that defines the gang lifestyle, prosecutors clarified the public record at the murder trial of his assailants. They noted, several days after his death, that Derrion was an "honor student," an "innocent bystander."

But while journalists were distracted by spectacular violence and initially mischaracterized Derrion as a gang member, it is important to point out exactly where this coverage fell short: Reporters failed to see that Derrion's beating cannot be understood outside of the encompassing contexts that shape local groups. More precisely, his death exemplifies the way that larger external forces are molding emergent generations of Chicagoans, everything from the "war on drugs," to a stagnant economy, to the kind of manufacturing loss that characterizes post-industrial decay.[1]

It is the relationship between these larger social forces and each individual's volition that William Julius Wilson famously described through his theory of "social isolation."[2] What distinguishes the popular conception of the inner city as a space of crime, danger, and tempestuous vice from Wilson's idea of the "socially isolated" ghetto is that his category of analysis does not merely refer to an inner-city enclave. The theory hinges on the five key factors that led a subclass of blacks to live in seclusion in America's largest cities starting in the 1970s. To restate matters briefly, these factors are an inadequate integration into community institutions; an increase in crime due to high unemployment; the out-migration of socially mobile residents; a lack of people willing to replenish the departed population; and an inability to find livable wages as the U.S. economy shifted from manufacturing to service industries.[3]

The idea of the isolated ghetto has been indispensable as a way to capture a post-industrial moment of concentrated poverty. That fact is undeniable. But throughout *Renegade Dreams*, I've been articulating another iteration of a theory of isolation, in the hopes of developing a successively closer approximation of what inner-city injury looks like at present, and to grapple with its interconnections with governmental and community institutions as well as its relationship to various social and historical processes. Unearthing alternate frames—that is, taking time to tease out multiple interpretations of urban life—is critical in this regard, especially because the footage of the gang fight captures details that would be easy for even the most attentive ethnographer to miss. In these blurred frames, black urban youth maim and murder with the fragmented debris from a defunct railway system.

Chicago's railway system was erected in the 1880s, when George Pullman built a company town that manufactured railroad cars. The twinned roles of boss and landlord proved lucrative for Pullman until 1894, when white and black workers alike objected to his business practices of laying off employees, lowering wages, and raising rent prices in his company homes.[4] Pullman's workers organized America's first union before orchestrating a national strike, and the fortunes of Chicago's urban labor market have risen and fallen with the manufacturing industry ever since. There were no video cameras then, but there are sketches of the willingly out of work, lines of strikers standing on dirt-compacted gravel that held the tracks of the nascent railway, refusing to budge. The wooden picket signs clutched by workers during the Pullman Strike point to the tragedy of the century that followed, as more and more city dwellers were out of work because of economic scarcity, rather than principled objection—as the railroad ties once cemented in Chicago's urban landscape loosened from lack of use.

In the 1970s and 1980s, when manufacturing jobs were all but disappearing in communities like Eastwood, the railroad industry underwent a long period of bankruptcies and mergers; both the national and regional rail systems were realigned. In 1976—five years before the Pullman Company manufactured its last railroad car—29 different railroad routes and branch lines crisscrossed inner-city Chicago. By 2006 the majority of these routes were defunct: 31 segments of the branch lines had been abandoned totally, and another 20 were cut back or downgraded. Lines were abandoned throughout Illinois, but, according to a recent report, "diminished rail service has been especially noticeable on the South Side of Chicago," where Derrion Albert was slain.[5] Even though the train in black popular culture has long served as a hopeful metaphor for African Americans leaving the South in their quest for work, the fact that the railroad ties used to slay Derrion were once synonymous with labor is not just a metaphorical convenience.[6] In Chicago these wooden railroad ties symbolize both Derrion's death and one of the most storied strikes in American history. The two events are grounded in the same material reality.

In this era of abandoned rail lines, the popular and scholarly frameworks that connect us to the inner city reinscribe a familiar and often thoughtless idea of the inner city. This is how the camera phone facilitates global circulation and urban stagnation, simultaneously. And this is why it should be clear that the frames captured by our web browsers are themselves at work, efficiently reproducing the enduring trope of the "socially isolated" ghetto, over and over again.

Two years before Derrion died, a monthly publication, *Chicago Magazine*, reported that another body was found lifeless in inner-city Chicago. This time it was a white high school student, Michael York, who died of a heroin overdose. York passed away in St. Charles, in a suburban mansion; and to add insult to injury, his peers loaded his dead body in a car and then dumped his corpse in a West Side neighborhood, North Lawndale, where they purchased the drugs. *Chicago Magazine*'s report on this incident is indicative of the way that black communities like North Lawndale and Eastwood are often portrayed as frozen both in time and morality.

"Geographically," reporter Bryan Smith starts, "the town of St. Charles lies about 40 miles from the alley where the body was found. In every other respect—income, appearance, demographics, outlook—St. Charles, population 33,000, floats as distant as the planets. The Chicago neighborhood of North Lawndale is 94 percent black and dirt poor." After quoting someone who described this neighborhood as "an industrial slum without the industry," Smith continues to defame this neighborhood: "Drug dealers, as brazen as gutter rats," he claims, "hawk their wares from corner hangouts and parked cars."[7]

In this excerpt, the frame of the isolated ghetto allows for another framing of the more sinister sort—the "TV crime drama" kind of framing, in which a criminal produces false evidence against the innocent so that they seem guilty. By abandoning York's dead body in an empty alleyway, his friends frame an entire community, making the neighborhood itself culpable for his death. Entailed in transforming the noun *frame* into a verb that depicts an unlawful act is an assessment about what belongs in the picture and what does not.[8]

Of course, this distinction between the perilous ghetto and the safe suburbs is largely overstated. As long as the black urban poor have inhabited America's inner cities, more privileged whites from nearby have traveled to the ghetto in the pursuit of forbidden pleasure.[9] Still, setting such clandestine interactions aside, today American cities are increasingly following patterns of Latin American cities like São Paulo and European cities like Paris, in which poverty is pushed from the city center into the periphery or *banlieue*.[10] The result of all this migration is a messy merger between urban communities and their encompassing contexts.[11] That is to say, the social phenomenon that causes privileged populations to gravitate toward the inner city is not unidirectional. Urban blacks travel throughout their respective cities for work, and at times for pleasure as well, inspiring incidents that are far more controversial than Michael York's crime scene.

Picture that desolate highway. It led from Hollywood to the inner-city streets of Compton—that relentlessly framed but not often visited place where gangs reside. Recall the three minutes of video footage taken along that highway of an unarmed motorist, Rodney King—the video of a black body being beaten that didn't even need the Internet to go viral. Recall, further, how that footage inspired the L.A. riots, as it was used to show how a body, even as it was being bludgeoned with nightsticks, could still be a threat. This sleight of logic, Judith Butler has argued, relies for its success on a sense of endangerment. In 1992 twelve jurors listened to defense attorneys argue that the policemen who beat Rodney King were themselves victims.[12]

To prove their point, they slowed down the footage. Then they sped it up, flooding the jury with thousands of frames per second. They sought to show that King was continuing to fight back, that King was in fact the aggressor. But speeding up the film also created a different possibility: a slow-motion effect, in which cultural presuppositions about urban blacks and their place in society filled in the gaps between the frames, rendering the texture of the grainy footage culturally clear, even as the actual picture became blurred beyond recognition. That framing is what allowed the jury to invert their perception of danger, correcting the imbalance concerning what the film evidently showed (police with wooden sticks beating an unarmed man) and what they already believed: We should fear urban blacks, and policemen should protect us from that fear.[13]

Lewis Gordon has termed this duality the simultaneous invisibility and hypervisibility of blackness. Rodney King, the person, becomes invisible, his actual reality subsumed by an "illicit appearance." The spotlight on black criminality (this "illicit appearance"), in other words, becomes so intense as to be blinding: hypervisibility leads to invisibility, "where to see a black person as such means there is nothing more to be known, seen, or learned." The viewer reverts to the glaring stereotype of the angry black man. This angry man is in "total control" of the situation, as one juror put it, even as he is beaten next to lifelessness—beaten in a way, might I add, that makes Derrion Albert's killers seem meek.[14]

The idea that urban blacks are always already threatening, prior to any video manipulation, enables the jury to inhabit multiple roles at once. They are witnesses; the lens of the video camera separates them from the site of danger, where the police protect them. At the same time, they *are* the police—endowed with responsibility, through the power to convict, to serve and protect, to enforce the law and order. Additionally, they are the injured body, only a whitewashed version of that body. The blows that King takes are the blows they would suffer—that society would suffer, from their perspective—without the police's protection. They identify with King's vulnerability, in other words, but construe it as their own.[15] This is how the viral footage of Derrion's death and others (like the more recent one of a black girl being pummeled by a bus driver) morph the assailant and the injured into one black body, making it easier to see all black bodies as dangerous, even as they are beaten into submission.[16]

We need not search far to see the logic of inverted fear at work. After all, we live in a historical moment in which New York City's stop-and-frisk policies, Arizona's anti-immigration interrogations, and Florida's "stand your ground" laws are vigorously defended—laws stating that a person may justifiably use "deadly force" in self-defense when there is "reasonable" belief of a threat—laws that put the burden on families to prove that their dead children were not justifiably menacing. George Zimmerman didn't wait for his jury-selection notice. On the night of February 26, 2012, he witnessed "danger" as he kept the streets of Sanford, Florida, safe. He assumed that a bulging pocket full of Skittles in Trayvon Martin's hoodie was a gun; he inhabited the role of the police; and in the name of watching over the community and protecting his own alleged vulnerability, he hunted and killed an unarmed black teenager from less than a foot away.

Well before the controversial acquittal of George Zimmerman created a national uproar about race relations in the United States, legal scholar Patricia Williams commented on the failure of the Sanford police to classify the incident as a homicide or even to arrest Zimmerman until months after the murder, after they were submerged in a sea of public outcry:

"The failure to investigate was not just lazy, not just sloppy, not just unprofessional," she writes, "it flouted basic tenets of our jurisprudence." Next Williams argues that the police's conclusion that there was "nothing" to disprove Zimmerman's version of events can only be substantiated by one of two explanations: "Either they blindly and unethically deferred to the word of the confessed killer and thus abandoned reference to any community standard at all," she says, "or else they instinctively shared Zimmerman's vision and thus instantiated 'being frightened to death' of a young black man as a reasonable community norm."[17]

Williams's quote helps to explain how injury becomes "reasonable," pointing us to the frameworks we take for granted. Even as violent crimes in our nation decrease, viral videos of black bodies being beaten remind us about black danger. Such videos are just the latest—but arguably the most visceral, the most effective—in a long line of fear-stoking depictions of urban life. These depictions are malleable in their mean-ings and used for multiple purposes. Some teens likely use these videos for bragging rights, as proof of their own urban authenticity. For others, they are likely a means to mourn, proof of how a beloved community is falling apart. And for many people, these videos may seem evidence of a virus; they become a metaphor for contagion, proof that violence is seeping everywhere.[18] From this perspective, bolstered by abundant viral evidence, such contamination must be controlled, lest the rest of society is affected. Controlling inner-city contamination thus becomes a justi-fied practice of policing the poor.[19]

In reviewing the injurious moments throughout *Renegade Dreams*, my aim is to access the political potential of the frame, both for scholars as well as non-academics who have dedicated their lives to addressing urban poverty—pastors like Tim Montgomery and activists like Eric Childs, community organizers like Mrs. Pearl and probation officers like Mr. Randall. These Eastwoodians bear witness in a different way than the jurors who acquitted Rodney's attackers and those who let Trayvon's killer go free. And the difference hinges on their proximity to what is typically framed as the problem. The Eastwoodians I've described are more like the person in the middle of the melee, holding the cell phone, than the person passing judgment from the jury stand or watching Der-rion's beating from his laptop. Some of them are Good Samaritans—like those teenage girls—who let their compassion and concern over-power their fear as they courageously helped Derrion to the doorway of that recreation center.

They address the forms of injury that plague their community by other means—not by subjecting bodies to violence or sanctioning bru-tality through verdicts of exoneration; they do so by dwelling in a space of injury and refusing to budge. The way Pastor Tim and the Eastwood Community Church address injury is through moral reform. Some-times this reform is evinced through the church's overarching belief that morally transforming residents is integral to community redevelop-ment; at other times it is evinced through more specific attempts to help addicts and HIV patients hone an illness narrative. Their take on moral transformation is not without controversy, as we have seen. It stifles the voices of other Eastwoodians who disagree with the church's vision for the community. For this reason, Eastwoodians like Justin address injury in another way. The anti-violence forum that he organized with the aid of a gang leader displays his attempts to refigure the community-wide perception of gang violence held by the church. His efforts demonstrate that the same social relationships that inspire vengeance can be transformed into social bonds that are a lot more peaceful.

We've seen gang elders like Mr. Otis grapple with the Divine Knights' political past as a means to lament the current state of affairs. We've similarly seen how, for a gang leader like Red Walker, the "renegade's" gym shoes serve as "sites of projection" that compensate for anxieties about the future.[20] We've seen, further, how Blizzard's attempts to vocalize his aspirations through the songs and poems he writes become a way for him to talk about the social repercussions of gang affiliation.

All that we've seen has given us another frame for understanding injury and the resilience that results from it. From Mrs. Dickerson and Amy O'Neal to Tamara Anderson and Mr. Otis, from young affiliates like Danny and Blizzard to seasoned members like Justin and Tosh, Eastwoodians who we've watched pursue their collective projects and individual pursuits have taught us how to harness injury. All of them, in their own way, have traded on the gang's image of violence, while understanding that it is exactly that—an image—which can be stripped of its veneer, its luminance dulled, so that the glare of gang involvement doesn't have to color who an urban resident is, always.

The alternative pathways we've watched Eastwoodians pursue in this book have demonstrated the frame's ability to disturb the senses. This is where the political potential of unyielding aspirations reside. The question is: How does a "renegade" like Danny or Tiko learn to hone and refine a personal story of struggle, like Amy or Justin have done? How does a person mobilize this pent-up potential? Butler addresses this concern metaphorically by reminding us of that playground game of "telephone," where children sit in a line and repeat a message to the person next to them.[21] The message is passed through the queue until, when the last player announces it to the group, errors have inevitably accumulated in the retellings. More often than not, the statement announced by the last player differs significantly from the one uttered by the first. (Some more adventurous players intentionally alter their retellings to ensure a changed story.)

Within the same critical space that allows world-altering dreams to take flight lies a broader framework for analyzing gangs and urban life. This new frame brazenly disrupts the interpretation of Derrion's death: With each new iteration we tell each other (often with our own phones), we can transform the message that the camera phone captures until the viral footage is no longer just a "savage" beating, but perhaps an inevitable consequence of post-industrial isolation. Or another potential retelling: Isolation itself is reproduced every time we refresh our web browser, helping to sustain an outmoded idea of the inner city and its inhabitants. We thus grow more distant even as we're more connected than ever before—close enough to purchase drugs from an unknown dealer and then frame a whole community for an overdose; and close enough to kill a hoodied stranger at close range as you "stand your ground."

My intent is not to deny or downplay the pioneering work that scholars like Wilson have made to disrupt entrenched American narratives. I just mean to suggest that, in addition to examining the factors that produce urban marginalization, we must also apprehend the inner city as part of an interconnected world in which people, objects, and ideas are rapidly changing and refuse to stay affixed.[22] Even before gentrification became commonplace in America's largest cities, it was debatable as to whether or not the inner city has ever been isolated economically. Ever since there's been a black inner-city population, they've stood as a low-wage reserve army, readily dismissed or pulled into a wider web of economic activity at the whim of the business cycle. Even the fleeting existence of Gangsta City Entertainment signals the fact that the artistic products created in the ghetto quickly become widely appropriated and appreciated; similarly, Derrion Albert's murder exemplifies that the forms of violence that seem to characterize "urban life" are quickly seized upon and circulated.[23]

Within this web of circulation, the products in which gangs traffic—particularly illegal drugs—are imported from multiple countries on multiple continents; indeed, a global infrastructure is needed to grow, package, and transport drugs like heroin—and yet the inner city is presumed to be divorced from our increasingly globalized marketplace. The economics of drug legislation is yet another example. Despite the fact that in 2011 President Obama's "drug-control" budget entailed a 13 percent increase in anti-drug spending for the Pentagon and an 18 percent increase for the Bureau of Prisons, the inner city is seen as estranged from the broader economy.[24] Of course, when most scholars speak about the inner city's economic isolation, they are not referring to the millions of government jobs that depend precisely on locking urban residents up. What they mean, here, is that the individuals who live in these communities are disconnected from opportunities in the *legal* labor market. True, indeed. But that disconnection, as we've seen, is embedded with its own interconnections. The fact that an inner-city neighborhood like Eastwood can become an international hub for the heroin trade and the fact that Eastwood residents comprise an alarming 30 percent of the entire prison population of the state of Illinois must also be part of how we frame the story—these interconnections help to explain the estrangement that is implicated in a theory of isolation; it helps us understand how thousands of young people like Danny and Blizzard wind up in jail, why black bodies with blurred faces brandish railroad ties.

While illuminating the texture of social life in Eastwood, we have seen, again and again, the perils of highlighting so-called legitimate networks at the expense of the hidden or less formal ones. There are numerous examples of how these formal and informal networks intersect and give shape to one another.[25] Take the relationship between block club presidents like Tamara and gang leaders like Red, for example, or the relationship between commodities like gym shoes and institutions like the West Side Detention Center, or social relationships between wounded ex–gang members like Tosh and active affiliates like Blizzard who may serve as their caretakers.

What I mean to say, in closing, is that these hidden connections reveal much about how injury is experienced and reimagined as a means to overcome. By focusing on dilapidated houses, gym shoes, blue lights, canes, wheelchairs, tattoos of the deceased, and railroad ties, I have attempted to extend the implications of an isolation theory by showing the resilience through which Eastwoodians' dynamic histories and their own means of healing come to life. The point of it all is to present a new frame as a resource for scholarship; and this analytic frame is fortified from the collapsing of other frames. As a frame of "senseless" violence collapses onto the frame of the isolated ghetto, "renegade dreams" emerge from the wreckage. The vignettes full of footworkin' gang members who shatter glass, picket signs of greystones that reframe what development should mean, interpretive dances that stave off the Grim Reaper, and poems that cling to wishes are all varied examples of the alternate frame employed by Eastwoodians to survive global and historical shifts wholly beyond their control, and to recast their fate.

"Renegade dreamers" refuse to be immobilized by injury, even when they're paraplegics. Like Tosh's goal to write a book in which he portrays a scene about leaving his hospital bed behind and walking out of the trauma center, the capacities to connect through writing and to imagine a different future are lights at the end of the tunnel, hopeful desires that lead resourceful urban residents to say: "We are not isolated. In fact, we're so connected that everyone reading about our dreams should feel culpable for the injuries that exist in the society we share." We live in a society in which black urbanites are subject to myriad forms of injury, indeed; but if the long-standing tradition of examining the inner city should stem from and foster collaboration—from a sincere, engaged effort by all of us to see the struggles particular to every neighborhood in light of the global struggles that we all must reckon with—if we can manage such collaboration, then the world won't be disappointed. It might just see the weapons wielded by urban blacks become train tracks, once again.

A RENEGADE DREAM COME TRUE

It didn't happen in the space above her jewelry shop. But it happened, nonetheless. In the summer of 2012, Eastwoodians erected a gang museum. And that museum amassed a level of support that Mr. Otis and Tamara Anderson probably didn't think possible in those early days of planning, three years prior. Little did they know, they weren't the only Eastwoodians with the unashamed dream of showcasing the Divine Knights' civil rights roots. In the end, Mr. Otis and other longtime members of the Divine Knights teamed up with a reputable local university and Chicago's Museum of Contemporary Culture to reveal a past that was buried beneath the endless news reports that bemoaned gang violence.

The Divine Knights Gang exhibit was sobering compared to the sensationalism that accompanies those cosmetic portrayals of urban life, but not merely because it strove to fulfill some sort of "positive" image. It was sobering in its routine recollection of a past that should've never been forgotten; it was sobering in the same way that young Eastwoodians now describe a present that shouldn't be so—like when you listen to a teenager chronicle her walk home from school, and in the midst the conversation you realize that for her, safety is provisional. Early death, the loss of limbs—the whole rotten ordeal—could come as easily as a spell of rain or a bout of sunshine. There's a matter-of-fact timbre to the way a young Eastwoodian depicts injury, so much less glossy, so much more tangible, than the footage of gang fights that circulate so often. One doesn't need much hyperbole in a description of violence, in other words, when just walking home requires a certain vigilance in order to stay alive. And because of this, Mr. Otis and the other Divine Knights who organized this exhibit didn't have to embellish either their gang's present-day exploits or its peaceful history to show how much things have changed: in their striking portrayal of a gang's civic engagement, the pictures spoke for themselves.

In the face of contemporary experiences of injury, the museum exhibit suggested an alternative pathway of what Eastwoodian streets could look like. It offered photographs of the recreation center and the small businesses the Divine Knights established in the 1960s, when service to the gang had nothing to do with heroin, back when a gang member's duties were centered on the hard toil of writing grants to governmental agencies. Four decades later, the exhibit that celebrated the gang's legacy of community service mirrored its method of fund-raising. This exhibit attracted funders as varied and influential as educational organizations, such as the Illinois Arts Administration, the state legislature of Illinois, and even one of the largest funders of community-based programs in the United States, the Public Humanities Consortium.

The advertisements for the exhibit promoted it as a "Report to the Public" in which everyone was invited to learn about the history of the Divine Knights, to meet former members, and to listen to their stories. "Consider the history and potential of gang members as community organizers," it beckoned. The evolving, multi-sited exhibit showcased cultural artifacts of the Divine Knights' political past in the vacant lots that usually serve as meeting places for feuding gang sets to carve out their territory; the exhibit also reclaimed the lots that now served as desolate bridges between boarded-up greystone buildings in Eastwood. And in doing so, this community-based project enlivened isolated spaces with artifacts from a vibrant gang archive—especially when the curators installed Mr. Otis's precious photographs in these otherwise abandoned lots. In the photographs on display, I saw Mr. Otis's black utopia being realized at last: clean-shaven, gang members in cardigans wielding long wooden brooms, instead of railroad ties. They were sweeping the same cracked concrete that too many Divine Knights now push themselves over in wheelchairs. In the exhibit's images, members of the Divine Knights, past and present, were articulating a vision for their neighborhood that wasn't imposed on them by the local government.

It was certainly true that, from the beginning, local politicians doubted the Divine Knights' intentions to transform themselves into a constructive community organization. It was also true that, as gang members in the 1970s aligned with the SCLC and the Black Panthers, some of those politicians feared that the vision of a revolutionary gang would come to fruition. With the gang's long political history in mind, the core question this exhibit asked was as resonant as any I've ever heard in Eastwood: "What would it take for today's gang members to bring peace to the neighborhood?"

One of the Divine Knights' oldest members dedicated seventy-four years on this earth to addressing that question. Finally, the cultural artifacts of the "good ol' gang" that he held on to for so many years in his basement fulfilled a collective purpose. When heroin took over, Mr. Otis continued to talk about the gang's political contributions, even though no one would listen. He never shied away or felt ashamed of his history, even during the heyday of the drug trade in the 1980s and 1990s when it seemed absurd, if not blasphemous, to speak of a "constructive" gang.

It was for these reasons—that he helped resurrect a forgotten history; that he insisted on squabbling with pastors, with policemen, with credulous scholars like me—that when Justin called in February 2013 to tell me Mr. Otis had passed away, I wasn't stricken with grief. In fact, thinking back on those late-night conversations with Mr. Otis, watching gang members from his stoop in the haze of the blue light, I couldn't help but smile.

As Justin told me of the big memorial service that neighbors had planned, I finally realized: the image of the gang that Mr. Otis hoped to change wasn't some sort of nightmarish apparition. Every gang member that floated in the street—so many ghosts of the gang's political past—

carried a glow that Mr. Otis could see; and he cherished that elusive light, he continued to see it even when most were convinced that it had been extinguished, or believed that such light never existed in the first place. Inside of each member—each battered, injured, surprisingly resilient poor young black resident—he saw his renegade dream. I was just glad that toward the end of his life he "had a breath left," as Blizzard would say, to make at least one of his dreams come true.

In Memory of **Otis Ball**

ACKNOWLEDGMENTS

✳

The people of Eastwood have made this book possible. I want to express my sincerest gratitude to every Eastwoodian who was gracious enough to spend time with me and share their thoughts. I learned countless lessons from you all; and hopefully I have conveyed at least some of the most important of these many lessons to the wider public.

Outside of Eastwood, this book has benefited from a talented cadre of advisers, friends, and family members who were kind enough to read my manuscript and were especially gracious with their commentary and support. I am also grateful for invitations to participate in seminars and symposia where chapters or sections of the book were first drafted and critiqued including, especially, the University of Pennsylvania's Anthropology Colloquium in 2013, Harvard University's New Faculty Lunch at the Mahindra Humanities Center in 2012, the University of Toronto's Centre for Diaspora and Transnational Studies in 2011, and the University of Cambridge's Center for Research in the Arts, Social Sciences and Humanities in 2011.

Membership at the Institute for Advanced Study in 2012–13 was invaluable in bringing this project to completion. I want to thank the faculty in the School of Social Science, especially Didier Fassin, Danielle Allen, and Joan Scott for offering feedback on my work-in-progress. I am also indebted to Vincent Dubois, Neve Gordon, Jens Meierhenrich, Nicola Perugini, and João Biehl for offering generous comments on different aspects of my work. I am especially grateful to my friend Lucas Bessire for reading and commenting on multiple iterations of my chapters.

My work and life have been greatly enriched by the conviviality and intellectual community of Harvard University's Department of African and African American Studies. I thank my colleagues Robin Bernstein, Lawrence Bobo, Jean Comaroff, Marla F. Frederick, Henry Louis Gates Jr., Evelyn Brooks Higginbotham, Michèle Lamont, Ingrid Monson, Marcyliena Morgan, Tommie Shelby, James Sidanius, and David Williams for their support and for critical comments offered in the course of conversations. I owe a special debt to William Julius Wilson, who has been more than a colleague, but also a mentor during my time at Harvard. Thank you for taking the time to read my manuscript and offer critical feedback on how it might improve. Your insights have been extremely helpful. I also thank my colleagues at Harvard University's Department of Anthropology, especially Theodore Bestor, Steve Caton, Kerry Chance, Peter Der Manuelian, Rowan Flad, Byron Good, Nicholas Harkness, Michael Herzfeld, Arthur Kleinman, Mary Steedly, Ajantha Subramanian, Lucien Castaing Taylor, and Gary Urton. I profited greatly from the discussions about my research material that I had with all of you. These discussions have substantially informed the arguments that take shape in this ethnography.

I would like to thank the Department of African and Afro-American Studies at the University of Michigan for offering me the Du Bois-Mandela-Rodney Post-Doctoral fellowship. I owe a great deal of thanks to Brandi Hughes and Rocío Magaña, who were very encouraging and supportive writing partners during my time in Ann Arbor.

Distinguished teachers have fundamentally informed this book. Thank you, John L. Comaroff, for always being available no matter where you are in the world. Thanks for helping to develop my ethnographic research and writing skills through your close tutelage. You were an ideal adviser during my graduate school years, and I am especially fortunate to have you and Jean as colleagues now. Thank you, Stephan Palmié, for your close readings and for our candid exchanges about how to traverse the theoretical minefields at the nexus

of anthropology and African American culture. Thank you, Michael Silverstein, for your teachings and the discussions and laughs we have shared. Your lessons have been invaluable in helping me capture the semiotics of gang life. Thank you, Joseph Masco, for convincing me to trust in my writerly instincts. I am truly grateful.

A number of professors have served as informal mentors. Early in my graduate school career, Cathy Cohen afforded me the opportunity to work on her Black Youth Project as a research assistant. Thank you. I learned countless lessons about how to engineer a research project from collaborating with you. I would also like to thank John Hagedorn. Soon after meeting him in 2006, John went out of his way to share his experiences about gang research in Chicago with me. I appreciate you taking me under your wing and helping to get my research started. I also thank you for your comments on this book. Your suggestions truly enhanced this ethnography. I am deeply grateful to Karla Slocum for her acumen and advice and for helping me develop an interest in anthropology as an undergraduate student.

To my friends at the University of Chicago—especially Stephanie Allen, Lily Chumley, Theodore Francis, Marina Mikhaylova, Jonathan Rosa, and Elizabeth Todd—thank you for investing time and energy into reading drafts of my work and offering critical feedback. Additionally, Jason Ruiz, Heidi Ardizzone, Jean Beaman, Denise Challenger, James Ford, Jessica Graham, Nicole Ivy, Richard Pierce, and Dianne Pinderhughes offered their insights on my research during my stay at the University of Notre Dame as an Erskine Peters Dissertation Fellow. I owe you all a great deal of gratitude. I would also like to thank a host of friends and colleagues: Megan Francis, Eva Haldane, Marica Lopes, Kevin Lewis O'Neill, Jessica Welburn, Leah Wright, and especially Juli Grigsby. I am thankful for the opportunity to share my work with you at conferences, retreats, and informal settings. I appreciate all of your hard work on my behalf.

I have been most fortunate to work with T. David Brent at the University of Chicago Press, and I thank him for his support and encouragement throughout the publication process. Also at the Press, I am grateful to Priya Nelson for her editorial guidance. I am grateful to the book's anonymous reviewers for their comments and suggestions, which helped immensely. I am also grateful to Lee Ellis and David Lobenstine for reading my work and offering careful and generous feedback. I am grateful to Eve Ewing for her tireless work as an indexer. A great deal of gratitude is due to Kehinde Wiley for allowing me to include his beautiful artwork in this book.

Finally, I would like to thank my family for instilling the value of education in me from an early age. Thank you, Michael Ralph Sr., Lynette Ralph, and Wolé Ralph for being voracious readers and outstanding academicians in your own right. A special thanks is due to Michael Ralph Jr. for leading me to the field of anthropology, the University of Chicago, and, most of all, for being the biggest fan of my work.

NOTES

Preface

1. African American Vernacular English (AAVE) is a variation of American English. It is commonly linked to varieties of English dialects that are spoken in the North American South. The most commonly identified distinctions between AAVE and Standard American English (SAE) are as follows:

1) AAVE has discernible pronunciation features from Creoles and dialects rooted in West Africa.
2) AAVE has a distinctive vocabulary. An example of a distinctive vocabulary word would be "finna"—as in "I'm finna go to the store." (In SAE the sentence would be "I'm getting ready to go to the store.")
3) AAVE has a distinctive use of verb tenses. An example of this distinctive use of verb tense would be AAVE's use of the phase auxiliary verb "been" to indicate the habitual—as in "He been living on that street." (In SAE the sentence would be "He has lived on that street for a while.")
4) AAVE speakers frequently use double negatives. An example of the use

of double negatives would be "I didn't go nowhere around that house." (In SAE the sentence would be "I didn't go anywhere around that house.")

For item (1), see John Dillard, *A History of American English* (New York: Longman, 1992); and Lisa Green, *African American English: A Linguistic Introduction* (Cambridge: Cambridge University Press, 2002). For item (2), see Dillard, *A History*; Green, *African American English*; and Charles DeBose, "Codeswitching: Black English and Standard English in the African-American Linguistic Repertoire," in *Codeswitching*, ed. Carol M. Eastman (Philadelphia: Multilingual Matters, 1992), 157–67. For item (3), see William Labov, *Language in the Inner City: Studies in Black English Vernacular* (Philadelphia: University of Pennsylvania Press, 1972); Joan Fickett, "Tense and Aspect in Black English," *Journal of English Linguistics* 6, no. 1 (1972): 17–19; and Green, *African American English*. For item (4), see Green, *African American English*. For a broader examination on the political context of AAVE, see Marcyliena Morgan, "US Language Planning and Policies for Social Dialect Speakers," in *Sociopolitical Perspectives on Language Policy and Planning in the USA*, ed. Kathryn Anne Davis (Philadelphia: J. Benjamins, 1999).

2. Some of my other collaborators did not feel comfortable with me disclosing the name of the gang either. Members of the Crippled Footprint Collective, for example, never mention the gangs to which they used to belong because they don't want to "advertise" their former affiliations. This was a major source of conflict with Justin, and one of the reasons he never attempted to officially join the group. He felt that it was important to use the gang's name to let young people know that their organization has not always been associated with violence.

Introduction

1. "Rahm Emanuel Mourns 260 Chicago Children Killed by Violence," *Huffington Post: Chicago Impact*, November 2, 2011, http://www.huffingtonpost .com/2011/11/02/rahm-emanuel-parents-mour_n_1071247.html (accessed October 2, 2013).

2. This statistic on "Violence-Induced Injury" is from the National Spinal Cord Injury Database: http://www.spinalcord.uab.edu (accessed June 11, 2013).

3. Alex Kotlowitz. "The Price of Public Violence," *New York Times*, Febru-

ary 23, 2013, http://www.nytimes.com/2013/02/24/opinion/sunday/the-price
-of-public-violence.html?pagewanted=all (accessed October 2, 2013).

4. In the history of anthropological thought, dreams have been used to think
about the separation between body and soul. In the Asian, African, and European cultural traditions, dreams have been regarded as expressions of inner
desires that travel through the mind (or soul) until the body is awakened,
prompting people to reimagine the way their social world is configured. See,
for example, Kelley Bulkeley, *Dreaming in the World's Religions: A Comparative History* (New York: New York University Press, 2008): Sandra T. Barnes,
ed., *Africa's Ogun: Old World and New* (Bloomington: Indiana University Press,
1989); Carl O'Nell, *Dreams, Culture, and the Individual* (San Francisco: Chandler & Sharp, 1975).

As early as the fourth century b.c., philosophers began to blur the lines between dreams and reality by speculating about whether or not the "real" world
was itself an illusion. See Chitrarekha Kher, *Buddhism as Presented by the Brahmanical Systems* (Delhi, India: Sri Satguru Publications, 1992): René Descartes,
Medications on First Philosophy: With Selections from the Objections and Replies
(Oxford: Oxford University Press, 2008).

Perhaps Sigmund Freud's psychoanalytic theory of dreams has had the
greatest impact on anthropology. He theorized that dreams reflect people's
unconscious mind. Freud, *New Introductory Lectures on Psycho-Analysis* (New
York: Norton, 1933). While, for Freud, the vast majority of dream content was
sexual in nature, he also considered how trauma and injury could influence
dreams. Expanding Freud's theories, Carl Jung argued that a dream reflects
the unconscious mind's attempt to recall glimpses of the past. For Jung, the
fact that some dreams constantly reoccured suggested that the dreamer was
neglecting an important issue that was in need of attention. Jung, *Children's
Dreams: Notes from the Seimnar Given in 1936–1940* (Princeton, NJ: Princeton
University Press, 2008).

These psychological theories of dreams are significant to my analysis insofar as they inform the way people understand their social position in society.
The difference between a Freudian analysis of dreams and my own is that I am
interested in how individual aspiration becomes a *conscious* attempt to navigate
one's place in the world. In this sense, the dreamers I am referring to are fully
aware that, as Jung insists, these visions for the world are important issues that
demand attention.

5. Taylor Branch, *Parting the Waters: America in the King Years, 1954–63* (New York: Simon and Schuster, 1988).

6. Barack Obama, *Dreams of My Father: A Story of Race and Inheritance* (New York: Random House, 1995).

7. The Rev. James T. Meeks, pastor of the House of Hope at Salem Baptist Church of Chicago and former member of the Illinois Senate, recently espoused the "crisis of the black male" rhetoric in a *Chicago Tribune* opinion piece entitled "It Starts with the Family: How to Save a Lost Generation of Black Males." In the article Meeks argues that due in large measure to the lack of two-parent households in Chicago's black communities, many African American males are growing up in a fatherless homes, and this has had "a negative impact on their psyche." In this familiar construction, Meeks links the social and economic disparities disproportionately impacting African American men and boys to the 361 homicide victims in Chicago in 2012, of which 287 were African American males between the ages of fifteen and thirty-five. James Meeks, "It Starts with the Family: How to Save a Lost Generation of Black Males," *Chicago Tribune*, April 10, 2013, http://articles.chicagotribune.com/2013-04-10/opinion/ct -perspec-0410-streets-20130410_1_gun-black-males-african-american-males (accessed October 2, 2013). For a nuanced scholarly analysis of the "crisis of the black male" framework, see Alford Young, *The Minds of Marginalized Black Men: Making Sense of Mobility, Opportunity, and Future Life Chances* (Princeton, NJ: Princeton University Press, 2004).

8. Cf. João Biehl and Peter Locke, "Deleuze and the Anthropology of Becoming," *Current Anthropology* 51 (2010): 317–51.

9. The notion of "renegade dreams" is informed by Cathy Cohen's important work on black youth. Her most recent work, *Democracy Remixed: Black Youth and the Future of American Politics* (New York: Oxford University Press, 2010), finds that black youth want, in large part, what most Americans want—a good job, a fulfilling life, safety, respect, and equality. But while this generation has much in common with the rest of America, they also believe that equality does not yet exist, at least not in their lives. What's more, for many urban black youth, the future seems bleak when they look at their neighborhoods, their schools, and even their own lives and choices. A "renegade dream" is to imagine a different future for yourself and your community even when living a life that's at odds with the dignity of your aspirations. The idea of "renegade dreams" is also influenced by Vincent Brown's compelling study of Atlantic slavery in which

the dead remain both a vital presence and a social force. In Brown's analysis, death is as generative as it is destructive since it cultivates essential aspects of social life among slaves. In fact, the act of summoning the dead, Brown shows, furthers people's desires and ambitions. Brown, *The Reaper's Garden: Death and Power in the World of Atlantic Slavery* (Cambridge, MA: Harvard University Press, 2008). Finally, the concept of "renegade dreams" is especially inspired by João Biehl's work *Vita: Life in a Zone of Social Abandonment* (Berkeley: University of California Press, 2004), and the "anthropology of becoming" that he and Peter Locke develop from Gilles Deleuze's philosophical theories. This idea of "becoming" is meant to challenge theories of social domination and popular modes of medical and political intervention by discussing the unexpected ways that people escape forms of knowledge and power, all the while expressing their desires in a way that might be "world altering." From this theoretical orientation, large structural and institutional processes and their material effects are rendered visible through an ethnographic engagement with people's "neglected human potentials." Biehl and Locke, "Deleuze and the Anthropology of Becoming."

10. For more on this topic, see Steven D. Levitt and Sudhir Alladi Venkatesh's analysis of the drug finances of a Chicago gang. This article includes a discussion section on the social and economic costs of policing drug territory or "turf." Levitt and Venkatash, "An Economic Analysis of a Drug-Selling Gang's Finances," *Quarterly Journal of Economics* 115, no. 3 (2000): 755–89.

11. See, for example, Anthony Bryk et al., *Organizing Schools for Improvement: Lessons from Chicago* (Chicago: University of Chicago Press, 2010); John Hagedorn, *A World of Gangs: Armed Young Men and Gangsta Culture* (Minneapolis: University of Minnesota Press, 2008); Bradford Hunt, *Blueprint for Disaster: The Unraveling of Public Housing* (Chicago: University of Chicago Press, 2009); Derek S. Hyra, *The New Urban Renewal: The Economic Transformation of Harlem and Bronzeville* (Chicago: University of Chicago Press, 2008); Natalie Moore and Lance Williams, *The Almighty Black P. Stone Nation: The Rise, Fall, and Resurgence of an American Gang* (Chicago: Lawrence Hill Books, 2011); Mary Pattillo, *Black on the Block: The Politics of Race and Class in the City* (Chicago: University of Chicago Press, 2007); Lawrence Vale, *Purging the Poorest: Public Housing and the Design Politics of Twice-Cleared Communities* (Chicago: University of Chicago Press, 2013); and Sudhir Venkatesh, *Gang Leader for a Day* (New York: Penguin, 2008).

12. This statistic on the poverty rate in Eastwood is compared to 16.9 percent for the city of Chicago and 9.6 percent nationally.

13. John L. Comaroff, "Dialectical Systems, History and Anthropology: Units of Study and Questions of Theory," *Journal of Southern African Studies* 8, no. 2 (1982): 146.

14. On the second great migration, see Nicholas Lemann, *The Promised Land: The Great Black Migration and How It Changed America* (New York: Knopf, 1991): 81; and William Julius Wilson, *When Work Disappears: The World of the New Urban Poor* (New York: Knopf, 1996), 29–30.

15. Eric Wolf, *Europe and the People without History* (Berkeley: University of California Press, 1982), 11.

16. William Julius Wilson, *The Truly Disadvantaged: The Inner City, the Underclass, and Public Policy* (1987; reprint, University of Chicago Press, 1990), 60–62. Wilson's approach can be placed within a larger genealogy of research associated with the Chicago school of sociology. Instead of defining the gang problem as primarily a criminal one, many early sociologists tried to analyze what had "gone amiss" that fostered slums. This notion was embraced most notably by Frederic Milton Thrasher, author of the classic *The Gang: A Study of 1,313 Gangs in Chicago* (1927; abridged ed., Chicago: University of Chicago Press, 1963).

17. John Hagedorn, "Gangs, Institutions, Race, and Space: The Chicago School Revisited," in *Gangs in the Global City: Alternatives to Traditional Criminology* (Urbana: University of Illinois Press, 2007), 17.

18. In *Code of the Street: Decency, Violence, and the Moral Life of the Inner City* (1990; reprint, New York: Norton, 2000), for example, Elijah Anderson argues that the strong, loving, and "decent" family was the most powerful force in counteracting inner-city impoverishment (37–45). In discussing how urban residents cope with crime and delinquent behavior, he contends that two distinct groups inhabit today's inner cities. Those in the first group—who are oriented toward "decent" values—attend church, participate in social institutions like schools and labor markets, and in general accept the laws and ethical codes of mainstream society. Those in the second group (whom he labels as "street") view education and hard work as futile. As opposed to mainstream social standards, they are willing to use violence to settle disputes. These people, Anderson argues, abide by the "law of the jungle" (84). Notice that Anderson's work assumes the existence of two types of societies: one in which *order* is maximized

because social relations are suffused with value consensus; and another in which *disorder* predominates over order because social relations are deranged by competing values. Such an approach pays attention to particular social relations (such as "the nuclear family") but neglects other kinds of kinship bonds as well as social and economic networks that proliferate via unconventional means. See Sudhir Venkatesh, *Off the Books: The Underground Economy of the Urban Poor* (Chicago: University of Chicago Press, 2006).

19. Philippe Bourgois, *In Search of Respect: Selling Crack in El Barrio* (Cambridge: Cambridge University Press, 1995); Anderson, *Code of the Street*; Mike Davis, *City of Quartz: Excavating the Future in Los Angeles* (London: Verso, 1990); and Venkatesh, *Off the Books*.

20. Here, I'm referring to Comaroff's dialectic between local and encompassing contexts. Comaroff argues that while the notion of a "traditional" or secluded society is no longer acceptable, an equally egregious approach is to view local communities as purely subject to external forces. He proposes an examination of the ways in which "internal forms" and "external forces" help constitute one another. This is because as sociohistorical processes shape a number of competing ideologies and orientations within an organization, the way in which members of that organization make sense of sociohistorical change has material consequences for the reality they are referencing. Comaroff, "Dialectical Systems, History and Anthropology."

21. Sudhir Alladi Venkatesh and Steven D. Levitt, for instance, show that as opportunities for illicit revenue generation opened up in the 1980s, many gang families stood as a variegated "composition of individuals with different biographies, relationships to social institutions, and personal interests, the sum of which manifested in cleavages amongst the membership." At the same time, the encompassing context in America was shifting in a post-industrial climate such that the gang struggled to ensure its collective integrity and reconfigure its place amid a changing urban landscape. The debates in which gang members engaged about the outlook and orientations to collective action (and especially how to reconstitute the organization's mission as either a "family" or "corporation") were dialectically related to the post-industrial restructuring and ascension of the corporatist ideology in American society, according to the authors. Venkatesh and Levitt, "'Are We a Family or a Business?': History and Disjuncture in the Urban American Street Gang," *Theory and Society* 29, no. 4 (2000): 430.

22. My attempt to expand a theory of inner-city isolation is inspired by the work of like-minded anthropologists who, in their given ethnographic contexts, have also demonstrated the limits of regarding ethnographic subjects as either people inhabiting a bounded cultural world or as people wholly captured by the logic of state power. Rather, the people whom I describe in *Renegade Dreams* are desperately attempting to constitute themselves as political subjects through their aspirations. For another compelling ethnographic example, see Ajantha Subramanian, *Shorelines: Space and Rights in South India* (Stanford, CA: Stanford University Press, 2009).

23. More specifically "governmentality" is associated with advanced liberal democracies (or the kind of democracies that are based on the predominance of market mechanisms and of the restriction of the action of the state). It refers to the practices (mentalities, rationalities, and techniques) through which subjects are governed as they enter different disciplinary institutions (schools, hospitals, psychiatric clinics, etc.) throughout the course of their lives. These institutions enact a new form of power upon subject's bodies. But for Foucault, power is not merely the hierarchical, top-down power of the state. Power also pertains to the forms of knowledge that societal institutions and government bureaucracies produce—such as the crime statistics of a particular population or even how populations are constituted in the first place. Michel Foucault, *Discipline and Punish* (1975; reprint, New York: Vintage, 1995). Because of its ability to grasp what's at stake for people as they grapple with new rational-technical state interventions, governmentality has been especially useful for anthropologists working in a variety of contexts. See, for example, Didier Fassin, *When Bodies Remember: Experiences and Politics of AIDS in South Africa* (Berkeley: University of California Press, 2007); James Ferguson, *Global Shadows: Africa in the Neoliberal World Order* (Durham, NC: Duke University Press, 2006); Anne Lovell, "Addiction Markets: The Case of High-Dose Buprenorphine in France," in *Global Pharmaceuticals: Practices, Markets, Ethics*, ed. Adriana Petryna, Andrew Lakoff, and Arthur Kleinman (Durham, NC: Duke University Press, 2006), 136–70; Aihwa Ong and Stephen J. Collier, eds., *Global Assemblages: Technology, Politics, and Ethics as Anthropological Problems* (Malden, MA: Blackwell, 2005); and Paul Rabinow and Nikolas Rose, "Biopower Today," *Biosocieties* 1 (2006): 195–217.

In Foucault's scheme, power can manifest itself by producing knowledge and certain discourses that get internalized by individuals and guide the behavior in a given society. Indeed, power arrangements are not simply normalizing.

They can also help constitute how people manage their households, raise their families, and how they think about sexuality. Foucault, *The History of Sexuality* (1976; reprint, New York: Vintage, 1990). These diffuse and pervasive power arrangements lead to more efficient forms of social control. Put another way, Foucault is interested in the ways in which governmental categories, techniques of surveillance, and political discourses—to name a few modes of governance— impact self-control and self-fashioning. In this way, the concept of governmentality is not merely a tool for thinking about government and governing, but also incorporates how and what people in a given society think about the way they are governed. Mitchell Dean, *Governmentality: Power and Rule in Modern Society* (London: Sage, 1999).

Similar to other theories of "social domination" (such as Freud's "unconscious" or Bourdieu's "habitus" or Agamben's "bare life"), the major critique of Foucault's concept of governmentality is that his focus on rationalities, discourses, technologies of power, and subject making paints a myopic portrait of society. Many have argued that such a portrait overdetermines a person's fate and discounts the ways in which people search for life alternatives even within constricted social fields. See, for example, Lila Abu-Lughod, *Writing Women's Worlds: Bedouin Stories* (Berkeley: University of California Press, 1993); Gilles Deleuze, *Essays Critical and Clinical* (Minneapolis: University of Minnesota Press, 1997); Sherry Ortner, "Power and Projects: Reflections on Agency," in *Anthropology and Social Theory: Culture, Power, and the Acting Subject* (Durham: Duke University Press, 2006); and Biehl and Locke, "Deleuze and the Anthropology of Becoming."

24. Here I am referring to the anthropological concept of "structural violence." One of the earliest usages of the concept is attributed to peace scholar Johan Galtung, who used the term to describe the social factors and institutions that produce injury and prevent people from attaining basic needs. For Galtung, institutionalized elitism, ethnocentrism, classism, racism, sexism, nationalism, heterosexism, and ageism were all forms of structural violence that could result in premature death and disability. Galtung, "Violence, Peace, and Peace Research," *Journal of Peace Research*, 6, no. 3 (1969). Structural violence has been popularized in the discipline of anthropology through the work of medical anthropologists, such as Paul Farmer. His approach to examining people's susceptibility to various diseases and illnesses was to not see these afflictions as a product of a person's culture or their individual will. Rather, he views such

susceptibility as a "historically given (and often economic driven) process that conspires to constrain individual agency." For Farmer, the force of structural violence impacts people whose position in society prevents them from accessing health care and even knowledge about the ways particular diseases are transmitted. Farmer, *The Uses of Haiti* (Monroe, ME: Common Courage Press, 1994); Farmer, *Infections and Inequalities: The Modern Plagues* (Berkeley: University of California Press, 2001); and Paul Farmer, Margaret Conners, and Janie Simmons, *Women, Poverty, and AIDS: Sex, Drugs, and Structural Violence* (Monroe, ME: Common Courage Press, 1996).

Other anthropologists, like Philippe Bourgois and Nancy Scheper-Hughes, have also been drawn to the concept of structural violence because of the way it views forms of injustice in the context of wider social phenomena. These scholars have all argued that the violence that produces inequitable social arrangements is not inevitable. Thus, by better understanding the institutions and processes that produce this violence, scholars can help experts (such as medical professionals and policy makers) understand and eventually alter the social forces behind a disease, illness, or disability. Bourgois, *In Search of Respect*; and Nancy Scheper-Hughes, *Death without Weeping: The Violence of Everyday Life in Brazil* (Berkeley: University of California Press, 1992). The major critique of structural violence is that it commonly serves as a macro concept that, in the process of explaining large-scale phenomena, reduces the micro sphere of everyday experience. Kenneth Parsons, "Structural Violence and Power," *Peace Review: A Journal of Social Justice*, 19 (2007): 173–81. Similar to Foucault's governmentality, when deployed as an umbrella term to describe forms of domination, marginalization, exploitation, and inequality, this concept can seem to wholly determine people's fate. In these ways, this concept is commonly taken up and applied, which often does not account for collective and individual striving as well as the potential for transformation. Biehl and Locke, "Deleuze and the Anthropology of Becoming."

25. This approach is similar to Renato Rosaldo's conception in *Culture and Truth: The Remaking of Social Analysis* (Boston: Beacon Press, 1989), 20. While problematizing the emphasis on structure in classical ethnography, Rosaldo notes that many ethnographies are unable to account for the open-ended human processes in the informal settings of everyday life that occur outside a circumscribed sphere of social life. Because culture is an open and "porous

array of intersections where distinct processes crisscross from within and beyond its borders," Rosaldo argues for a focus on the intersections of "cultural
borderlands."

26. Michel-Rolph Trouillot, *Silencing the Past: Power and the Production of
History* (Boston: Beacon Press, 1997), 5.

27. Ibid.

28. John Comaroff and Jean Comaroff, *Ethnography and the Historical Imagination* (Boulder, CO: Westview Press, 1992), 27.

Chapter One

1. Karen Umemoto has noted that many long-term community residents
in Los Angeles also believe that attention to gang violence is part of a conspiracy between the police and real estate speculators, who would benefit from
an exodus of low-income residents. Umemoto, *The Truce: Lessons from an L.A.
Gang War* (Ithaca, NY: Cornell University Press, 2006), 6.

2. This is a pseudonym for one of the two most popular gang alliances in the
United States.

3. When it comes to law enforcement in Chicago, scandals abound. Part of
the reason that these agencies are prone to problems is because, just as in other
states where there is a substantial gang presence, systems of law enforcement
are multilayered. There are a number of different agencies responding to gang
violence (e.g., police, city attorney, district attorney, departments of probation
and parole). It follows that "each agency has its own mission, powers, tasks, incentive structures, decision-making processes, leadership and institutional culture, range of discretion, and specific policy instruments" that may differ from,
and are not accountable to, one another. Umemoto, *The Truce*, 120.

4. See Malcolm W. Klein, *The American Street Gang: Its Nature, Prevalence,
and Control* (New York: Oxford University Press, 1995), 207, on the ways in
which gang representations circulate beyond the boundaries of particular urban
neighborhoods.

5. One common reason why teenagers are in the "wrong" part of town is because of policy changes that happen periodically.

6. See also Japonica Brown-Saracino, *A Neighborhood that Never Changes:
Gentrification, Social Preservation, and the Search for Authenticity* (Chicago: Uni-

versity of Chicago Press, 2009); and Derek S. Hyra, *The New Urban Renewal: The Economic Transformation of Harlem and Bronzeville* (Chicago: University of Chicago Press, 2008).

7. Mary Pattillo, *Black on the Block: The Politics of Race and Class in the City* (Chicago: University of Chicago Press, 2007).

8. I mentioned, in the preface, that "Pastor Tim" is a composite of more than one pastor in Eastwood. The common attributes among these pastors are as follows: (1) They are white males operating in a neighborhood that is predominately (over 90 percent black); (2) they are from outside of the community; (3) their churches are engaged in a number of social-reform initiatives, particularly redevelopment.

9. For another striking ethnographic example of the ways in which the threat of dislocation triggers the construction of the past and the role of religion in daily life amidst a myriad of social actors, see Michael Hertzfield, *Evicted from Eternity: The Restructuring of Modern Rome* (Chicago: University of Chicago Press, 2009).

10. In the conclusion to *Renegade Dreams*, I explore the prevalent idea that the inner city is "socially isolated" and far removed in time, space, and morality from the middle class.

11. Pattillo, *Black on the Block*, 141. See also Hyra, *The New Urban Renewal*, 50–51.

12. Similarly to cities like Los Angeles, in Chicago the sources of disadvantage and the means of getting ahead differ greatly among the city's variegated ethnic groups. The construction industry is one among a growing number in which the city's low-skilled black workers are increasingly marginalized.

13. In her study of four distinct communities—the Chicago neighborhoods of Andersonville and Argyle and the New England towns of Provincetown and Dresden—Japonica Brown-Saracino discusses a new breed of gentrifiers. Her thoughtful study finds that they exhibit an acute self-consciousness about their role in the process and think deeply about longtime residents as well as the character of the community to which they hope to move. The gentrifiers in Brown-Saracino's study cherish the "unique and fragile," and would likely view a greystone, for example, as an authentic aspect of Eastwood that should remain in place. In Eastwood, the Greystone Project seems to be catering to the demand of newcomers who actually want to live in a community that is uniquely special and attractive. Unlike the institutions that Mindy Fullilove

describes in the context of urban renewal—the institutions that seek simply to destroy and rebuild—organizations in Eastwood have incorporated in their mission the more nuanced idea of redevelopment to which the work of Japonica Brown-Saracino gestures. But, as we'll see, these beliefs still do not privilege the voices and perspectives of poor urban residents. Mindy Thompson Fulli-love, *Rootshock: How Tearing Up City Neighborhoods Hurts America and What We Can Do about It* (New York: Ballantine/One World, 2004); Brown-Saracino, *A Neighborhood that Never Changes.*

14. See chapter 2 for a broader discussion of "renegades."

15. Pierre Bourdieu, *Outline of a Theory of Practice* (Cambridge: Cambridge University Press, 1977).

16. Here Eric Childs is referencing the distinction between the "house Negro" and the "field Negro" that Malcolm X made famous in a speech to the Student Nonviolent Coordinating Committee (SNCC) in Selma, Alabama, on February 4, 1965:

[Back during slavery] there was two kinds of slaves. There was the house Negro and the field Negro. The house Negroes—they lived in the house with master, they dressed pretty good, they ate good 'cause they ate his food—what he left. They lived in the attic or the basement, but still they lived near the master; and they loved their master more than the master loved himself. They would give their life to save the master's house quicker than the master would. The house Negro, if the master said, "We got a good house here," the house Negro would say, "Yeah, we got a good house here." Whenever the master said "we," he said "we." That's how you can tell a house Negro.

If the master's house caught on fire, the house Negro would fight harder to put the blaze out than the master would. If the master got sick, the house Negro would say, "What's the matter, boss, we sick?" We sick! He identi-fied himself with his master more than his master identified with himself. And if you came to the house Negro and said, "Let's run away, let's escape, let's separate," the house Negro would look at you and say, "Man, you crazy. What you mean, separate? Where is there a better house than this? Where can I wear better clothes than this? Where can I eat better food than this?" That was that house Negro. In those days he was called a "house nigger." And that's what we call him today, because we've still got some house nig-gers running around here.

Malcolm X, "Message to the Grass Roots," speech, November 10, 1963, Detroit, MI. Available at http://xroads.virginia.edu/~public/civilrights/a0147.html (accessed September 30, 2013).

17. This point is inspired by Herbert Gans's classic study, *The Urban Villagers: Group and Class in the Life of Italian-Americans* (New York: Free Press Glencoe, 1962). In it, Gans depicts "urban villagers" as close-knit Italian families living in South Philadelphia who were, by and large, hardworking. Yet the large buildings in which they lived made it easy for onlookers to characterize them as good-for-nothing slum dwellers. In Eastwood, dilapidated houses inspire similar kinds of interpretive work as the large buildings in Gans's study. They make it easy for outsiders to claim that the people who live there deserve any form of violence that the city government chooses to inflict upon them.

18. I should note that this perspective is indicative of the "crisis of the black male" framework mentioned in the introduction.

19. Scholars who studied poor African American communities in the 1940s, 1950s, and 1960s contended that the residents of these neighborhoods had a different set of standards from those who lived in "straight" or "mainstream" society. In recent decades this perspective has been debunked. We now see that poor urban residents are in pursuit of the American dream just as their suburban counterparts. Poor residents may even be more wedded to the ideals of meritocracy, for example. Still, the popular image of the gang remains influenced by the idea that they have a radically different code of ethics, a set of "moral standards" that depart from the norm. The gang members in Eastwood are fully aware that they are perceived as being morally bankrupt and "dangerous." Here, we see how they strategically deploy the gang's image of violence to their political advantage. Gans, *The Urban Villagers*.

20. Ken Auletta's *The Underclass* (New York: Vintage, 1982) is a classic example of the notion that the "urban poor" are alienated from political institutions. See also Laurence Friedman, *The Horizontal Society* (New Haven, CT: Yale University Press, 1999).

21. It should be pointed out that the women of the Neighborhood Coalition are avid churchgoers. Some of them even attend the Eastwood Community Church. But like the women in Marla Frederick's heralded study, *Between Sundays: Black Women and Everyday Struggles of Faith* (Berkeley: University of California Press, 2003), spirituality emerges as a space for creative agency, of vital importance to the ways in which these women interpret, inform, and reshape

their social conditions. The actions of the spiritual leaders in Frederick's study as well as my own should be understood in the context of the larger history that Evelyn Brooks Higginbotham famously articulated. In *Righteous Discontent: The Women's Movement in the Black Baptist Church* (Cambridge, MA: Harvard University Press, 1993), she demonstrates that between 1880 and 1920 women were largely responsible for making the church a force for self-help in the black community. In her account, we see how the efforts of women enabled the church to build schools, provide food and clothing to the poor, and offer a host of social welfare services. The women of the Eastwood Neighborhood Coalition are interesting in light of Higginbotham's work. Unlike the black Baptist women whom she describes, the women in Eastwood do not employ a "politics of respectability" to solve community problems. See also Johnetta Betsch Cole and Beverly Guy-Sheftall, *Gender Talk: The Struggle for Women's Equality in African American Communities* (New York: One World, 2003).

22. The actions of Eastwood residents recall Michel De Certeau's distinction between strategies and tactics. While the former refers to forms of practice employed by power holders, the latter, he argues, are tools of the weak. De Certeau, *The Practice of Everyday Life* (Berkeley: University of California Press, 1984), 37. Most of the victories of tactics over strategies are temporary and must constantly be fought. See also Steffen Jensen for gang life and "redevelopment" in the South African Capetown flats. Jensen, *Gangs, Politics and Dignity in Cape Town* (Chicago: University of Chicago Press, 2008), 7.

Chapter Two

1. The intergenerational approach to examining urban life in my study resonates with David Harding's analysis in *Living the Drama: Community, Conflict, and Culture among Inner-City Boys* (Chicago: University of Chicago Press, 2010). This influential study examines the ways in which a person's life is shaped in Boston by their street address. In it, Harding finds that older boys who can navigate the streets serve as role models, teaching younger boys how to protect their neighborhood. My work complicates Harding's analysis in the following respect: In Eastwood, it is not merely that young residents look up to older generations uncritically. There are a host of intergenerational contestations that have to do with the problems that the community faces at any given historical moment. Hence, the fact that gym shoes carry very different meanings depend-

ing on the generation to which you belong adds nuance to the idea of a role model by pointing to the structural imbalances in the street that weigh heavily on the formation of identities today.

2. The use of the twinned adjectives "his and her" begs the question of gender. I do not mean to paint a portrait of the Divine Knights as exclusively male. Even though it is predominately male, I deal specifically with the issue of gender relationships within the gang in chapter 3.

3. See also Mary Pattillo-McCoy, *Black Picket Fences: Privilege and Peril among the Black Middle Class* (Chicago: University of Chicago Press, 1999), 156–59; and Elizabeth Chin, *Purchasing Power: Black Kids and American Consumer Culture* (Minneapolis: University of Minnesota Press), 126–27.

4. My analysis of shoe culture is meant to point out that, indeed, poor urban youth are influenced by the same consumption trends as many segments of American youth. In this regard, my work is indebted to Carl Nightingale, Al Young, and John Hagedorn. In arguing against the "culture of poverty" thesis, they have pointed out that poor urban youth are not beholden to an "oppositional" or "street" culture, but are deeply affected by the contradictions of American culture. The difference between them and their more privileged peers is that they have less resources and far fewer choices. Carl Nightingale, *On the Edge: A History of Poor Black Children and Their American Dreams* (New York: Basic Books, 1993); Young, *The Minds of Marginalized Black Men*; John Hagedorn, *People and Folks: Gangs, Crime, and the Underclass in a Rustbelt City* (Chicago: Lake View Press, 1988).

5. These price points are taken from the websites of the brands that manufacture each shoe.

6. This price point is an average of the three most popular signatures, as determined by twenty-five teenage gang members from Eastwood. At the time (December 2008), the most popular signature shoes (besides Jordans) were LeBron James's, Kobe Bryant's, and Derrick Rose's.

7. The prices of Jordans vary from year to year. This price point is a bit of an outlier because it represents the 2008 model, which was an anniversary edition shoe. Still, I felt it important to flag this price because they were especially coveted, precisely because of their historic status.

8. On the sense of gratification for young Chicagoans purchasing Jordans, in particular, see Pattillo-McCoy, *Black Picket Fences*, 156–59. It should also be noted that this brand, which boasts a substantial variety of designs, offers the

owner of the shoe a chance for a bit of personal distinction. Any of the twenty-three versions of Jordans that Nike has released since 1985 can be purchased online, each of which are always in style. On sight, a Jordan connoisseur can identify a particular style based on its release.

9. Svetlana Boym, *The Future of Nostalgia* (2001; reprint, New York: Basic Books, 2006), xiii.

10. Ibid., 3–4.

11. Ibid., xiv.

12. Mr. Otis's words resonate with Hagedorn's influential study, *People and Folks*, in which he interviews the founding members of Milwaukee's street gangs.

13. On ghosts, see Boym, *The Future of Nostalgia*, 3. Here, Mr. Otis's discussion of ghosts is meant to capture what Hagedorn has previously referred to as a sense of alienation among gang members. Crucially, the feelings of nostalgia and alienation that both Hagedorn and I reference are linked to a context of economic restructuring in which deindustrialization and social forces such as mass incarceration have changed the urban landscape, making it hard for urban youth to find their place in the world. Hagedorn, *People and Folks*.

14. For gangs as social clubs and delinquents, see Frederic Milton Thrasher, *The Gang: A Study of 1,313 Gangs in Chicago* (1927; abridged ed., Chicago: University of Chicago Press, 1963).

15. David Dawley, *A Nation of Lords: The Autobiography of the Vice Lords*, 2nd ed. (Long Grove, IL: Waveland Press, 1992), 103.

16. Ibid, 103.

17. Quoted in Dawley, *A Nation of Lords*, 109.

18. Ibid, 1.

19. Ibid, 110.

20. Andrew J. Diamond, *Mean Streets: Chicago Youths and the Everyday Struggle for Empowerment in the Multiracial City, 1908–1969* (Berkeley: University of California Press, 2009), 265–67.

21. The Chicago Freedom Movement lasted from mid-1965 to early 1967. Led by the SCLC, one of the primary goals of the movement was to end slums in American cities. It organized tenants' unions, assumed control of a Chicago housing project, and rallied black and white Chicagoans to march into segregated areas of the city. Some of the movement's major demands were to have real estate boards and brokers issue public statements that all of their properties

would be available on a non-discriminatory basis; to have banks and savings institutions issue public statements pertaining to non-discriminatory mortgage policies; to create an ordinance giving ready access to the names of people who owned and invested in slum properties; and to institute a requirement that elected officials live in the precincts in which they were elected. James R. Ralph, *Northern Protest: Martin Luther King, Jr., Chicago, and the Civil Rights Movement* (Cambridge, MA: Harvard University Press, 1993).

22. Another severe blow to community investment came when major industries and employers began to close their doors. International Harvester Tractor Company closed in 1969, causing a loss of an estimated 3,400 jobs. In 1974 Sears Roebuck moved its headquarters to downtown Chicago, significantly reducing its Eastwood facility. Ten years later, they completely pulled out of the community. During the 1970s, 80 percent of the manufacturing jobs in the community disappeared. Most have never been replaced.

23. Notice here that the riots become a pivotal moment in the subjective history that Mr. Otis tells. City planners similarly use the riots of the 1960s to make the implicit claim that black urban residents have destroyed their own community—a community whose local economy was robust in the 1960s when working-class white immigrants lived on Chicago's West Side. It's important to point out that, like Mr. Otis's, this rendering is also nostalgic. Amanda Seligman's study *Block by Block: Neighborhoods and Public Policy on Chicago's West Side* (Chicago: University of Chicago Press, 2005) brilliantly demonstrates that the deterioration in West Side neighborhoods began well before black inhabitants moved in to communities like Eastwood. She argues that the riots that erupted on Chicago's West Side stemmed from "the legacy of accumulated neglect after decades of white occupancy"—not merely from the tribulations specific to urban blacks.

24. See Mercer L. Sullivan, *"Getting Paid": Youth Crime and Work in the Inner City* (Ithaca, NY: Cornell University Press, 1989), 245. Sullivan, for example, suggests that despite the addictive collective spirit of the civil rights movement, a substantial number of gangs remained governed by their own parochial and selfish concerns.

25. The Divine Knights Gang is split into segments, referred to by gang members as "sets." Gang sets have many of the characteristics of the gang itself: each has its distinctive name (e.g., the Orthodox Knights, the Roving Knights, the Anonymous Knights, etc.), its common sentiment (as expressed in gang

literature, such as "The Divine Knights Constitution"), and its unique territory (though the area controlled by one gang set need not be clearly divided
from another). Since 2000 there have been approximately eight gang sets of
the Divine Knights dispersed throughout Chicago. These subgroups are over-
whelmingly male and African American. There are four major gang sets in
Eastwood. Each of these gang sets control a ten- to fifteen-square-block territory and range from 30–40 members. Of this membership, crews of 4–6 members serve as "foot soldiers," responsible for street-level dealing in open-air
markets. Approximately 8–10 members fulfill other drug-related duties (e.g.,
runners, muscle, treasurers). The rest of the affiliates may or may not have an explicit connection to the gang's drug-distribution network. For them, the gang
is primarily a social group.

26. My focus here on the political history of the Divine Knights Gang is
meant to demystify the organization and write against the notion that gangs
are inherently pathological. Martin Sánchez-Jankowski and John Hagedorn
have also worked to humanize gang members in earlier studies of gang participation and organization. Sánchez-Jankowski, *Islands in the Street: Gangs and
American Urban Society* (Berkeley: University of California Press, 1991); Hagedorn, *People and Folks*.

27. Sudhir Alladi Venkatesh and Steven D. Levitt, "'Are We a Family or
a Business?': History and Disjuncture in the Urban American Street Gang,"
Theory and Society 29, no. 4 (2000): 427–62.

28. It is important to remember that while the "violent gang" has remained a
dominant perception for the general public, the "rigid organizational structure"
that I am using to describe the Divine Knights places this group within a relatively small category of "supergangs." As Klein (1995) has noted, these "large
and effective confederations of local gangs" are anomalous in their ability to
develop coordinated chapters, commercial enterprises and political affiliations,
along with written oaths and constitutions. For the Divine Knights, the ranks
that are specifically related to their heroin-distribution network have traditionally included the following: (1) *the Supreme Chief,* who serves as the head of the
central leadership committee; (2) *the central leadership committee* (also known as
universal elites)—a group of authority figures who collect dues, oversee recruit-
ment, allocate punishments, and serve as community liaisons; (3) *gang leaders*
(also known as *precinct kings* or *chiefs*), who oversee local gang collectivities
and pay fees to central leadership in return for protection, access to wholesale

drugs, and the possibility of becoming part of the central leadership committee; (4) *enforcers* (also known as *ministers of command* or *muscle*), who ensure safety of group members; (5) *treasurers*, who are responsible for liquid assets; (6) *runners*, who transport large quantities of drugs and money to and from the supplier; (7) *foot soldiers*, street-level dealers who report to enforcers; and (8) *rank and file*, who have little responsibility for drug dealing but pay dues in order to receive protection and the status afforded by membership (cf. Venkatesh and Levitt "'Are We a Family or a Business?'"). See also James W. Wagner et al., eds., *The Chicago Crime Commission Gang Book: A Detailed Overview of Street Gangs in the Chicago Metropolitan Area* (Chicago: Chicago Crime Commission, 2006).

29. On the making of the business-oriented or "corporate" gang, see Francis Ianni, *Black Mafia: Ethic Succession Organized in Crime* (New York: Simon and Schuster, 1974); Steven D. Levitt and Sudhir Alladi Venkatesh, "An Economic Analysis of a Drug-Selling Gang's Finances," *Quarterly Journal of Economics* 115, no. 3 (2000): 755–89; Michael J. Olivero, *Honor, Violence and Upward Mobility: A Case Study of Chicago's Street Gangs during the 1970s and 1980s* (Edinburg, TX: Pan American Press, 1991); and Felix Padilla, *The Gang as an American Enterprise* (New Brunswick, NJ: Rutgers University Press, 1992).

30. Jennifer Hamer's study of East St. Louis, *Abandoned in the Heartland: Work, Family, and Living in East St. Louis* (Berkeley: University of California Press, 2011), also addresses what happens to a region when industry has abandoned it. Like Eastwood, East St. Louis is bereft of jobs, quality schools, and city services. Although Hamer examines a suburb and I am focused on inner-city life, we both are dealing with the ways that people cope with the social costs of government abandonment and survive amidst an infrastructure that has been crumbling for decades.

31. Sudhir Venkatesh, *Off the Books: The Underground Economy of the Urban Poor* (Chicago: University of Chicago Press, 2006), 283.

32. Venkatesh and Levitt, "'Are We a Family or a Business?,'" 430.

33. Christian Parenti, *Lockdown America: Police and Prisons in the Age of Crisis* (London: Verso, 1999), 57; Loïc Wacquant, "Deadly Symbiosis: Rethinking Race and Imprisonment in Twenty-First Century America," *Boston Review* (2002); Wacquant, "Three Pernicious Premises in the Study of the American Ghetto," *International Journal of Urban and Regional Research* (July 1997): 341–53.

34. Marc Mauer and the Sentencing Project (U.S.), *Race to Incarcerate*, 2nd

ed. (New York: New Press, 2006), 93. See also Robin D. G. Kelley, *Yo' Mama's Disfunktional!: Fighting the Culture Wars in Urban America* (Boston: Beacon Press, 1997), 99.

35. Nancy G. La Vigne, Cynthia A. Mamalian, Jeremy Travis, and Christy Visher, *A Portrait of Prisoner Reentry in Illinois: Research Report* (Washington, DC: Urban Institute Justice Policy Center, April 2003).

36. Ibid.

37. Ibid.

38. As a number of scholars have discussed, only two years after Reagan's 1984 crime bill (one of the most severe anti-crime measures since the Nixon era), legislation that affected the inner-city poor reached new heights. Politicians reacted abrasively to the arrival of a new drug: crack cocaine. The most significant piece of legislation implemented to deter drug dealers was the Federal Anti-Drug Abuse Act of 1986, which imposed a total of twenty-nine harsh new sentence guidelines for drug-related offenses. The community of Eastwood was greatly impacted by longer sentences because they targeted the specific form of "rock" cocaine most often sold by street-level dealers. The alarming frequency of arrests and imprisonment starting in the mid-1980s caused the Divine Knights' leadership structure to become increasingly decentralized. As the gang lost its centralized structure, by the late 1990s it shifted into a diffuse organization comprised of competitive gang factions. What is more, Venkatesh and Levitt, "'Are We a Family or a Business?,'" discuss how Chicago gangs splintered into a number of subgang "sets" to fill the void in central leadership in the mid-1990s as the "franchise model" gained popularity. Under this economic structure, each faction controls its own drug sales and wages, while competing with other "sets."

39. Sánchez-Jankowski, *Islands in the Street*, 24–26; John Hagedorn, "Homeboys, New Jacks, and Anomie," *Journal of African American Studies* 3, no. 1 (1997): 7–28; Venkatesh and Levitt, "'Are We a Family or a Business?,'" 440.

40. In this regard, it is fitting that these troublesome affiliates are deemed renegades. Ever since the term was coined, it has referred to the impossibility of belonging to a group in a way that is deemed "traditional," especially after the circumstances that once bolstered that tradition have changed. The renegade first emerged at the end of the sixteenth century, when English travelers to Ottoman territories confronted an increasing amount of formerly Christian converts and bristled at the thought of an Islamic future. These "renegades"—

from the Spanish *renegado*, literally meaning "Christian turned Muslim"—not only saddened but frightened visitors because with the Turkish army on the rise, English natives worried that they might eventually become Muslim subjects, forced to renounce their faith and nationalist tradition. By the beginning of the seventeenth century, unfaithful renegades so grew in number that English dramatists, writers, and poets felt the need to portray this unsavory figure in mythical tales that reaffirmed the comforts of traditional life. These artists used sartorial emblems to magnify the "heinous" way that renegades renounced their Englishness and the tranquility of national belonging. The turbans worn by many renegades were the most obvious, though not the only, evidence of how these men and women rebuked English identity and pride in favor of Muslim mores. Indeed, the contrast between the English hat and Turkish turban captured the tension between the irreproachable Christian and the dangerous renegade, whose capitulation to Islam stood in for a rapidly changing and terribly uncertain present. N. I. Matar, "The Renegade in English Seventeenth-Century Imagination," *Studies in English Literature, 1500–1900*, 33, no. 3 (1993): 489–505.

41. It's crucial to point out that since there are so many nonprofit organizations in Eastwood, the window hecklers are not exactly socially isolated, despite their marginalization. In this regard, we can think of their response to Career Day in terms of Alford Young's work on marginalized black men who live in Chicago. He argues that poor urban youth have been exposed to more privileged Americans to varying degrees. He finds that men who have regular interactions with privileged Americans have met a substantial amount of racism and hostility. As a result, they are less likely to believe that their country provides equal opportunities to all citizens. The window hecklers are clearly used to seeing professionals come to their school. Young's work suggests that their previous experiences likely shape the context for their resentment. Young, *The Minds of Marginalized Black Men: Making Sense of Mobility, Opportunity, and Future Life Chances* (Princeton, NJ: Princeton University Press, 2004). See also Paul Willis, *Learning to Labor: How Working-Class Kids Get Working-Class Jobs* (New York: Columbia University Press, 1977); and Jay MacLeod, *Ain't No Making It: Aspirations and Attainment in a Low-Income Neighborhood* (Boulder, CO: Westview, 1995).

42. The neighborhood's unemployment rate and high school dropout rate were both mentioned in publications advertising Career Day. As noted in the

introduction, over the course of my fieldwork, Eastwood's unemployment rate was 13 percent—three times as much as the rest of Chicago. Thirty-four percent of residents between eighteen and twenty-four years of age lacked a high school diploma or GED, and 70 percent of the population never finished high school.

43. In the 1945 introduction to *Black Metropolis*, Richard Wright framed the problems of African Americans living in Chicago in terms of this lack of "fulfillment." St. Clair Drake and Horace R. Clayton, *Black Metropolis: A Study of Negro Life in a Northern City* (New York: Harcourt, Brace, 1945).

Chapter Three

1. The analysis of rap lyrics and poems in *Renegade Dreams* is indebted to Steven Caton's approach in *Peaks of Yemen I Summon*. Similarly to the ethnographic context that Caton describes, I see rap music as both a creation of art and a political and social act—an act that depends in large measure on the charisma and spontaneity of the artist. In Eastwood, as in Yemeni society, the poet/rapper has the power to motivate his or her audience. But, as we will see, this power is linked to a discourse of authenticity. That is, in order for that poet/rapper's power to be realized, he or she must be viewed by the audience as authentic. Steven Caton, *Peaks of Yemen I Summon: Poetry as Cultural Practice in a North Yemeni Tribe* (Berkeley: University of California Press, 1990). See also John Jackson, *Harlemworld: Doing Race and Class in Contemporary Black America* (Chicago: University of Chicago Press, 2003); John Jackson, *Real Black: Adventures in Racial Sincerity* (Chicago: University of Chicago Press, 2005); and Marcyliena Morgan, *The Real Hiphop: Battling for Knowledge, Power, and Respect in the LA Underground* (Durham, NC: Duke University Press, 2009).

2. For Jay-Z as a corporate mogul, see Jay-Z, *Decoded* (New York: Spiegel & Grau, 2010); and Mark Healy, "Jay-Z: Renaissance Mogul," *GQ Magazine* (2006): 286–358. For hip hop moguls in general, see Lisa DePaulo, "50 Cent: Big Shot," *GQ Magazine* (2005): 289–360; Paul Gilroy, "All about the Benjamins: Multicultural Blackness—Corporate, Commercial, and Oppositional," in *Between Camps: Nations, Cultures and the Allure of Race* (New York: Routledge Press, 2004); Ice-T, *Ice: A Memoir of Gangster Redemption* (New York: Ballantine, 2011), 1–13, 89–179; Keith Negus, "The Business of Rap: Between the Street and the Executive Suite," in *That's the Joint!: The Hip hop Studies Reader*, ed. Mark Anthony Neal and Murray Forman (New York: Routledge, 2004); Imani Perry,

"Bling Bling . . . and Going Pop: Consumerism and Co-optation in Hip Hop," in *Prophets of da Hood: The Politics and Poetics of Hip Hop* (Durham, NC: Duke University Press, 2004), 191–204; and Christopher Holmes Smith, "'I Don't Like to Dream about Getting Paid': Representations of Social Mobility and the Emergence of the Hip Hop Mogul," *Social Text* 21, no. 4 (2003): 69–97.

3. Tricia Rose, *Black Noise: Rap Music and Black Culture in Contemporary America* (Hanover, NH: Wesleyan University Press, 1994).

4. See also Jackson, *Real Black*.

5. Michael Eric Dyson, *Holler If You Hear Me: Searching for Tupac Shakur* (New York: Basic Civitas Books, 2001), 217.

6. Tricia Rose, *The Hip Hop Wars: What We Talk about When We Talk about Hip Hop* (New York: Basic Civitas, 2008), 134.

7. The term "vulgar money-getters" is a quote from W. E. B. Du Bois in *The Souls of Black Folk*. I make use of this term to signal a notion of racial uplift. For Du Bois, the ability to put idealism ahead of pragmatism was the trademark of the authentic race leader. As much as anywhere else in *The Souls of Black Folk*, Du Bois highlights the imperatives of the authentic race leader in the fifth chapter, "Of the Wings of Atalanta." In this chapter Du Bois discusses how, in the pursuit of material wealth, the city of Atlanta runs the risk of forfeiting its role as a region that produces great intellectuals and academic institutions:

Atlanta must not lead the south to dream of material prosperity as the touchtone of all success; already the fatal might of this ideal is beginning to spread; it is replacing the finer type of Southerner with vulgar money-getters; it is burying the sweeter beauties of Southern life beneath pretense and ostentation.

As this quote suggests, for Du Bois, the material prosperity is a "fatal" and potentially debilitating illusion that distracts leaders of the black community. Materialism needs quelling since it could motivate a shift in priorities in which the racially conscious Southerner could easily morph into a "vulgar money-getter." Later in this chapter, Du Bois highlights the dangers of pursuing "pretense and ostentation" by turning to Greek mythology. Symbolizing his own intellectual virtuosity, and inhabiting the figure of the race leader he implores others to become, Du Bois takes for granted that his audience "knows the tale" of Atalanta. It is the myth of a beautiful but elusive maiden who would only marry the man who could outrun her in a footrace. Knowing that she would never lose, Atalanta raced and outran all of her suitors except for Hippomenes. Armed with three golden apples, the deceptive charlatan dropped them one at a time to distract Atalanta. She was able to regain her lead even after recovering the first two golden apples, but when she stopped to scoop the third, Hippomenes beat her and won her hand in marriage. Du Bois uses this allegory to convince race leaders that the city of Atlanta, then a beacon of black intellect, should not be tempted by money. The city should retain its core ideals. Given that *The Souls of Black Folk* has become a foundational text for the field of African American studies, and given that the study of hip hop is couched within this discipline, I want to modernize Du Bois's allegory. He writes: "If Atlanta be not named for Atalanta, she ought to have been." Following this tradition, today one might say: "If Hip hop be not named for Hippomenes, it ought to have been." Du Bois, *The Souls of Black Folk* (1903; reprint, New York: Vintage, 1990).

8. See Earnest Allen Jr., "Making the Strong Survive: The Contours and Contradictions of Message Rap," in *Droppin' Science: Critical Essays on Rap Music and Hip Hop Culture*, ed. William Eric Perkins (Philadelphia: Temple University Press, 1996); Cheryl L. Keyes, *Rap Music and Street Consciousness* (Urbana: University of Illinois Press, 2002); and Mark Anthony Neal, *Soul Babies: Black Popular Culture and the Post-Soul Aesthetic* (New York: Routledge, 2002).

9. Cf. João Biehl and Peter Locke, "Deleuze and the Anthropology of Becoming," *Current Anthropology* 51 (2010): 317–51; and Gilles Deleuze, *Essays Critical and Clinical* (Minneapolis: University of Minnesota Press, 1997), 61.

10. Cornell West, *Race Matters* (Boston: Beacon Press, 1993), 128.

11. This analysis of the drug trade in Eastwood follows ethnographic studies of complex social institutions that organize the internal culture and dynamics of local markets in the context of globalization. See, for example, Theodore Bestor, *Tsukiji: The Fish Market at the Center of the World* (Berkeley: University of California Press, 2004). For other compelling anthropological examples of the ways in which global and national policies shape everyday practices within local markets, see Arjun Appadurai, "Introduction: Commodities and the Politics of Value," in *The Social Life of Things: Commodities in Cultural Perspective*, ed. Arjun Appadurai (Cambridge: Cambridge University Press, 1986); and Karla Slocum, *Free Trade and Freedom: Neoliberalism, Place, and Nation in the Caribbean* (Ann Arbor: University of Michigan Press, 2006).

12. Richard Askwith, "How Aspirin Turned Hero," *Sunday Times* (London), September 13, 1998.

13. Philippe Bourgois and Jeff Schonberg speak about the difference between black and white heroin users in San Francisco in which the former inject through the vein or "shoot up" and the latter inject through the muscle or "skin pop." Bourgois and Schonberg, *Righteous Dopefiend* (Berkeley: University of California Press, 2009), 111.

14. Tracy Swartz, "Chicago's Heroin Zones," *RedEye*, February 24, 2010.

15. It is a long-standing fact that opium and coca production has thrived in areas that have been the focal points of U.S. intervention abroad. For decades, the Golden Triangle (the area that encompasses the mountains of Burma, Vietnam, Laos, and Thailand, Asia's main opium-producing region) has been heavily affected by U.S. occupation and sponsorship. In the late 1960s and early 1970s, the CIA supported anti-Communist Chinese Nationalists settled near the Sino-Burmese border. This helped the development of opium production in the region because Burma's transitional government was unwilling to address the basic needs of local farmers. As a result, peasants began to grow opium and forged alliances with illegal actors for protection. Likewise, the Soviet war in Afghanistan in the 1970s led to increased drug production in the Pakistani-Afghani border regions when the United States backed mujahedin militants who raised money for arms by selling opium.

16. United Nations Office on Drugs and Crime, *2008 World Drug Report* (United Nations, 2008).

17. For nuanced examples of hip hop and its "negative" representations of crime, see Paul Butler, *Let's Get Free: A Hip Hop Theory of Justice* (New York: New Press, 2009), 1–56, 123–46; Stephen J. Dubner, "Toward a Unified Theory of Black America," *New York Times Magazine*, March 20, 2005; Ice-T, *Ice*; Perry, *Prophets of da Hood*, 102–17; Rose, *Black Noise*, 146–82; and Samantha M. Shapiro, "Hip Hop Outlaw," *New York Times*, February 18, 2007.

18. This analysis of heroin addicts is informed by Alisse Waterson's powerful work *Street Addicts in the Political Economy* (Philadelphia: Temple University Press, 1997) on the economic, political, and ideological forces that shape the nature of street-addict life. Waterson's classic text disputes the view that hardcore, low-income drug users are situated in deviant subcultures. She does so by depicting their relations with family, friends, and lovers, while connecting ethnographic data with a macro-level understanding of the political economy.

19. In *Real Black*, John Jackson distinguishes between racial sincerity and authenticity. These concepts, he argues, have very different ways of imagining "keeping it real." Authenticity usually refers to how social and cultural "guidelines for proper and improper behavior" delimit people's options in life. Sincerity, on the other hand, has to do with the characteristics by which people measure someone's genuineness. Jackson's call to look at race, and hip hop, in terms of sincerity as well as authenticity informs my analysis. Yet I focus on authenticity because I am specifically interested, as Jackson puts it, in the relationship "between subjects (who authenticate) and objects (dumb, mute, and inorganic) that are interpreted and analyzed from the outside, because they cannot simply speak for themselves." In my study the authenticators are not merely gang members, and the "objects" are not simply drugs and rap music. I am also making an argument about the role that social scientists play in objectifying black urban youth through arguments about authenticity, rendering them "dumb, mute, and inorganic" in the process.

20. Steven D. Levitt and Sudhir Alladi Venkatesh, "An Economic Analysis of a Drug-Selling Gang's Finance," *Quarterly Journal of Economics* 115, no. 3 (2000): 755–89.

21. Sudhir Venkatesh, *Off the Books: The Underground Economy of the Urban Poor* (Chicago: University of Chicago Press, 2006).

22. My analysis of rap explores the relationship between theories of labor and value. I draw on scholarship that has investigated how value is measured in capitalist and non-capitalist societies. See, for example, Jean Baudrillard, *The Mirror of Production* (St. Louis: Telos Press, 1975); Diane Elson, ed., *Value: The Representation of Labour in Capitalism* (London: CSE Books, 1979); David Graeber, *Toward an Anthropological Theory of Value: The False Coin of Our Own Dreams* (New York: Palgrave, 2001); Lisette Josephides, *The Production of Inequality: Gender and Exchange among the Kewa* (New York: Tavistock, 1985); Marcel Mauss, *The Gift* (1967; reprint, New York: Norton, 1990); Georg Simmel, *The Philosophy of Money* (Boston: Routledge & Kegan Paul, 1978); Annette Weiner, *Women of Value, Men of Renown: New Perspectives in Trobriand Exchange* (Austin: University of Texas Press, 1976); and Annette Weiner, *Inalienable Possessions: The Paradox of Keeping-While-Giving* (Berkeley: University of California Press, 1992).

More specifically, I'm interested in the link that scholars have made between capitalism and morality/value(s)—how conceptions of "hard work" and "legitimate work" are infused into normative assessments of "the good" in various societies. Raymond Firth, "Work and Value: Reflections on the Ideas of Karl Marx," in *Social Anthropology of Work*, ed. Sandra Wallman (London: Academic Press, 1979); David Harvey, "Labor, Capital and Class Struggle around the Built Environment in Advanced Capitalist Societies," in *Urbanization and Conflicts in Market Societies*, ed. K. R. Cox (New York: Methuen, 1978); Erik Schwimmer, "The Self and the Product: Concepts of Work in Comparative Perspective," in *Social Anthropology of Work*, ed. Sandra Wallman (London: Academic Press, 1979); Richard Sennett, *The Corrosion of Character: The Personal Consequences of Work in the New Capitalism* (New York: Norton, 1998); E. P. Thompson, "The Moral Economy of the English Crowd in the Eighteenth Century," in *Customs in Common* (New York: New Press, 1991); Bettylou Valentine, *Hustling and Other Hard Work: Life Styles in the Ghetto* (New York: Free Press, 1978); Thorstein Veblen, *The Vested Interests and the Common Man: The Modern Point of View and the New Order* (1919; reprint, New York: Augustus M. Kelley, 1964); and Max Weber, *The Protestant Ethic and the Spirit of Capitalism* (New York: Charles Scribner's Sons, 1958).

23. Philippe Bourgois, *In Search of Respect: Selling Crack in El Barrio* (Cambridge: Cambridge University Press, 1995), 50.

24. This is especially true when the legal system is viewed as partially responsible for a group's substandard living conditions. Perhaps this helps to explain why criminal figures have long been the concern of those writing social histories as well as scholars writing in the anthropological folkloristic tradition. This analysis of rap music as born out of the African American folklore tradition is, of course, indebted to Henry Louis Gates Jr.'s classic study, *The Signifying Monkey: A Theory of Afro-American Literary Criticism* (New York: Oxford University Press, 1988). This study explores the relationship between the African and African American vernacular traditions and black literature, elaborating a new critical approach located *within* this tradition that allows the black voice to speak for itself. See also Eric Hobsbawm, *Bandits* rev. ed. (New York: New Press, 2000); Zora Neale Hurston, *Mules and Men* (New York: Negro Universities Press, 1969); Paul Radin, *The Trickster: A Study in American Indian Mythology* (New York: Schocken Press, 1988); and John W. Roberts, *From Trickster to Badman: The Black Folk Hero in Slavery and Freedom* (Philadelphia: University of Pennsylvania Press, 1989).

25. Roberts, *From Trickster to Badman*.

26. For Crouch's perspective on rap authenticity, see Michael Eric Dyson, *Holler if You Hear Me: Searching for Tupac Shakur* (New York: Basic Civitas Books, 2001), 217.

27. Walter Benjamin, "The Critique of Violence," in *Reflections: Essays, Aphorisms, Autobiographical Writings* (New York: Harcourt Brace Jovanovich, 1978), 281.

28. Donald Goines wrote sixteen books (some under the pen name of Al C. Clark). His most prominent works include *Dopefiend* (1971), *Black Girl Lost* (1974) (also the title of a rap song by Nas), *Eldorado Red* (1974), and *Kenyatta's Escape* (1974). To get a sense of his influence in hip hop, several rap references to his works are listed below.

Brand Nubian, "Who Can Get Busy Like This Man . . . ," *One for All* (1990): "The skills go back to the days of flippin' coins / Past time readin' books by my man Donald Goines." Gravediggaz, "Defective Trip (Trippin')," *6 Feet Deep* (1994): "But like a Dopefiend character of Donald Goines." AZ, "Rather Unique," *Doe or Die* (1995): "Too hard to follow, you took a bite but couldn't swallow / Your mind's boggled, but I'm as deep as Donald Goines' novels." 2Pac, "Tradin War Stories," *All Eyez on Me* (1996): "Machiavelli was my tutor, Donald Goines my father figure / Moms sent me to go play with the drug dealers." Nas, "Escobar '97" *Men in Black Soundtrack* (1997): "Eldorado Red, sippin' Dom [Pérignon] out the bottle / My life is like a Donald Goines novel." MF Grimm, "Take Em to War," *Scars and Memories* (2005): "If Donald Goines wrote my life, my name would be Kenyatta / I don't choose to kill a brother, but to stay alive right now I gotta." In addition to these lyrics and many more, there is a rapper named Donny Goines. Also, one of the members from the rap group Pitch Black goes by the name of D.G. after the influential author.

29. In mentioning this, I mean to highlight the fact that oftentimes, when something or someone is presumed to be inauthentic, the debate itself obscures the ways in which a "substitute" or "imitation" becomes just as dangerous as the original.

30. Tosh's dream is another way of interpreting the "real" since, Tosh says, it haunts even his waking hours. In Eastwood, authenticity works similarly to Tosh's vision. The fake is always on the verge of becoming real, and the real on the verge of becoming fake. Here, the dialectic between the real and its impostor surfaces by examining the intersection between heroin trafficking and rap music production, and how gang members relate to both industries. In this

vein, Blizzard and Tosh—their past hardships, their daily struggles, and their relationship to the "real"—reveal differing efforts to live amidst the gang. Even though Blizzard is a card-carrying gang member, he is seen as a "studio gangsta": someone who raps in the first person about crimes that he has not committed. Thus, his difficulty in getting out of the game stems from being part of a gang that is notorious for heroin trafficking while restricting his own relationship to such violence to fictive musical narratives. Meanwhile, Tosh is not an active gang member and yet is considered authentic because he wears his battle wounds. His ability to get out of the game comes only from his *dis*ability—this, an honorable discharge for services rendered when a gunshot wound left him paralyzed. In Eastwood, the different possibilities for people like Blizzard and Tosh, Kemo and Shawn, to be authentic gang members—to prove their "truthteller" credentials—involve nonstop, perpetual effort.

Chapter Four

1. These numbers are from the "Annual Crime Statistics" released by the Federal Bureau of Investigation in May 2010. http://www.fbi.gov/stats-services /crimestats (accessed March 14, 2013).

2. Again, as mentioned in the introduction, at the time this number was viewed as especially tragic as it had surpassed the 2007–8 total (twenty-seven) by more than eleven teenagers.

3. This statistic on violence-induced injury is from the National Spinal Cord Injury Database: http://www.spinalcord.uab.edu (accessed June 11, 2013).

4. James W. Wagner et al., *The Chicago Crime Commission Gang Book: A Detailed Overview of Street Gangs in the Chicago Metropolitan Area* (Chicago: Chicago Crime Commission, 2006).

5. See Khalil Gibran Muhammad, *The Condemnation of Blackness: Race, Crime, and the Making of Modern Urban America* (Cambridge, MA: Harvard University Press, 2010). See also Christian Parenti, *Lockdown America: Police and Prisons in the Age of Crisis* (London: Verso, 1999).

6. Robin D. G. Kelley, *Yo' Mama's Disfunktional!: Fighting the Culture Wars in Urban America* (Boston: Beacon Press, 1997).

7. For an early critique of biologically based theories of innate dysfunction, see Franz Boas, *Changes in Bodily Form of Descendants of Immigrants* (Washington, DC: United States Immigration Commission, 1910). For a prominent ex-

ample of a "culture of poverty" thesis, see Daniel Patrick Moynihan, *The Negro Family: The Case for National Action* (Washington, DC: Office of Policy Planning and Research, U.S. Department of Labor, 1965).

8. Philippe Bourgois and Jeff Schonberg, *Righteous Dopefiend* (Berkeley: University of California Press, 2009).

9. In "The Prosthetic Imagination," Sarah S. Jain demonstrates the mutual constitution between wounding and enabling. Although she focuses on how futuristic fantasies associated with prostheses simultaneously wound and enable, her analysis is also useful in thinking about where and how disability is located in a gang. Contemplating what it means to be wounded—and conversely enabled—by a gang allows us to examine both the relationships that are formed through the trade in injury and the discourse on disability that gang members produce as a consequence of it. Jain, "The Prosthetic Imagination: Enabling and Disabling the Prosthesis Trope," *Science, Technology & Human Values* 24, no. 1 (1999): 31–54.

10. Sudhir Venkatesh, *Off the Books: The Underground Economy of the Urban Poor* (Chicago: University of Chicago Press, 2006).

11. Here, I do not mean to endow the notion of disability with a negative moral valence. Rather, the disabled subject, found at the intersection of race and socioeconomics, signals how certain risks—morbidity, unemployment, incarceration, and mortality rates—are funneled toward young black Chicagoans who are far more likely than most people reading this book to be crippled by a stray bullet shot from a gang member's gun. For early Chicago examples of territoriality and ordered segmentation, see Gerald Suttles, *The Social Order of the Slum: Ethnicity and Territory in the Inner City* (Chicago: University of Chicago Press, 1968).

12. Even though the rate of incarceration for women in Chicago was on the rise, in most cases the prototypical problem child was a young black male.

13. I am pointing to the ways in which disabled ex-gang members redeploy the stigma surrounding their disability. On stigma and social identity, see Erving Goffman, *Stigma: Notes on a Spoiled Identity* (New York: Simon and Schuster, 1963).

14. Ronald Berger and Melvin Juette, *Wheelchair Warrior: Gangs, Disability, and Basketball* (Philadelphia: Temple University Press, 2008), 10.

15. See Tobin Anthony Siebers, *Disability Theory* (Ann Arbor: University of Michigan Press, 2008).

222 † NOTES TO PAGES 126–130

16. For a comprehensive history and critique of Western medicine, see Byron Good, *Medicine, Rationality and Experience: An Anthropological Perspective* (Cambridge: Cambridge University Press, 1994).

17. Arthur W. Frank, *The Wounded Storyteller: Body, Illness, and Ethics* (Chicago: University of Chicago Press, 1995), 5. Likewise, in *Crip Theory*, Robert McRuer brilliantly demonstrates how, by turning a story of suffering into testimony, disabled activists who "come out crip" endow the pejorative slur "crippled" with a positive valence. McRuer, *Crip Theory: Cultural Signs of Queerness and Disability* (New York: New York University Press, 2006).

18. Arthur Kleinman and Joan Kleinman, "How Bodies Remember: Social Memory and Bodily Experience of Criticism, Resistance, and Delegitimation Following China's Cultural Revolution," *New Literary History* 25 (1994): 710–11.

19. On the heterogeneity within communities of the stigmatized, see Michael Warner, *The Trouble with Normal* (New York: Free Press, 1999).

20. The exchange reminds me of Erving Goffman's observation that stigma is not only embarrassing for the stigmatized person, but for those who are confronted with stigma as well. It is not just that the stigmatized person has to avoid embarrassing himself by being out of control in situations where physical control is expected. He must also avoid embarrassing others, who should be protected from having to witness the loss of physical control. Goffman, *Stigma*; and Frank, *The Wounded Storyteller*, 50.

21. Kleinman and Kleinman, "How Bodies Remember." See also Frank, *The Wounded Storyteller*.

22. Didier Fassin and Richard Rechtman, *The Empire of Trauma: An Inquiry into the Condition of Victimhood* (Princeton, NJ: Princeton University Press, 2009).

23. Frank, *The Wounded Storyteller*, 1.

24. On race and the production of medical and scientific knowledge, see Sharla Fett, *Working Cures: Healing, Health, and Power on Southern Slave Plantations* (Chapel Hill: University of North Carolina Press, 2002); Londa Schiebinger, *Nature's Body: Gender in the Making of Modern Science* (Boston: Beacon Press, 1993); Rebecca Skloot, *The Immortal Life of Henrietta Lacks* (New York: Crown, 2010); and Harriet A. Washington, *Medical Apartheid: The Dark History of Medical Experimentation on Black Americans from Colonial Times to the Present* (New York: Anchor Books, 2006).

25. For the gang as a stand-in family, see Scott H. Decker and Barrik van Winkle, *Life in the Gang: Family, Friends, and Violence* (New York; Cambridge: Cambridge University Press, 1996). For the geography of gang territories, see Martin Sánchez-Jankowski, *Islands in the Street: Gangs and American Urban Society* (Berkeley: University of California Press, 1991).

26. On disability and gun violence, see Berger and Juette, *Wheelchair Warrior*; Patrick J. Devlieger, Gary L. Albrecht, and Miram Hertz, "The Production of Disability Culture among Young African-American Men," *Social Science & Medicine* 64, no. 9 (2007): 1948–59; and John Rich, *Wrong Place, Wrong Time: Trauma and Violence in the Lives of Young Black Men* (Baltimore: Johns Hopkins University Press, 2009).

27. Though not a central concern of *Renegade Dreams*, I use Marcus's description of his neighborhood, and the recollections of his mother's warnings, to gesture toward the fact that it is one's family members—oftentimes, those who condemn gang life the most—who become the primary caretakers for black urban youth who are disabled. See Devlieger, Albrecht, and Hertz, "The Production of Disability Culture among Young African-American Men."

28. I cannot mention the name of this book for reasons of confidentiality.

Chapter Five

1. See Eric Cazdyn, *The Already Dead: The New Time of Politics, Culture, and Illness* (Durham, NC: Duke University Press, 2012), 5.

2. This analysis of HIV and AIDS is indebted to Cathy Cohen's groundbreaking study, *The Boundaries of Blackness: AIDS and the Breakdown of Black Politics* (Chicago: University of Chicago Press, 1999), which looks at the cultural impact of AIDS on the African American community. By focusing on the different fault lines and analyzing the ensuing struggles and debates about disease, she reveals the ways in which the epidemic fractured rather than united the black community. Here I take a similar approach to examining the ways in which ministers, congregants, health workers, and patients grapple with disease, while paying attention to what it means for the community at large.

3. In Chicago, there is evidence that the link between HIV and drug use is becoming more pronounced over time. In 2008, when Mark made this statement, 47.5 percent of HIV patients reported using illicit drugs. In 2011, when I sent a draft of this chapter to Mark for him to review, he wrote in the margins

that the number had risen to almost 53 percent. He later pointed me to the following study: Chicago Department of Public Health, *HIV Risk and Prevention Behaviors among Men Who Have Sex with Men, Chicago, 2008 and 2011* (Chicago: City of Chicago, 2012).

4. João Biehl, *Will to Live: AIDS Therapies and the Politics of Survival* (Princeton, NJ: Princeton University Press, 2007), 353.

5. Ibid., 353, 361.

6. João Biehl makes this point in *Will to Live*. This landmark study was released while I was in the throes of completing my fieldwork. At the time, I was unsure of how to think about the HIV and AIDS patients I met in Eastwood. Many were like Amy. They had recently found out that they were HIV positive and emerged with resiliency from an initial bout of depression, after health workers informed them that HIV was no longer a death sentence. I found points of comparison with Biehl's ethnography, which describes how Brazil became the first developing country to universalize access to lifesaving AIDS therapies. Although AIDS remained lethal, these therapies allowed people to live longer, to move back to their old neighborhoods, become parents, and search for jobs. The return of aspiration among AIDS patients, Biehl writes, was largely due to the fact that antiretroviral therapies had taken root in the everyday. The quote that encapsulates the underlying sentiment in Biehl's study comes from an AIDS patient named Evilasio, as he describes the role of a strong will in managing AIDS: "I know that I have trespassed God's laws. When one mistreats oneself, this is the art of Satan. Even though I suffer, God knows that I have this will to live." While Evilasio's quote speaks to the strength and resiliency of an AIDS patient, it also betrays a potential barrier to adherence for those who do not share his beliefs. Evilasio's will to adhere is tied to his faith in God. But what does this mean for someone like Amy? Although she does not believe in God, honing a will to adhere is critical to her survival. This is where the church comes in. With only a few places in the community available to talk openly about what it feels like to live with HIV, the church has taken on an important role in her struggle to stay healthy. Hence, even though she considers herself an atheist, the church is a site where she can develop the will to do battle with a life-threatening disease.

7. Mark Dybul et al., "Guidelines for Using Antiretroviral Agents among HIV-Infected Adults and Adolescents," *Annals of Internal Medicine* 137 (2002): 381-433.

8. In non-Western contexts, researchers have identified several barriers to adherence, among them are the following: Those with the disease may have to travel a long distance from rural areas to medical treatment centers to receive drugs; they may have a lack of faith in Western medicine and health care professionals based on long histories of colonial oppression; and they may prefer local healers and spiritual methods of treatment rather than prescription drugs.

Beyond this, the African literature on HIV and antiretrovirals, on dance, and on the relationship between them reminds us that the redemptive mode itself can be its own kind of barrier, that HIV produces particular healing narratives, possibilities, and silences within churches. For example, Vinh Kim Nguyen, *The Republic of Therapy: Triage and Sovereignty in West Africa's Time of AIDS* (Durham, NC: Duke University Press, 2010); Paul Geissler and Ruth Jane Prince, *The Land Is Dying: Contingency, Creativity and Conflict in Western Kenya* (New York: Berghahn Books, 2010); Hansjorg Dilger, Abdoulaye Kane, and Stacey A. Langwick, eds., *Medicine, Mobility, and Power in Global Africa: Transnational Health and Healing* (Bloomington: Indiana University Press, 2012).

9. See Kevin Lewis O'Neill, "The Reckless Will: Prison Chaplaincy and the Problem of Mara Salvatrucha," *Public Culture* 22 (2010): 67–88.

10. When preliminary research in Eastwood began in 2006, there were more than 22,000 people living with HIV/AIDS in Chicago; over half of whom were living with HIV and had not progressed to AIDS. The number of people living with HIV/AIDS continues to grow as new HIV and AIDS cases are diagnosed every year and less people die as a result of HIV. Since 2000, over 1,000 new HIV (not AIDS) diagnoses are made each year. The rate of HIV infection has now surpassed the number of AIDS diagnoses. Of the nearly 1,500 diagnosed HIV infections made in 2006, 80 percent were males and 20 percent were females. Close to three out of every four HIV infection diagnoses were among blacks and Hispanics. While the overall number of infections has declined by close to 20 percent in the six years preceding 2006, not all demographic and risk groups have experienced the same trend. For instance, adolescent and young adults (15–24), who accounted for 16 percent of newly diagnosed HIV infections in 2006, experienced an increase of over 40 percent between 2000 and 2006. In contrast, people aged 35–44, who accounted for 83 percent of HIV infections in 2006, experienced a 34 percent decline in the number of diagnosed HIV infections during the same time period. http://www

.cityofchicago.org/city/en/depts/cdph/provdrs/pol_plan_report/svcs/chicago
_hiv_aidsbriefs.html (accessed on January 24, 2013).

11. "Juke music" is a subset of "house music," an electronic dance music that
originated in Chicago in the late 1970s and early 1980s. It was initially popularized in mid-1980s discothèques catering to the African American, Latino, and
gay communities, first in Chicago and then in New York City and Detroit. It
eventually reached Europe before becoming infused into mainstream pop and
dance music worldwide. House is strongly influenced by elements of soul- and
funk-infused varieties of disco. It generally mimics disco's percussion, especially the use of a prominent bass drum on every beat, but may feature a prominent synthesizer bass line, electronic drums, electronic effects, funk and pop
samples, and enhanced vocals. Using the template of classic Chicago House
music, "juke music" typically adds sexually explicit lyrics that are repeated in
various ways throughout the musical track.

12. Emile Durkheim, *The Elementary Forms of Religious Life* (1912; reprint,
New York: Free Press, 1995), xxxiv.

13. Considering that footworkin' focuses on the facility by which you can
flick your feet (and gym shoes often highlight your personal style, in this regard), many footworkers are also renegades (even if the reverse is not true).
Gang leaders like Red, for instance, often refer to footworkin' with disdain,
since street dancers also privileged possessing the most stylish gym shoes. According to him, it is the ultimate pastime of "renegades."

14. In this way, the dance that Fatima choreographed is typical of the skits
performed at Youth Night. They all entail three crucial elements through which
a sense of willingness is fashioned: a moment of stability, a moment of rupture,
and a moment of transformation. The beginning of the dance sequence sets up
a moment of stability where the protagonist's life is secure due to her close relationship with Christ. During this period the Christ figure essentially plays
the role of a puppeteer. This is meant to disavow the notion that you are the
sole controller of your own fate. Rather, as a believer in Christ, you rely on his
will for balance of mind. The next part of the performance portrays moments of
rupture that threaten a person's initial closeness to Christ. All of the temptations that Fatima has experienced (from the young man who lays money at her
feet to the young woman who encourages her to contemplate suicide) have led
her to this point: standing with a gun barrel pointed at her own head, waiting to
pull the trigger. The climax of the performance is when, after a series of poten-

tially fatal events, Fatima experiences a moment of transformation in which God gives her the strength to fight her enemies. Even though she is in worse shape than when she left him—clothes in tatters, bloodied, and bruised—the way he puts his hand on her cheek, lovingly, indicates that he forgives without reservation.

15. The analysis of pain in this chapter draws upon anthropological theories of emotion. The following texts are especially informative to my analysis of the ways in which the injury becomes embodied and then articulated emotionally: Veena Das and Ranendra K. Das, "How the Body Speaks: Illness and the Lifeworld among the Urban Poor," in *Subjectivity: Ethnographic Investigations*, ed. João Biehl, Byron Good, and Arthur Kleinman (Berkeley: University of California Press, 2007): 66–97; Robert Desjarlais, *Body and Emotion: The Aesthetics of Illness and Healing in the Nepal Himalayas* (Philadelphia: University of Pennsylvania Press, 1992); Laurence Kirmayer, "Landscapes of Memory: Trauma, Narrative and Dissociation," in *Tense Past: Cultural Essays on Memory and Trauma*, ed. Paul Antze and Michael Lambek (London: Routledge, 1996), 173–98; Catherine Lutz and Lila Abu-Lughod, eds., *Language and the Politics of Emotion* (Cambridge: Cambridge University Press, 1990); Elaine Scarry, *The Body in Pain: The Making and Unmaking of the World* (New York: Oxford University Press, 1985); Glenn H. Shephard, "Three Days of Weeping: Dreams, Emotions, and Death in the Peruvian Andes," *Medical Anthropology Quarterly* 16, no 2 (2002): 200–229; Maria Tapias, "Emotions and the Intergenerational Embodiment of Social Suffering in Rural Bolivia," *Medical Anthropology Quarterly* 20, no. 3 (2006): 399–415; and Christina Zarowsky, "Writing Trauma: Emotion, Ethnography, and the Politics of Suffering among Somali Returnees in Ethiopia," *Culture, Medicine and Psychiatry* 28, no. 2 (2004): 189–209.

Conclusion

1. For scholarship on the social impacts of deindustrialization in urban America, see Douglas S. Massey and Nancy A. Denton, *American Apartheid: Segregation and the Making of the Underclass* (Cambridge, MA: Harvard University Press, 1993); and Christine Walley, *Exit Zero: Family and Class in Postindustrial Chicago* (Chicago: University of Chicago Press, 2013).

2. William Julius Wilson, *The Truly Disadvantaged: The Inner City, the Underclass, and Public Policy* (1987; reprint, University of Chicago Press, 1990).

3. Ibid.

4. See Beth Tompkins Bates, *Pullman Porters and the Rise of Protest Politics in Black America* (Chapel Hill: University of North Carolina Press, 2001); and Shelton Schneirov and Nick Salvatore, *The Pullman Strike and the Crisis of the 1890s: Essays on Labor and Politics* (Urbana: University of Illinois Press, 1999).

5. "Transportation Facts," *Chicago Area Transportation Study*, April 2007.

6. Christopher Lehman, *A Critical History of "Soul Train" on Television* (Jefferson, NC: McFarland, 2008).

7. Bryan Smith, "Trashed: The Death of Michael York and How Heroin Has Invaded the Chicago Suburbs," *Chicago Magazine*, November 2009, http://www.chicagomag.com/Chicago-Magazine/November-2009/The-death-of-Michael-York-and-how-heroin-has-invaded-the-Chicago-suburbs/ (accessed on May 29, 2010).

8. It is telling that in their reportage, *Chicago Magazine* finds it fitting to portray Eastwood residents as "brazen" black "gutter rats," who sustain themselves by essentially devouring (otherwise irreproachable) cadavers like Michael's. It is no mere semantics that in the same way that local reporters speak of the "savagery" associated with Derrion's death, this journalist deploys *Savage Inequalities*, a study that was authored almost twenty years ago, to depict the community in the contemporary moment; these invocations both fuel a perception of black inner-city communities as stagnant and immobile. Ironically enough, this is the same logic that motivated York's "friends" to abandon his body in an alley in urban Chicago.

9. In his autobiography, Malcolm X (then "Detroit Red") reminds us of the white aristocrats and reefer lovers who visited Harlem—"their sin-den, their fleshpot"—under the cloak of night: "They stole off among the taboo of black people," Malcolm writes, "and took off whatever antiseptic, important, dignified masks they wore in their white world." With Malcolm's words in mind, it can be said that York's friends were following this tradition of thrill-seeking in the slums. Malcolm X, *The Autobiography of Malcolm X* (New York: Grove Press, 1965), 122.

10. On the São Paulo "periphery," see Teresa Caldeira, *City of Walls: Crime, Segregation, and Citizenship in São Paulo* (Berkeley: University of California Press, 2000). On the *banlieues* of Paris, see Didier Fassin, *La Force de L'Ordre: Une Anthropologie de la Police des Quartiers* (Paris: Seuil, 2011).

11. See John L. Comaroff, "Dialectical Systems, History and Anthropology:

Units of Study and Questions of Theory," *Journal of Southern African Studies* 8, no. 2 (1982).

12. Although the jury was composed of ten Caucasians, one Latino, and one Asian American, this was a racially charged environment. Here, I agree with Judith Butler that "whiteness as an episteme operates despite the existence of two nonwhite jurors," so that the vulnerability of whiteness helps all of the jurors, collectively, to refigure the black body as a threat. Butler, "Endangered/Endangering: Schematic Racism and White Paranoia," in *Reading Rodney King/Reading Urban Uprising*, ed. Robert Gooding-Williams (New York: Routledge, 1993).

13. Ibid., 8.

14. Lewis Gordon, "Of Illicit Appearance: The L.A. Riots/Rebellion as a Portent of Things to Come," *Truthout*, October 2013, http://truth-out.org /news/item/9008-of-illicit-appearance-the-la-riots-rebellion-as-a-portent-of -things-to-come (accessed on October 4, 2013).

15. Butler, "Endangered/Endangering," 8.

16. See the following link for the girl beaten by bus driver: http://www .huffingtonpost.com/2012/10/12/bus-uppercut-punch-cleveland-driver-teen -girl-video-_n_1961527.html (accessed on March 11, 2012).

17. Patricia Williams, "The L.A. Riots/Rebellion as a Portent of Things to Come," *Transition Magazine* (Cambridge: The W. E. B. Du Bois Institute, forthcoming).

18. Barbara Browning, *Infectious Rhythm: Metaphors of Contagion and the Spread of African Culture* (New York: Routledge, 1998), 105–40.

19. It should be no surprise for those familiar with the crack cocaine laws of the 1980s, which have disproportionately affected poor people of color, that Michael York's death is being mobilized to petition for harsher laws concerning the sale (and notably not the purchase) of heroin. If they are passed, these laws will undoubtedly result in stricter police surveillance in communities like Eastwood.

20. On "object culture" and "sites of projection," see Bill Brown, "Reification, Reanimation, and the American Uncanny," *Critical Inquiry* 32, no. 2 (2006): 175–207; and Bill Brown, "Objects, Others, and Us (The Refabrication of Things)," *Critical Inquiry* 36, no. 2 (2010): 183–217.

21. Judith Butler, *Frames of War: When Is Life Grievable?* (2009; reprint, London: Verso, 2010). Special thanks to Tomas Matza for pointing me to this

analogy in his 2012 talk at the American Anthropological Association meetings in San Francisco. His presentation was entitled "Relationality, Circulation, Ownership."

22. It is important to note that Wilson's theory of isolation was never meant to be all-encompassing. He was referring to the social and economic isolation of urban residents in a relative sense—i.e., with regards to their estrangement from community institutions and jobs in the legal labor market.

23. Ibid.

24. Eric Wyckoff Williams, "Will Obama Support Marijuana Legalization in His 2nd Term?," *The Root*, http://www.theroot.com/views/what-will -obama-do-about-marijuana (accessed on December 10, 2012).

25. For a critique of the concept of "informal economies," see Janet Roitman, *Fiscal Disobedience: An Anthropology of Economic Regulation in Central Africa* (Princeton, NJ: Princeton University Press, 2005).

BIBLIOGRAPHY

✳

Abu-Lughod, Lila. *Writing Women's Worlds: Bedouin Stories.* Berkeley: University of California Press, 1993.

Allen, Earnest, Jr. "Making the Strong Survive: The Contours and Contradictions of Message Rap." In *Droppin' Science: Critical Essays on Rap Music and Hip Hop Culture,* edited by William Eric Perkins. Philadelphia: Temple University Press, 1996.

Anderson, Elijah. *Code of the Street: Decency, Violence, and the Moral Life of the Inner City.* 1990. Reprint, New York: Norton, 2000.

Appadurai, Arjun. "Introduction: Commodities and the Politics of Value." In *The Social Life of Things: Commodities in Cultural Perspective,* edited by Arjun Appadurai. Cambridge: Cambridge University Press, 1986.

Ards, Angela. "Organizing the Hip-Hop Generation." *The Nation,* July 26, 1994.

Askwith, Richard. "How Aspirin Turned Hero." *Sunday Times* (London), September 13, 1998.

Auletta, Ken. *The Underclass.* New York: Vintage, 1982.

Barnes, Sandra, ed. *Africa's Ogun: Old World and New.* Bloomington: Indiana University Press, 1989.

Bates, Beth Tompkins. *Pullman Porters and the Rise of Protest Politics in Black America.* Chapel Hill: University of North Carolina Press, 2001.

Bates, Karen. "Profile: Importance of the Movie 'The Spook Who Sat by the Door' on the Release of a 30th-Anniversary DVD." *All Things Considered*, NPR, March 2004.

Baudrillard, Jean. *The Mirror of Production.* St. Louis: Telos Press, 1975.

Benjamin, Walter. "The Critique of Violence." In *Reflections: Essays, Aphorisms, Autobiographical Writings.* New York: Harcourt Brace Jovanovich, 1978.

Berger, Ronald, and Melvin Juette. *Wheelchair Warrior: Gangs, Disability, and Basketball.* Philadelphia: Temple University Press, 2008.

Bestor, Theodore. *Tsukiji: The Fish Market at the Center of the World.* Berkeley: University of California Press, 2004.

Biehl, João. *Vita: Life in a Zone of Social Abandonment.* Berkeley: University of California Press, 2004.

———. *Will to Live: AIDS Therapies and the Politics of Survival.* Princeton, NJ: Princeton University Press, 2007.

Biehl, João, and Peter Locke. "Deleuze and the Anthropology of Becoming." *Current Anthropology* 51 (2010): 317–51.

Boas, Franz. *Changes in Bodily Form of Descendants of Immigrants.* Washington, DC: United States Immigration Commission, 1910.

Bourdieu, Pierre. *Outline of a Theory of Practice.* Cambridge: Cambridge University Press, 1977.

Bourgois, Philippe. *In Search of Respect: Selling Crack in El Barrio.* Cambridge: Cambridge University Press, 1995.

Bourgois, Philippe, and Jeff Schonberg. *Righteous Dopefiend.* Berkeley: University of California Press, 2009.

Boym, Svetlana. *The Future of Nostalgia.* 2001. Reprint, New York: Basic Books, 2006.

Branch, Taylor. *Parting the Waters: America in the King Years, 1954–63.* New York: Simon and Schuster, 1988.

Brown, Bill. "Objects, Others, and Us (The Refabrication of Things)." *Critical Inquiry* 36, no. 2 (2010): 183–217.

———. "Reification, Reanimation, and the American Uncanny." *Critical Inquiry* 32, no. 2 (2006): 175–207.

Brown, Vincent. *The Reaper's Garden: Death and Power in the World of Atlantic Slavery.* Cambridge, MA: Harvard University Press, 2008.

Browning, Barbara. *Infectious Rhythm: Metaphors of Contagion and the Spread of African Culture.* New York: Routledge, 1998.

Brown-Saracino, Japonica. *A Neighborhood that Never Changes: Gentrification, So-*

cial Preservation, and the Search for Authenticity. Chicago: University of Chicago Press, 2009.

Bryk, Anthony, et al. *Organizing Schools for Improvement: Lessons from Chicago*. Chicago: University of Chicago Press, 2010.

Bulkeley, Kelley. *Dreaming in the World's Religions: A Comparative History*. New York: New York University Press, 2008.

Butler, Judith. "Endangered/Endangering: Schematic Racism and White Paranoia." In *Reading Rodney King/Reading Urban Uprising*, edited by Robert Gooding-Williams. New York: Routledge, 1993.

———. *Frames of War: When Is Life Grievable?* 2009. Reprint, London: Verso, 2010.

Butler, Paul. *Let's Get Free: A Hip-Hop Theory of Justice*. New York: New Press, 2009.

Caldeira, Teresa. *City of Walls: Crime, Segregation, and Citizenship in São Paulo*. Berkeley: University of California Press, 2000.

Caton, Steven. *Peaks of Yemen I Summon: Poetry as Cultural Practice in a North Yemeni Tribe*. Berkeley: University of California Press, 1990.

Cazdyn, Eric. *The Already Dead: The New Time of Politics, Culture, and Illness*. Durham, NC: Duke University Press, 2012.

Chicago Department of Public Health. *HIV Risk and Prevention Behaviors among Men Who Have Sex with Men, Chicago, 2008 and 2011*. Chicago: City of Chicago, December 2012.

Chin, Elizabeth. *Purchasing Power: Black Kids and American Consumer Culture*. Minneapolis: University of Minnesota Press, 2001.

Cohen, Cathy. *The Boundaries of Blackness: AIDS and the Breakdown of Black Politics*. Chicago: University of Chicago Press, 1999.

———. *Democracy Remixed: Black Youth and the Future of American Politics*. New York: Oxford University Press, 2010.

Cole, Johnnetta Betsch, and Beverly Guy-Sheftall. *Gender Talk: The Struggle for Women's Equality in African American Communities*. New York: One World, 2003.

Comaroff, John L. "Dialectical Systems, History and Anthropology: Units of Study and Questions of Theory." *Journal of Southern African Studies* 8, no. 2 (1982): 146.

Comaroff, John, and Jean Comaroff. *Ethnography and the Historical Imagination*. Boulder, CO: Westview Press, 1992.

Cose, Ellis. *The Envy of the World: On Being a Black Man in America*. New York: Washington Square Press, 2002.

Das, Veena, and Ranendra K. Das. "How the Body Speaks: Illness and the Lifeworld among the Urban Poor." In *Subjectivity: Ethnographic Investigations*, edited by João Biehl, Byron Good, and Arthur Kleinman. Berkeley: University of California Press, 2007.

Davis, Mike. *City of Quartz: Excavating the Future in Los Angeles*. London: Verso, 1990.

———. *From Prisoners of the American Dream*. 1986. Reprint, New York: Verso, 1999.

Dawley, David. *A Nation of Lords: The Autobiography of the Vice Lords*. 2nd ed. Long Grove, IL: Waveland Press, 1992.

Dean, Mitchell. *Governmentality: Power and Rule in Modern Society*. London: Sage, 1999.

DeBose, Charles. "Codeswitching: Black English and Standard English in the African-American Linguistic Repertoire." In *Codeswitching*, edited by Carol M. Eastman. Philadelphia: Multilingual Matters, 1992.

De Certeau, Michel. *The Practice of Everyday Life*. Berkeley: University of California Press, 1984.

Decker, Scott H., and Barrik van Winkle. *Life in the Gang: Family, Friends, and Violence*. New York: Cambridge University Press, 1996.

Deleuze, Gilles. *Essays Critical and Clinical*. Minneapolis: University of Minnesota Press, 1997.

———. *Two Regimes of Madness: Texts and Interviews, 1975–1995*. Los Angeles: Semiotext(e), 2006.

DePaulo, Lisa. "50 Cent: Big Shot." *GQ Magazine* (2005): 289–360.

Derrida, Jacques. "The Force of Law: The 'Mystical Foundations of Authority.'" In *Acts of Religion*. 1989. Reprint, New York: Routledge, 2002.

Descartes, René. *Meditations on First Philosophy: With Selections from the Objections and Replies*. Oxford: Oxford University Press, 2008.

Desjarlais, Robert. *Body and Emotion: The Aesthetics of Illness and Healing in the Nepal Himalayas*. Philadelphia: University of Pennsylvania Press, 1992.

Devlieger, Patrick J., Gary L. Albrecht, and Miram Hertz. "The Production of Disability Culture among Young African-American Men." *Social Science & Medicine* 64, no. 9 (2007): 1948–59.

Diamond, Andrew J. *Mean Streets: Chicago Youths and the Everyday Struggle for Empowerment in the Multiracial City, 1908–1969*. Berkeley: University of California Press, 2009.

Dilger, Hansjorg, Abdoulaye Kane, and Stacey A. Langwick, eds. *Medicine, Mobility, and Power in Global Africa: Transnational Health and Healing*. Bloomington: Indiana University Press, 2012.

Dillard, John. *A History of American English*. New York: Longman, 1992.

Dirks, Nicolas B., Geoff Eley, and Sherry B. Ortner, eds. Introduction to *Culture/Power/History*. Princeton, NJ: Princeton University Press, 1994.

Drake, St. Clair, and Horace R. Clayton. *Black Metropolis: A Study of Negro Life in a Northern City*. New York: Harcourt, Brace, 1945.

Dubner, Stephen J. "Toward a Unified Theory of Black America." *New York Times Magazine* March 20, 2005.

Du Bois, W. E. B. *The Souls of Black Folk*. 1903. Reprint, New York: Vintage, 1990.

Duneier, Michelle. *Slim's Table: Race, Respectability, and Masculinity in America*. Chicago: University of Chicago Press, 1992.

Durkheim, Emile. *The Elementary Forms of Religious Life*. 1912. Reprint, New York: Free Press, 1995.

Dybul Mark, et al. "Guidelines for Using Antiretroviral Agents among HIV-Infected Adults and Adolescents." *Annals of Internal Medicine* 137 (2002): 381–433.

Dyson, Michael Eric. *Holler If You Hear Me: Searching for Tupac Shakur*. New York: Basic Civitas Books, 2001.

Elson, Diane, ed. *Value: The Representation of Labour in Capitalism*. London: CSE Books, 1979.

Farmer, Paul. *Infections and Inequalities: The Modern Plagues*. Berkeley: University of California Press, 2001.

———. *The Uses of Haiti*. Monroe, ME: Common Courage Press, 1994.

Farmer, Paul, Margaret Conners, and Janie Simmons. *Women, Poverty, and AIDS: Sex, Drugs, and Structural Violence*. Monroe, ME: Common Courage Press, 1996.

Fassin, Didier. *La Force de L'Ordre: Une Anthropologie de la Police des Quartiers*. Paris: Seuil, 2011.

———. *When Bodies Remember: Experiences and Politics of AIDS in South Africa*. Berkeley: University of California Press, 2007.

Fassin, Didier, and Richard Rechtman. *The Empire of Trauma: An Inquiry into the Condition of Victimhood*. Princeton, NJ: Princeton University Press, 2009.

Fanon, Frantz. *Black Skin White Masks*. New York: Grove Press, 1967.

Fett, Sharla. *Working Cures: Healing, Health, and Power on Southern Slave Plantations*. Chapel Hill: University of North Carolina Press, 2002.

Ferguson, James. *Global Shadows: Africa in the Neoliberal World Order*. Durham, NC: Duke University Press, 2006.

Fickett, Joan. "Tense and Aspect in Black English." *Journal of English Linguistics* 6 (1972): 17–19.

Firth, Raymond. "Work and Value: Reflections on the Ideas of Karl Marx." In *Social Anthropology of Work*, edited by Sandra Wallman. London: Academic Press, 1979.

Foucault, Michel. *Discipline and Punish*. 1975. Reprint, New York: Vintage, 1995.

————. *The History of Sexuality.* 1976. Reprint, New York: Vintage, 1990.

Frank, Arthur W. *The Wounded Storyteller: Body, Illness, and Ethics.* Chicago: University of Chicago Press, 1995.

Frazier, Franklin E. *The Negro Family in Chicago.* Chicago: University of Chicago Press, 1932.

Frederick, Marla. *Between Sundays: Black Women and Everyday Struggles of Faith.* Berkeley: University of California Press, 2003.

Freud, Sigmund. *New Introductory Lectures on Psycho-Analysis.* New York: Norton, 1933.

Friedman, Laurence. *The Horizontal Society.* New Haven, CT: Yale University Press, 1999.

Fullilove, Mindy Thompson. *Rootshock: How Tearing Up City Neighborhoods Hurts America and What We Can Do about It.* New York: Ballantine/One World, 2004.

Galtung, Johan. "Violence, Peace, and Peace Research." *Journal of Peace Research* 6, no. 3 (1969).

Gans, Herbert. *The Urban Villagers: Group and Class in the Life of Italian-Americans.* New York: Free Press Glencoe, 1962.

Gates, Henry Louis, Jr. *The Signifying Monkey: A Theory of Afro-American Literary Criticism.* New York: Oxford University Press, 1988.

Geissler, Paul, and Ruth Jane Prince. *The Land Is Dying: Contingency, Creativity and Conflict in Western Kenya.* New York: Berghahn Books, 2010.

Gilroy, Paul. "All about the Benjamins: Multicultural Blackness—Corporate, Commercial, and Oppositional." In *Between Camps: Nations, Cultures and the Allure of Race.* New York: Routledge Press, 2004.

Goffman, Erving. *Stigma: Notes on a Spoiled Identity.* New York: Simon and Schuster, 1963.

Good, Byron. *Medicine, Rationality and Experience: An Anthropological Perspective.* Cambridge: Cambridge University Press, 1994.

Gordon, Lewis. "Of Illicit Appearance: The L.A. Riots/Rebellion as a Portent of Things to Come." *Truthout.* October 2013, http://truth-out.org/news/item/9008 -of-illicit-appearance-the-la-riots-rebellion-as-a-portent-of-things-to-come (accessed on October 4, 2013).

Graeber, David. *Toward an Anthropological Theory of Value: The False Coin of Our Own Dreams.* New York: Palgrave, 2001.

Gramsci, Antonio. *The Prison Notebooks.* 1971. Reprint, New York: International Publishers, 1999.

Green, Lisa. *African American English: A Linguistic Introduction.* Cambridge: Cambridge University Press, 2002.

Hagedorn, John. "Gangs, Institutions, Race, and Space: The Chicago School Revisited." In *Gangs in the Global City: Alternatives to Traditional Criminology.* Urbana: University of Illinois Press, 2007.

———. "Homeboys, New Jacks, and Anomie." *Journal of African American Studies* 3, no. 1 (1997): 7–28.

———. *People and Folks: Gangs, Crime, and the Underclass in a Rustbelt City.* Chicago: Lake View Press, 1988.

———. *A World of Gangs: Armed Young Men and Gangsta Culture.* Minneapolis: University of Minnesota Press, 2008.

Hamer, Jennifer. *Abandoned in the Heartland: Work, Family, and Living in East St. Louis.* Berkeley: University of California Press, 2011.

Harding, David. *Living the Drama: Community, Conflict, and Culture among Inner-City Boys.* Chicago: University of Chicago Press, 2010.

Harvey, David. "Labor, Capital and Class Struggle around the Built Environment in Advanced Capitalist Societies." In *Urbanization and Conflicts in Market Societies,* edited by K. R. Cox. New York: Methuen, 1978.

Healy, Mark. "Jay-Z: Renaissance Mogul." *GQ* Magazine (2006): 286–358.

Hertzfield, Michael. *Evicted from Eternity: The Restructuring of Modern Rome.* Chicago: University of Chicago Press, 2009.

Higginbotham, Evelyn Brooks. *Righteous Discontent: The Women's Movement in the Black Baptist Church.* Cambridge, MA: Harvard University Press, 1993.

Hobsbawm, Eric. *Bandits.* Rev. ed. New York: New Press, 2000.

hooks, bell. *We Real Cool: Black Men and Masculinity.* New York: Routledge, 2004.

Hunt, Bradford. *Blueprint for Disaster: The Unraveling of Public Housing.* Chicago: University of Chicago Press, 2009.

Hurston, Zora Neale. *Mules and Men.* New York: Negro Universities Press, 1969.

Hyra, Derek S. *The New Urban Renewal: The Economic Transformation of Harlem and Bronzeville.* Chicago: University of Chicago Press, 2008.

Ianni, Francis. *Black Mafia: Ethic Succession Organized in Crime.* New York: Simon and Schuster, 1974.

Ice-T. *Ice: A Memoir of Gangster Redemption.* New York: Ballantine, 2011.

Jackson, John. *Harlemworld: Doing Race and Class in Contemporary Black America.* Chicago: University of Chicago Press, 2003.

———. *Real Black: Adventures in Racial Sincerity.* Chicago: University of Chicago Press, 2005.

Jain, Sarah S. "The Prosthetic Imagination: Enabling and Disabling the Prosthesis Trope." *Science, Technology & Human Values* 24, no. 1 (1999): 31–54.

Jay-Z. *Decoded.* New York: Spiegel & Grau, 2010.

Jensen, Steffen. *Gangs, Politics and Dignity in Cape Town.* Chicago: University of Chicago Press, 2008.

Josephides, Lisette. *The Production of Inequality: Gender and Exchange among the Kewa*. New York: Tavistock, 1985.

Jung, Carl. *Children's Dreams: Notes from the Seimnar Given in 1936–1940*. Princeton, NJ: Princeton University Press, 2008.

Kelley, Robin D. G. *Yo' Mama's Disfunktional!: Fighting the Culture Wars in Urban America*. Boston: Beacon Press, 1997.

Keyes, Cheryl L. *Rap Music and Street Consciousness*. Urbana: University of Illinois Press, 2002.

Kher, Chitrarekha. *Buddhism as Presented by the Brahmanical Systems*. Delhi: Sri Satguru Publications, 1992.

Kirmayer, Laurence. "Landscapes of Memory: Trauma, Narrative and Dissociation." In *Tense Past: Cultural Essays on Memory and Trauma*, edited by Paul Antze and Michael Lambek. London: Routledge, 1996.

Kitwana, Bakari. *The Hip Hop Generation: Young Blacks and the Crisis of African-American Culture*. New York: Basic Civitas Books, 2002.

———. *Why White Kids Love Hip-Hop: Wankstas, Wiggas, Wannabes, and the New Reality of Race in America*. New York: Basic Civitas Books, 2005.

Klein, Malcolm W. *The American Street Gang: Its Nature, Prevalence, and Control*. New York: Oxford University Press, 1995.

Kleinman, Arthur. "The Art of Medicine: Catastrophe and Caregiving: The Failure of Medicine as Art." *The Lancet* 371 (2008).

———. "From Illness as Culture to Caregiving as Moral Experience." *New England Journal of Medicine* 368 (2013): 15.

Kleinman, Arthur, and Joan Kleinman, "How Bodies Remember: Social Memory and Bodily Experience of Criticism, Resistance, and Delegitimation Following China's Cultural Revolution." *New Literary History* 25 (1994): 710–11.

Kotlowitz, Alex. "The Price of Public Violence." *New York Times*, February 23, 2013.

Labov, William. *Language in the Inner City: Studies in Black English Vernacular*. Philadelphia: University of Pennsylvania Press, 1972.

———. *Sociolinguistic Patterns*. Philadelphia: University of Pennsylvania Press, 1972.

La Vigne, Nancy G., Cynthia A. Mamalian, Jeremy Travis, and Christy Visher. *A Portrait of Prisoner Reentry in Illinois: Research Report*. Washington, DC: Urban Institute Justice Policy Center, April 2003.

Lehman, Christopher. *A Critical History of "Soul Train" on Television*. Jefferson, NC: McFarland, 2008.

Lemann, Nicholas. *The Promised Land: The Great Black Migration and How It Changed America*. New York: Knopf, 1991.

Levitt, Steven D., and Sudhir Alladi Venkatesh. "An Economic Analysis of a

Drug-Selling Gang's Finances." *Quarterly Journal of Economics* 115, no. 3 (2000): 755–89.

Liebow, Elliot. *Tally's Corner: A Study of Negro Streetcorner Men.* Boston: Little, Brown, 1967.

Lovell, Anne. "Addiction Markets: The Case of High-Dose Buprenorphine in France." In *Global Pharmaceuticals: Practices, Markets, Ethics*, edited by Adriana Petryna, Andrew Lakoff, and Arthur Kleinman. Durham, NC: Duke University Press, 2006.

Lutz, Catherine, and Lila Abu-Lughod, eds. *Language and the Politics of Emotion.* Cambridge: Cambridge University Press, 1990.

MacLeod, Jay. *Ain't No Making It: Aspirations and Attainment in a Low-Income Neighborhood.* Boulder, CO: Westview Press, 1995.

Maine, Henry. *Ancient Law.* Boston: Beacon Press, 1963.

Malcolm X. *The Autobiography of Malcolm X.* New York: Grove Press, 1965.

Marx, Karl. *Capital: A Critique of Political Economy.* 3 vols. 1867. Reprint, New York: International Publishers, 1967.

———. "Economic and Philosophic Manuscripts of 1844." In *The Marx-Engels Reader* 2nd ed., edited by Robert C. Tucker. New York: Norton, 1978.

Masco, Joseph. "Counterinsurgency, the Spook, and Blowback." In *Anthropology and Global Counterinsurgency*, edited by John D. Kelly, Beatrice Jaregui, Dean T. Mitchell, and Jeremy Walton. Chicago: University of Chicago Press, 2010.

Massey, Douglas S., and Nancy A. Denton. *American Apartheid: Segregation and the Making of the Underclass.* Cambridge, MA: Harvard University Press, 1993.

Matar, N. I. "The Renegade in English Seventeenth-Century Imagination." *Studies in English Literature, 1500–1900*, 33, no. 3 (1993): 489–505.

Mauer, Marc, and the Sentencing Project (U.S.). *Race to Incarcerate.* 2nd ed. New York: New Press, 2006.

Mauss, Marcel. *The Gift.* 1967. Reprint, New York: Norton, 1990.

McRuer, Robert. *Crip Theory: Cultural Signs of Queerness and Disability.* New York: New York University Press, 2006.

Meeks, James. "It Starts with the Family: How to Save a Lost Generation of Black Males." *Chicago Tribune*, April 10, 2013.

Memmi, Albert. *The Colonizer and the Colonized.* Boston: Beacon Press, 1965.

Moore, Natalie, and Lance Williams. *The Almighty Black P. Stone Nation: The Rise, Fall, and Resurgence of an American Gang.* Chicago: Lawrence Hill Books, 2011.

Morgan, Marcyliena. *The Real Hiphop: Battling for Knowledge, Power, and Respect in the LA Underground.* Durham, NC: Duke University Press, 2009.

———. "US Language Planning and Policies for Social Dialect Speakers." In

Sociopolitical Perspectives on Language Policy and Planning in the USA, edited by Kathryn Anne Davis. Philadelphia: J. Benjamins, 1999.

Moynihan, Daniel Patrick. *The Negro Family: The Case for National Action*. Washington, DC: Office of Policy Planning and Research, U.S. Department of Labor, 1965.

Muhammad, Khalil Gibran. *The Condemnation of Blackness: Race, Crime, and the Making of Modern Urban America*. Cambridge, MA: Harvard University Press, 2010.

Neal, Mark Anthony. *Soul Babies: Black Popular Culture and the Post-Soul Aesthetic*. New York: Routledge, 2002.

Negus, Keith. "The Business of Rap: Between the Street and the Executive Suite." In *That's the Joint!: The Hip-Hop Studies Reader*, edited by Mark Anthony Neal and Murray Forman. New York: Routledge, 2004.

Nguyen, Vinh Kim. *The Republic of Therapy: Triage and Sovereignty in West Africa's Time of AIDS*. Durham, NC: Duke University Press, 2010.

Nightingale, Carl. *On the Edge: A History of Poor Black Children and Their American Dreams*. New York: Basic Books, 1993.

Obama, Barack. *Dreams from My Father: A Story of Race and Inheritance*. New York: Random House, 1995.

Olivero, Michael J. *Honor, Violence, and Upward Mobility: A Case Study of Chicago's Street Gangs during the 1970s and 1980s*. Edinburg, TX: Pan American Press, 1991.

O'Neill, Kevin Lewis. "The Reckless Will: Prison Chaplaincy and the Problem of Mara Salvatrucha." *Public Culture* 22 (2010): 67–88.

O'Nell, Carl. *Dreams, Culture, and the Individual*. San Francisco: Chandler & Sharp, 1975.

Ong, Aihwa, and Stephen J. Collier, eds. *Global Assemblages: Technology, Politics, and Ethics as Anthropological Problems*. Malden, MA: Blackwell, 2005.

Ortner, Sherry. "Power and Projects: Reflections on Agency." In *Anthropology and Social Theory: Culture, Power, and the Acting Subject*. Durham, NC: Duke University Press, 2006.

Padilla, Felix. *The Gang as an American Enterprise*. New Brunswick, NJ: Rutgers University Press, 1992.

Parenti, Christian. *Lockdown America: Police and Prisons in the Age of Crisis*. London: Verso, 1999.

Parsons, Kenneth. "Structural Violence and Power." *Peace Review: A Journal of Social Justice* 19 (2007): 173–81.

Pattillo, Mary. *Black on the Block: The Politics of Race and Class in the City*. Chicago: University of Chicago Press, 2007.

Pattillo-McCoy, Mary. *Black Picket Fences: Privilege and Peril among the Black Middle Class*. Chicago: University of Chicago Press, 1999.

Perry, Imani. "Bling Bling . . . and Going Pop: Consumerism and Co-optation in Hip Hop." In *Prophets of da Hood: The Politics and Poetics of Hip Hop*. Durham, NC: Duke University Press, 2004.

Rabinow, Paul, and Nikolas Rose. "Biopower Today." *Biosocieties* 1 (2006): 195–217.

Radin, Paul. *The Trickster: A Study in American Indian Mythology*. New York: Schocken Press, 1988.

"Rahm Emanuel Mourns 260 Chicago Children Killed by Violence." *Huffington Post: Chicago Impact*, November 2, 2011, http://www.huffingtonpost.com /2011/11/02/rahm-emanuel-parents-mour_n_1071247.html.

Ralph, James R. *Northern Protest: Martin Luther King, Jr., Chicago, and the Civil Rights Movement*. Cambridge: Harvard University Press, 1993.

Reed, Adolph. *Posing as Politics and Other Thoughts on the American Scene*. New York: New Press, 2000.

Rich, John. *Wrong Place, Wrong Time: Trauma and Violence in the Lives of Young Black Men*. Baltimore: John Hopkins University Press, 2009.

Roberts, John W. *From Trickster to Badman: The Black Folk Hero in Slavery and Freedom*. Philadelphia: University of Pennsylvania Press, 1989.

Roitman, Janet. *Fiscal Disobedience: An Anthropology of Economic Regulation in Central Africa*. Princeton, NJ: Princeton University Press, 2005.

Rosaldo, Renato. *Culture and Truth: The Remaking of Social Analysis*. Boston: Beacon Press, 1989.

Rose, Tricia. *Black Noise: Rap Music and Black Culture in Contemporary America*. Hanover, NH: Wesleyan University Press, 1994.

———. *The Hip Hop Wars: What We Talk about When We Talk about Hip Hop*. New York: Basic Civitas, 2008.

Rousseau, Jean-Jacques. *The Social Contract*. New York: Hafner, 1947.

Said, Edward. *Orientalism*. New York: Vintage Books, 1978.

Sánchez-Jankowski, Martin. *Islands in the Street: Gangs and American Urban Society*. Berkeley: University of California Press, 1991.

Scarry, Elaine. *The Body in Pain: The Making and Unmaking of the World*. New York: Oxford University Press, 1985.

Scheper-Hughes, Nancy. *Death without Weeping: The Violence of Everyday Life in Brazil*. Berkeley: University of California Press, 1992.

Schiebinger, Londa. *Nature's Body: Gender in the Making of Modern Science*. Boston: Beacon Press, 1993.

Schneirov, Shelton, and Nick Salvatore. *The Pullman Strike and the Crisis of the 1890s: Essays on Labor and Politics*. Urbana: University of Illinois Press, 1999.

Schwimmer, Erik. "The Self and the Product: Concepts of Work in Comparative Perspective." In *Social Anthropology of Work*, edited by Sandra Wallman. London: Academic Press, 1979.

Scott, James. *Domination and the Arts of Resistance*. New Haven, CT: Yale University Press, 1990.

Shephard, Glenn H. "Three Days of Weeping: Dreams, Emotions, and Death in the Peruvian Andes." *Medical Anthropology Quarterly* 16, no. 2 (2002): 200–229.

Siebers, Tobin Anthony. *Disability Theory*. Ann Arbor: University of Michigan Press, 2008.

Seligman, Amanda. *Block by Block: Neighborhoods and Public Policy on Chicago's West Side*. Chicago: University of Chicago Press, 2005.

Sennett, Richard. *The Corrosion of Character: The Personal Consequences of Work in the New Capitalism*. New York: Norton, 1998.

Shapiro, Samantha M. "Hip Hop Outlaw." *New York Times*, February 18, 2007.

Silverstein, Michael. "Monoglot 'Standard' in America: Standardization and Metaphors of Linguistic Hegemony." Working Papers and Proceedings of the Center for Psychological Studies 13 (1987).

Simmel, Georg. *The Philosophy of Money*. Boston: Routledge & Kegan Paul, 1978.

Skloot, Rebecca. *The Immortal Life of Henrietta Lacks*. New York: Crown, 2010.

Slocum, Karla. *Free Trade and Freedom: Neoliberalism, Place, and Nation in the Caribbean*. Ann Arbor: University of Michigan Press, 2006.

Smith, Bryan. "Trashed: The Death of Michael York and How Heroin Has Invaded the Chicago Suburbs." *Chicago Magazine*, November 2009. http://www.chicagomag.com/Chicago-Magazine/November-2009/The-death-of-Michael-York-and-how-heroin-has-invaded-the-Chicago-suburbs/. Accessed on May 29, 2010.

Smith, Christopher Holmes. "'I Don't Like to Dream about Getting Paid': Representations of Social Mobility and the Emergence of the Hip-Hop Mogul." *Social Text* 21, no. 4 (2003): 69–97.

Stack, Carol. *All Our Kin: Strategies for Survival in a Black Community*. New York: Harper, 1974.

Steedly, Mary. *Hanging without a Rope: Narrative Experience in Colonial and Postcolonial Karoland*. Princeton, NJ: Princeton University Press, 1993.

———. *Rifle Reports: A Story of Indonesian Independence*. Berkeley: University of California Press, 2013.

Stewart, Kathleen. *A Space on the Side of the Road*. Princeton, NJ: Princeton University Press, 1996.

Subramanian, Ajantha. *Shorelines: Space and Rights in South India*. Stanford, CA: Stanford University Press, 2009.

Sullivan, Mercer L. *"Getting Paid": Youth Crime and Work in the Inner City*. Ithaca, NY: Cornell University Press, 1989.

Suttles, Gerald. *The Social Order of the Slum: Ethnicity and Territory in the Inner City*. Chicago: University of Chicago Press, 1968.

Swartz, Tracy. "Chicago's Heroin Zones." *RedEye*, February 24, 2010.

Tapias, Maria. "Emotions and the Intergenerational Embodiment of Social Suffering in Rural Bolivia." *Medical Anthropology Quarterly* 20, no. 3 (2006): 399–415.

Thompson, E. P. "The Moral Economy of the English Crowd in the Eighteenth Century." In *Customs in Common*. New York: New Press, 1991.

Thrasher, Frederic Milton. *The Gang: A Study of 1,313 Gangs in Chicago*. 1927. Abridged ed. Chicago: University of Chicago Press, 1963.

"Transportation Facts." *Chicago Area Transportation Study*, April 2007.

Trouillot, Michel-Rolph. *Silencing the Past: Power and the Production of History*. Boston: Beacon Press, 1997.

Umemoto, Karen. *The Truce: Lessons from an L.A. Gang War*. Ithaca, NY: Cornell University Press, 2006.

United Nations Office on Drugs and Crime. *2008 World Drug Report*. United Nations, 2008.

Vale, Lawrence. *Purging the Poorest: Public Housing and the Design Politics of Twice-Cleared Communities*. Chicago: University of Chicago Press, 2013.

Valentine, Bettylou. *Hustling and Other Hard Work: Life Styles in the Ghetto*. New York: Free Press, 1978.

Veblen, Thorstein. *The Vested Interests and the Common Man: The Modern Point of View and the New Order*. 1919. Reprint, New York: Augustus M. Kelley, 1964.

Venkatesh, Sudhir. *Gang Leader for a Day*. New York: Penguin, 2008.

———. *Off the Books: The Underground Economy of the Urban Poor*. Chicago: University of Chicago Press, 2006.

Venkatesh, Sudhir Alladi, and Steven D. Levitt. "'Are We a Family or a Business?': History and Disjuncture in the Urban American Street Gang." *Theory and Society* 29, no. 4 (2000): 427–62.

Wacquant, Loïc. "Deadly Symbiosis: Rethinking Race and Imprisonment in Twenty-First Century America." *Boston Review* (2002).

———. "Three Pernicious Premises in the Study of the American Ghetto." *International Journal of Urban and Regional Research*, July 1997: 341–53.

Wagner, James W., et al. *The Chicago Crime Commission Gang Book: A Detailed Overview of Street Gangs in the Chicago Metropolitan Area*. Chicago: Chicago Crime Commission, 2006.

Walley, Christine. *Exit Zero: Family and Class in Postindustrial Chicago*. Chicago: University of Chicago Press, 2013.

Warner, Michael. *The Trouble with Normal.* New York: Free Press, 1999.

Washington, Harriet A. *Medical Apartheid: The Dark History of Medical Experimentation on Black Americans from Colonial Times to the Present.* New York: Anchor Books, 2006.

Waterson, Alisse. *Street Addicts in the Political Economy.* Philadelphia: Temple University Press, 1997.

Weber, Max. *Economy and Society.* Vols. 1 and 2. Berkeley: University of California Press, 1978.

———. *The Protestant Ethic and the Spirit of Capitalism.* New York: Charles Scribner's Sons, 1958.

Weiner, Annette. *Inalienable Possessions: The Paradox of Keeping-While-Giving.* Berkeley: University of California Press, 1992.

———. *Women of Value, Men of Renown: New Perspectives in Trobriand Exchange.* Austin: University of Texas Press, 1976.

Whyte, William Foote. *Street Corner Society.* Chicago: University of Chicago Press, 1943.

Williams, Eric Wyckoff. "Will Obama Support Marijuana Legalization in His 2nd Term?" *The Root,* http://www.theroot.com/views/what-will-obama-do-about-marijuana (accessed on December 10, 2012).

Williams, Patricia. "The Luminance of Guilt." *Transition Magazine.* Cambridge: The W. E. B. Du Bois Institute, forthcoming.

Willis, Paul. *Learning to Labor: How Working-Class Kids Get Working-Class Jobs.* New York: Columbia University Press, 1977.

Wilson, William Julius. *The Truly Disadvantaged: The Inner City, the Underclass, and Public Policy.* 1987. Reprint, Chicago: University of Chicago Press, 1990.

———. *When Work Disappears: The World of the New Urban Poor.* New York: Knopf, 1996.

Wolf, Eric. *Europe and the People without History.* Berkeley: University of California Press, 1982.

Young, Alford. *The Minds of Marginalized Black Men: Making Sense of Mobility, Opportunity, and Future Life Chances.* Princeton, NJ: Princeton University Press, 2004.

Zarowsky, Christina. "Writing Trauma: Emotion, Ethnography, and the Politics of Suffering among Somali Returnees in Ethiopia." *Culture, Medicine and Psychiatry* 28, no. 2 (2004): 189–209.

INDEX

✳

affordable housing, challenges with, 8, 22
African American Vernacular English (AAVE), 191n1
Air Force Ones, 58, 69, 83
Albert, Derrion, murder of, 167–70, 172, 174, 176, 178, 228n8
Albrecht, Gary L., 223nn26–27
Altgeld Gardens, 7
Americans with Disabilities Act of 1990, 126
Appadurai, Arjun, 215n11
authenticity, 93–94; and blackness, 217n19; in hip-hop, 89–92, 100–101, 107, 111, 213n1, 219n26, 219n30; through videos of violence, 176

banlieues. See suburbanization of poverty

Baudrillard, Jean, 217n22
Benjamin, Walter, 219n27, 102
Berger, Ronald, 221n14, 223n26
Bestor, Theodore, 215n11
Biehl, João, 194nn8–9, 198n23, 199n24, 215n9, 224nn4–6, 227n15
Black Panthers, 65, 183
black subjects: as biologically defective, 122; as culturally degenerate, 122, 204n19; as simultaneously invisible and hypervisible, 174; as threatening, 174–75
blight, governmental designation of, 29–30, 47, 49–51
block clubs, 9, 28, 49, 179
blue-light cameras, 62, 93, 97, 165, 179, 183
Boas, Franz, 220n7
Bourdieu, Pierre, 198n23, 203n15